Catherine McKinnon

(McDonald, Ballard) (1823-1904)

Figure 1. Catherine McKinnon (Photo courtesy of Angus MacDonald)

Cover: 'Leaving with "bounty" emigrants', 1844 (*Illustrated London News*, England, 27 July 1844, p.4).

Catherine's Story: From a Childhood on the Isle of Skye to Life in the Colony of New South Wales

Gail Barnes

Published by Gail Barnes, 2024.

CATHERINE'S STORY: FROM A CHILDHOOD ON THE ISLE OF SKYE TO LIFE IN THE COLONY OF NEW SOUTH WALES

First edition. August 16, 2024.

ISBN: 979-8227926043

Written by Gail Barnes.

Table of Contents

This story is dedicated to all the descendants of Catherine McKinnon.

This is also our story.

Acknowledgements

I would like to acknowledge the Traditional Custodians of the land where I live, and to pay my respect to their Elders past and present. I am on Arakwal land and the Arakwal Bumberlin people are part of the Bundjalung nation.

Even if my ancestors didn't directly perpetrate any crimes against the traditional owners, I want to acknowledge that they were, as I am, a beneficiary of colonisation and the historical violence and dispossession that took place and continues to play out to this day. The land was never ceded and a treaty has never been signed. There is no Aboriginal voice to the Federal parliament and First Nations people are not recognised in the Australian Constitution. First Nations people continue to die young, to experience unacceptable levels of violence, to be incarcerated at incredibly high rates, to have their children taken and put into out-of-home care and many lack the educational opportunities afforded to non-Aboriginal Australians, such as myself. From my heart, I am sorry.

At the same time, I want to recognise the great work which is being carried out within many Aboriginal communities to keep language alive and inspire connection to country in young people. As I have learned through undertaking this project, cultural identity is important.

I would also like to acknowledge a number of people who have supported me during the research and writing of this book. Fairly early in the writing process I connected with John Nolan, a distant cousin who is also researching his branch of our McKinnon family. Many thanks go to John who shared my excitement when we made progress uncovering buried information. Together we started a Facebook group called 'The McKinnons of Kendram, Skye'.

Much gratitude also goes to Angus MacDonald, Catherine's great grandson. His online genealogy pages were a great help and an inspiration at the beginning of my research and he supplied some of the photos. Jan Vizer shared family photos with me from an album which had been passed on to her by her mother, Audrey Vizer (nee Sargeant). The Glen Innes History Museum now holds the album as part of its collection. Amina Hussain, John

Gillies, Pamela Slater, Debbie Little and Amalia Samios also sent me photos. Ben Wrigley, a photographer and friend, helped restore some of the old images which appear in the book.

Amina Hussain, who started 'The Rosses of Kilmalaug' Facebook group, was incredibly generous with her assistance in clarifying facts and sharing her wonderful family stories which have been passed down through generations. Steve Taylor and Richard Stoddart from another Facebook group, called 'Lost Skye', were also very helpful and shared some great information with me about Tallanantain.

'Scotland's People' and the National Library of Australia's site 'Trove' were both invaluable internet sites for accessing information online, particularly during Covid-19, when travel wasn't possible. In May 2022, when the Australian border was reopened, I travelled to Skye in Scotland. When I was in Skye, I visited Armadale Castle, where the McDonald Family archives are kept. I am very appreciative of the assistance I received from the archivist at Armadale Castle on my visit and in follow-up communications. The 'Skye and Lochalsh Archive Centre' at Portree was also a great resource.

When I was on the Isle of Skye, I visited Kendram. Richard Connor helped me to look for the original McKinnon croft at Kendram where Catherine grew up. Richard's local knowledge was invaluable and, together with an 1878 ordinance map, I believe we found the original 'blackhouse'. I am very grateful to Richard for his help.

I would like to acknowledge the wonderful 'Land of the Beardies History House Museum and Research Centre' in Glen Innes, and Eve Chappell in particular for her help. Also, I'd like to thank Maureen Kingston from the Dungog Museum. Maureen connected me with the academic research undertaken by Glenda Strachan in the Dungog area.

I am very grateful to Alastair Greig, an academic and friend, who offered me feedback and support during the writing process. Alastair encouraged me to turn what had started as a family story, into something much bigger.

Finally, I want to acknowledge the unfailing support of my partner, Michael. Michael read drafts, offered feedback on my manuscript and helped me navigate the publishing process. He showed an enduring interest in my writing and enthusiastically engaged with the journey from its inception. Michael always supported and encouraged my research efforts, including accompanying me to Skye to stand on the land of my ancestors.

Introduction

Catherine's Story is a nineteenth century social history which is centred on the life of Catherine McKinnon. Catherine McKinnon is my great, great grandmother. I decided to write *Catherine's Story* because when I began to research my family history I found that the historical focus was mainly on the lives of men. Women were usually referred to as a particular man's wife, his daughter or his sister. Or, as can be seen on nineteenth century Australian census documents, men were named and women were represented only as the number of females in the household. During the nineteenth century in NSW, women couldn't vote in elections and married women had no legal identity of their own. They were subsumed under their husband's identity. Women were largely invisible, or relegated to an unnamed appendage to a man's story. Despite this invisibility, or in fact because of it, this story sits within a feminist framework which puts Catherine's life at the centre of the narrative.

The story also includes discussion of the relevant social and political events which were taking place as Catherine negotiated her life path. By connecting Catherine's life with the larger scale events taking place around her, we can transform, as Brissette describes, a 'microhistory into a narrative history with global themes, through a biographical lens' (Brissette, 2022). In this way, in *Catherine's Story* we are able to investigate some of the previously unexplored gaps in the colonial narrative, particularly in relation to the lives of marginalised, immigrant women in NSW.

Other authors have also focused on the lives of their own nineteenth century ancestors in NSW, and have told the stories that they uncovered. For instance, Don Watson's (1984) book *Caledonia Australis* is the story of his ancestor, Angus McMillan, who also emigrated to Australia from the Isle of Skye in 1838. Watson discusses the immigrant experience of the Scots from the Isle of Skye who left their ancestral land and came to Australia to make a new life on Aboriginal land. Watson points to the irony that the Scots, who were suffering dispossession in their own country, went about removing First Nations people from their land. This same irony exists in *Catherine's Story*.

Since the work of the historian Henry Reynolds in his 1981 book *The Other Side of the Frontier: Aboriginal Resistance to the European Invasion of Australia*, there has been a growing interest from white Australia in understanding what really happened on the Australian frontiers. Rather than the romanticised and thoroughly sanitised historical accounts that had previously been taught in the Australian education system, Reynolds and others have shown that many First Nations people people resisted invasion by the early white settlers and wars were fought. In some situations, the indiscriminate killing of Aboriginal men, women and children also took place.

Therefore, as a researcher writing about the colonial history of Australia, it is impossible to delve into this history without being prepared to uncover atrocities. This is even more relevant when writing about one's own ancestors. This was the case for Watson (1984) when he found McMillan, along with other early settlers in the Gippsland area, had massacred a number of the local Kurnai people. The author and journalist, David Marr, also recently uncovered his own shocking story of violence and brutality perpetrated by his ancestors who served with the Native Police in Queensland. Marr's (2023) book, *Killing for Country*, is another historical account of killings which were committed for the possession of land which belonged to First Nations people.

At this time, most of the white settlers would have known about the arbitrary killing of First Nations people. It was hidden in plain sight, at least until the Myall Creek massacre in 1838 (see Chapter 8). Once settlers were convicted and hung for killing Aboriginal people at Myall Creek, things changed. However, the killings didn't stop. As Watson (1984, p.xxiv) argues, the killings in Gippsland were kept out of official records because of what happened after Myall Creek. Marr (2023, p.87) suggests that after Myall Creek 'the men of the bush discovered more discreet ways to kill'. Poison was one popular method ('Native Blacks', 24 December 1838, p.2). Unlike Watson and Marr's books, *Catherine's Story* is not a book about the frontier wars, even though they were still being fought on the edges of many settlements when Catherine arrived in the colony. As we will see, not every new settler had to slaughter Aboriginal people for their land, for in many instances the land had already been taken.

Janet Spillman (2015) wrote an historical account of her ancestors, the Lords, which she called *Queensland Lords: Edward and Eliza Lord's Colonial Family*. Spillman, like myself, is the great, great grand-daughter of the main characters of her book. Spillman's ancestors were a wealthy immigrant family from Lancashire. Initially, the Lords - who were merchants - bought various blocks of land in NSW, including on the Paterson River.

Therefore, the Lords for a short period of time were practically neighbours of Catherine's when she was living at Dunmore Estate in the early 1840s. The Lords were buying and selling land and businesses, including the river steamships that sailed up the Paterson River. They lived in NSW until Edward Lord, like so many others in the early 1840s, became insolvent. Shortly after, in 1844, the Lord family moved to Queensland. Their story then focuses on their many business ventures and their contributions to the development of Queensland. Unlike Catherine, the Lords were born into wealth and privilege, they were far from being marginalised. So even though they were practically neighbours, they most likely would not have met. The story of Catherine's life is not about entrepreneurs and business ventures in the NSW colony. It is more a story of chance and fortune, both good and bad.

In an incredible stroke of good luck Catherine's husband, a poor tenant farmer named Angus McDonald (2) (there are four different males all called Angus McDonald in this story, so I have numbered them (1)-(4) from oldest to youngest, to try and avoid confusion), won the Bank of Australia lottery in 1849. His prize was a huge property near Dungog known as Underbank Estate. The newspapers at the time were full of discussion about the controversial lottery, but most did little more than name the winner, and they certainly didn't name his wife. Even though it was the first lottery ever held in Australia, there have only been a few accounts of it in the academic literature.

Both Sydney Butlin (1968) and Trevor Sykes (1998) have undertaken analysis about the economic circumstances and the questionable financial practices which preceded the failure of the Bank of Australia. Both authors also briefly mention the lottery, which was run in order to try to rescue the assets of the failed Bank. However, neither author mentions the lottery winner Angus McDonald, let alone his wife Catherine. Neil Radford (2017) describes the lottery and names Angus (2), but Radford suggests that his young son, Angus (4), owned the winning ticket. He also contends that the father, Angus (2), bought tickets for each of his four children. As will be suggested in Chapter 5, both of these arguments are highly unlikely.

The most recent account of the lottery can be found in Alastair Grieg's (2023) book, *The Road to Batemans Bay: Speculating on the South Coast of During the 1840s Depression*. Greig discusses the first lottery in relation to the merchants and land speculators, John Terry Hughes and John Hosking. When the Bank of Australia collapsed and called in its debts, the firm of Hughes & Hoskings, a major lender, couldn't pay back money they owed the Bank. They, like so many others at the time, became insolvent. Greig (2023, p.8) suggests that their insolvency 'shook the financial foundations of NSW' and their name became linked with the downfall of the Bank and the associated lottery. Greig details the circumstances of the lottery and names Angus (2) as the winner. He also mentions Angus's (2) death shortly after his win, but he doesn't name Catherine, or discuss the legal proceedings which followed over the ownership of Underbank.

Certainly, there has been nothing written in the academic literature about Catherine and her family, who they were, what became of them or Underbank Estate, in the decades after the lottery win. For the story doesn't end with the initial windfall: Underbank Estate was gambled on gold shares and was lost, meaning that in 1876 Catherine and her family had to leave the property. They started over from scratch in the bush at Red Range, near Glen Innes.

As women were largely invisible in the nineteenth century, so the recounting of history has also tended to ignore their experiences, particularly those of women like Catherine without any formal education. Catherine's voice cannot be heard. Because Catherine was unable to read or write there are no letters, descriptions or journal entries written in her voice. Therefore, it is impossible to know how she felt about particular people, or events in her life, or those happening in the wider world. We don't know how she felt about the people and the life she left behind, or the life she made for herself in NSW. We can only speculate about these things.

In many ways this makes it even more important that the story of Catherine's experience of leaving her homeland to make a new life in NSW is told. As such, *Catherine's Story* is the portrayal of one woman's rich life, but it is also much more than that. It is a story about our history and, therefore, it is also a story about our present and about our future. Without first trying to understanding where we came from, we cannot move forward.

Catherine's Story begins in Scotland on the Isle of Skye where Catherine was born. Initially in Chapter 1, we look at the Scots' culture on the Isle and the history of Clan MacKinnon. Catherine's name is Catherine McKinnon, meaning her paternal ancestry is associated with Clan MacKinnon. 'McKinnon' can also be spelt as 'MacKinnon', sometimes the 'K' is a capital letter and sometimes it is lower case. There are variations, as most of the population of Scotland in the nineteenth century did not read or write. So, it was up to the parish priest, registrar or clerk or whoever was writing the registration, as to how a person's name was spelt ('Surnames', 2022). I have noticed that many old records tend to write 'MacKinnon' whereas the more recent spelling appears to favour 'McKinnon'. The two are used interchangeably in this story.

The impacts of the Highland Clearances on poor tenant farmers, such as Catherine's family, are also discussed in this Chapter. Catherine's mother Flora was a Cameron, and the discussion explains her family history over several generations at a settlement called Tallanantain, which was owned by

Lord MacDonald's Estate. What's more, the Chapter describes the events which took place once the infamous Captain William Fraser bought the estate.

Flora Cameron married Catherine's father, Ewen McKinnon, and by the time Catherine was born in 1823 they had taken up a croft at Kendram. Kendram was also owned by Lord MacDonald and established as a crofting settlement not long after 1811. Kendram is described in Chapter 2 as the place of Catherine's childhood where she was surrounded by her parents, her siblings and her extended family. Some insights into life at Kendram are garnered from the reflections of her niece, Mary Ross. Following on from these reflections, the discussion in this chapter depicts how challenging life had become, particularly after the potato famine of 1836-37. It is clear, there was no future for Catherine on Skye.

The Rev Dr John Dunmore Lang went to Skye, talking up the prospects for good Protestant Highlanders like Catherine in the Australian colonies. As a result, Catherine, together with her older brother and his family, enlisted in Lang's Bounty Scheme and left their homeland. They sailed onboard the *Midlothian* across the world to the colony of New South Wales in search of a better life. However, as we will see, the journey to 'a better life' was not without its perils, particularly for a young woman.

Catherine's Story cannot be told without first recognising the dark history of the NSW colony where she was headed. Initially, Chapter 3 outlines the early beginnings of the colony as a penal settlement, where convicts from Britain were transported to serve time for breaking British law. We come to understand that the colony was built on the invasion of Aboriginal people's land. The ongoing abhorrent treatment of First Nations people by the colonists, particularly of Aboriginal women, is also discussed to highlight the fact that a better life for some was built on violence and dispossession for others.

Following a long and difficult journey, upon their arrival in NSW the group of Presbyterian Scots insisted to the authorities that they were to be settled as a group. After some initial issues, Catherine, her brother and the remaining passengers from the *Midlothian*, headed to Dunmore Estate. Dunmore Estate was a property owned by Andrew Lang, the brother of Rev Lang, who initiated the bounty scheme which brought them to Australia.

As we see in Chapter 4, Catherine and the passengers from the *Midlothian* are employed to fill labour shortages on Dunmore Estate by working as tenant farmers. At Dunmore, surrounded by other immigrants from her homeland, Catherine settles into family life with Angus McDonald (2), also a bounty immigrant from the *Midlothian*.

The Wonnarua are First Nations people who lived on the land in the area, including Dunmore Estate. However, the Wonnarua people began to suffer from starvation as they increasingly lost access to their traditional food sources and were pushed further and further to the margins. It is argued that the irony of this situation was probably lost on Catherine at the time.

The story then follows Catherine's path as a new settler in a recently colonised country. Bushrangers and the rising crime rate are explored, as young, free settler families like Catherine's look to establish themselves in the colony. Prostitution and homosexuality are also analysed in the context of concerns about the 'moral woes' of the colony, and the growing opposition to transportation. We see Catherine and Angus (2) marry and the arrival of more children. The importance of Catherine's reproductive and domestic labour, and that of other immigrant women like her, is discussed as essential to the development of the colony.

In Chapter 5, the squattocracy and the beginnings of democracy in the colony are described in order to set the scene for an astonishing windfall for Catherine and her family when they won Underbank Estate in Australia's first lottery. Some of the controversies which surrounded the lottery are considered, as is the tragic accident which befell Catherine's husband, Angus (2), before they had even moved to Underbank. It was an accident which left Catherine a widow with four young sons, and once the ownership of the estate was resolved, she also had a large property to manage.

8

The discussion includes the Gringai, who are the local Aboriginal people from the Underbank area and Dungog which is their new service town. Then, in 1851, two of Catherine's younger siblings arrive from Scotland, bringing a joyous family reunion and some help with running the estate. At about the same time as her siblings arrive, gold is discovered in NSW in payable quantities, starting a gold rush. The gold rush is considered with particular reference to the poorly treated, indentured Chinese workers, who get the impetus to abscond from their jobs as shepherds and join other hopefuls on the goldfields. As we will see, this so-called 'gold fever' helped shape the future of the colony, and that of Catherine's own family.

Chapter 6 begins with a reflection on Caroline Chisholm and her influence on the colony. Chisholm asserted the ideal of domesticity for respectable Christian women like Catherine. Catherine was expected to remarry, and in 1853 she married her second husband, Thomas Lewis Ballard. As Catherine and Thomas have their own children, the death of Catherine's sister, Dorcas and the deaths of three of Dorcas's children at Kendram are also discussed. The high infant mortality rates in the NSW colony are considered, along with birthing practices, with particular reference to the work of Glenda Strachan (2001 (b)). Strachan's research brings some insight into the birthing practices employed by colonial women in the Dungog area. Strachan makes the point that very little has been documented about how, where and with whom, women gave birth in the NSW colony.

Chapter 6, also discusses the slow advancement of suffrage in the colony and the introduction of three new *Acts* by the NSW government. These new *Acts* are the *Chinese Immigrants Regulation and Restriction Act 1861,* the *Crown Lands Act 1861* and the *Felons Apprehension Act 1865.* As encounters with bushrangers by settlers become relatively commonplace, this chapter finishes with the story of Ewen McDonald's close encounter with the bushranger Captain Thunderbolt.

In Chapter 7, Catherine's brother Angus and her son Ewen both marry. Then her first grandchild Albert is born to Ewen and his wife, Emily. The threads that bound Catherine and her family to Scotland and the Scottish culture are explored in this chapter. With the start of a new generation of Australian grandchildren and the deaths of Catherine's mother, father and her eldest brother, John, we see the loosening of her ties to Scotland.

Also in Chapter 7, Catherine's husband, Thomas Ballard and a party of local men from around Underbank, set off on an overland journey. Apart from having a great adventure, Thomas gets what is perhaps his first glimpse of the New England Tablelands area. The New England Tablelands, unbeknown to him at the time, will later become their home. In the meantime, the family have a happy life at Underbank and more of Catherine's children marry, bringing the prospect of more grandchildren. However, when the unthinkable happens and their home is lost, they all have to pack up and leave.

The last seven chapters of this story unfold at Red Range, near Glen Innes in NSW, during the last quarter of the nineteenth century and in the early days of the twentieth century. In Chapter 8, Catherine, Thomas and their four teenage sons move to Red Range where they purchase land under the *1861 Crown Lands Act*. They start over on a selection of 'virgin forest'. We learn of some of the other people who also settled in the area, as well as 'Black Tommy' a local bushranger, who they would have encountered. Chapter 8 describes their early days at Red Range, the traditional owners of the land where they settled, and the town of Glen Innes. Glen Innes was their local service town, a place which would become familiar to them. It was where they would go when they needed to buy goods and attend to business affairs.

Chapter 9 begins by acknowledging the death of Rev Lang. Some of his achievements and his impact on the NSW colony are explored, including his support for secular education, which led to the introduction of the *Public Instruction Act 1880*. This chapter also highlights some aspects of life on the 'Range'. This includes discussion of Thomas' mail run, the impact that settlement was having on the natural environment, and the likely employment of Aboriginal workers at Red Range. Some consideration is given to the local cricket matches and other social events that served to break up the long days of hard work at Red Range.

Chapter 10 suggests there were a number of family visits to Red Range to see Catherine and Thomas. One particular visit from their son and his family sees the arrival of another grandchild. This was not unusual at the time as babies were usually born at home. An analysis follows about the availability of health care, if and when it was needed.

The chapter also reflects on the downfall of Catherine's younger brother Angus McKinnon, after a terrible coach accident kills his wife. The wedding of Catherine's son, Malcolm McDonald, at Maclean on the Clarence River is described as it provided an opportunity for the family to get together and celebrate. However, the chapter ends with the distressing death of Catherine's brother, Angus by his own hand.

Chapter 11, explores the arrival of the steam train in Glen Innes and the ongoing development of Red Range. Red Range is growing into a strong community, a place of 'civilised society'. The Ballard family clearly feel that with this civilisation comes a civic responsibility to be involved and to engage in the politics of the day. As a result, they hold political meetings in their home, and we see the Temperance Movement emerging as a strong socio-political force within the colony.

As the nineteenth century progresses, Chapter 12 reflects on the growing sense of pride among those who were born in the colony. This is evident in Catherine's own family when her son, David Ballard and his wife Kitty, start a family. Their second child, a daughter, is known by the Aboriginal name 'Myee' which translates to 'born of this land'.

The chapter also addresses the idea of a 'national identity'. The 'typical Australian' which is being promoted in media such as *The Bulletin* magazine, appears as Federation looms on the horizon. However, this notion of a 'typical Australian' is not inclusive of everyone. Therefore, there is discussion of those who were excluded from this 'national identity', such as the women of the colony, the Chinese immigrants and First Nations people.

Life in the colony was fragile, and Chapter 13 suggests just how fragile it could be. Premature death was relatively common and, as the end of the nineteenth century approached, Catherine and her family suffered their share of losses, which included the death of six grandchildren, her son Edward and her son-in-law, James Cornish. At this time there was also a decline in birth rates in Australia and across the western world. Many women were taking active measures to limit the size of their families. A Royal Commission was held in NSW in 1903 to try to ascertain the cause of the falling number of births. Despite the suffering and grief experienced by the Ballard family, Chapter 13 also demonstrates an underlying strength and sense of humour which was inherent in Catherine's husband Thomas, when he appears in a court case over a stolen heifer.

As Catherine's final years approach, Chapter 14 addresses some of the many changes taking place in the new century. These changes include the death of Queen Victoria and the federation of the colonies into the Commonwealth of Australia, the development of the motor car and suffrage for British women in Australia. Suffrage is discussed as a socio-political movement which included feminists and the Women's Christian Temperance Union. Suffragists were hoping to improve the lives of women by achieving equal voting rights. Suffrage, however, was attained at the expense of Aboriginal men and women.

As the story of Catherine's life and the times in which she lived draws to a close, we see the end of an era in the Ballard family. Thomas Ballard dies in February 1904 and his passing is followed only months later in May by Catherine's own death. The discussion reflects on Catherine's life as a woman in nineteenth century colonial NSW. She was a central figure in the life of her large family, and yet her life was largely lived without public recognition or written record.

To tell *Catherine's Story*, I have used academic sources and nineteenth century newspapers articles. I have also drawn on archival records, both Australian and Scottish, including census reports, births, deaths and marriage records and various other primary sources. This narrative has taken a 'social reconstruction' (Strachan & Henderson, 2008, p.489) approach to telling the story of Catherine's life and the context in which it played out. As with any social reconstruction, it is the prerogative of the writer to focus on events and critique issues that the author sees as relevant. Therefore, I would like to acknowledge from the outset that this narrative, rather than claiming to be an objective complete biography, constitutes a subjective retelling of Catherine's life told through my twenty-first century lens.

Also, there may be inaccuracies, but I have attempted to cross-check information and I have used primary sources wherever it was possible to do so. However, if I have omitted any important events or family members or inadvertently misrepresented anyone, I apologise. Relying on sources such as newspaper articles from another period can also be problematic as journalists sometimes make mistakes. The men (and yes, they were mostly, if not all, men) writing for newspapers, carry their own politics and biases, including the exclusion, or side-lining of women and minority groups. They can also write with their own self-interest in mind.

I have included discussion of First Nations people throughout the book. First Nations people living traditional lives, those who worked with the colonisers, as well as those who had moved into towns were a part of everyday life in the colony. They were very visible to the new settlers, even though their long connection to the land and their history was generally rendered invisible. Catherine and her family would have built relationships with Aboriginal people living in the vicinity of their various homes at Dunmore Estate, Underbank and Red Range. Those relationships would have inevitably been influenced by the sociopolitical context in which they developed.

The discussion of the colonisation of the land, where First Nations people had lived for tens of thousands of years, is inevitably sensitive. I have attempted to use language which is considerate. I have avoided using 'Indigenous Australians', as this term is offensive to many First Nations people who feel that it categorises them as fauna and flora. Therefore, I have used 'First Nations people' and 'Aboriginal people' to refer to the original peoples and traditional custodians of the land. I hope this will not offend anyone.

Finally, the book includes a number of photographs. The photographs give a glimpse of the landscape and of people's lives, both on Skye and in the colony of NSW. Some of the early photographs have come from family albums which were saved by various relatives over the years, and others have come from libraries and museums. In particular, the photos of Catherine are invaluable for personalising her experience. As Lucy Frost (1984, p.13) argues, photographs 'give a visual shape to those silent women who left no words.'

We can't hear Catherine's own voice, but hopefully this book will make her life visible to those of us who came later.

Chapter 1
The Isle of Skye

The Isle of Skye - Clan McKinnon - Culloden - the Highland Clearances - Blackadder's Report to Lord MacDonald - Tallanantain - the infamous Captain William Fraser

The Isle of Skye

Catherine's life began on the Isle of Skye in Scotland. As we will see in this and the following chapter, both her maternal and paternal ancestors lived on Skye. Her ancestry on the island goes back at least hundreds of years and, most probably, thousands. Therefore, it is important to begin *Catherine's Story* by trying to understand more about the Isle of Skye and Catherine's connection to its people.

The exact origin of the name of the Isle of Skye is uncertain, although it is commonly believed that the name was anglicised from old Norse mythology. The word *Skuy* means 'misty or cloudy', describing the island's mist covered mountains. However, *an t-Eilean Sgitheanach* (pronounced *an tschehlan Skianach*) or 'the Winged Isle', is the traditional Gaelic name for the Isle of Skye, possibly due to the shape formed by the northern Trotternish and Waternish Peninsulas. *An t-Eilean* means 'island', so it is also possible that the name *Ski* came from traditional Gaelic (Gittings, 2012).

Skye is the largest island of the Western Isles or Hebrides Archipelago. The island is considered to be part of the Scottish Highlands and it sits within the historic county of Inverness-Shire. Portree (*Port an Righ*) is Skye's capital and its largest town. Skye is known for its many sea lochs and lobate peninsulas, which means that anywhere on Skye is never more than eight kilometres (approx. five miles) from the sea. The beautiful and rugged Cuillin Mountains sit 993 metres (3,257 feet) above sea level in the centre of the island. However, much of Skye is moorland. In Catherine's time the only access to mainland Scotland was by boat, and it is unlikely that she ever left the island until she emigrated.

Two years before Catherine was born, according to the 1821 census, the population of Skye was recorded as 20,627 people (Gittings, 2012). In Rev MacKinnon's (1899, p.8) account of life in nineteenth century Skye, he describes the people as 'sober, correct, charitable, hospitable, obedient and respectful'. Scots Gaelic is their traditional language and in the nineteenth century, when Catherine lived on Skye, everyone spoke Gaelic. Nevertheless, Rev MacKinnon (1899, p.8) suggests that by 1847, which was ten years after Catherine had left the island, the people of Skye had incorporated some English words into their vernacular.

The people on Skye had a rich culture and held strong beliefs which permeated their daily life. Rev John Lanne Buchanan (1793, p.79) described the music and dance of the Western Isles as both 'tasteful' and 'elegant'. He wrote that the people 'have a fine vein for poetry and music'. Furthermore, he suggested that even the most 'vulgar' of people, no less than the most refined, compose 'soft and tender strains of feeling and affection, that melt the soul with heart-felt sensibility and love, along with the most moving dirges and lamentations for their soft sweethearts and friends'.

Music, which was mostly played on the violin (the pipes were more often used in the fields for weddings, funerals and public meetings), as well as dance, poetry and the recounting of sagas were regularly enjoyed by those on Skye at 'ceilidhs'. Ceilidhs are 'visits' in Gaelic, which were often held at people's homes. They are social gatherings or parties, attended by both the young and the old, where participants from the community entertained each other. As most of the population were illiterate, the words to songs had to be memorised or composed on the spot (Watson, 1984). According to Watson (1984) apart from providing entertainment, ceilidhs encouraged hospitality and they engendered social skills. He says they were an enjoyable expression of Celtic culture which served to pass on traditions to the younger generations.

During the sixteenth century, the Protestant Reformation had resulted in the formation of the Church of Scotland, a mostly Calvinist Kirk, which adopted Presbyterian worship. Catherine and her family on Skye were members of the Church of Scotland (Catherine McKinnon, 1837). The Church of Scotland followed *Sabbatarianism* which was a mainstay of Presbyterianism and meant a strict, austere observance of the Sabbath as a day of rest. The Kirk also had control over the schools, and it shaped the conservative morals of the population ('Church of Scotland', 2022).

Little is known about the specific religious beliefs or practices on Skye before the arrival of Christianity. However, it is commonly thought that *Celtic Polytheism* was practiced by the Picts who had inhabited the area. It is believed that they worshipped well-spirits and other entities as sacred wells and springs were often sites of pilgrimage for the people on Skye (Dunbavin, 1998, p.41). MacKinnon (1899, p.3) points out that despite the spread of Christianity to the island, the people were still very superstitious and held 'a belief in Daoine shith or fairies; a belief in the influence of departed spirits over temporal affairs and second-sight'. He says that the main festivals celebrated by the people of Skye in 1899, when he was writing his account, were the ancient Celtic feasts of Beltane (*Bealtuinn*) on the 1st of May and Samhuin *(Samhuinn)* between 31st October and the 1st of November, which he suggests is 'indicative of their former idolatry'.

There was a strong clan system throughout Scotland, which was thought to originate in the Highlands. The word 'clan' derives from the Gaelic word *'clanna'* which means children or descendants, and refers to a close-knit family group (MacKinnon, 1899). Clans were generally organised in geographic areas and there was a heritable succession through the male line. Most clans had a head, or chief, and anyone who swore allegiance to the chief could join the clan, even if they were not related by blood. The chief was expected to look out for the clan members and make decisions on behalf of the group ('The Birth of Scottish Clan Culture', 2023).

Clans gave people a sense of kinship, identity and pride. They were also a symbol of strength and an important part of survival in times gone by when battles and disputes, from both outside invaders and neighbours, were frequent. The most powerful clans on the Isle of Skye were Clan McLeod of Dunvegan and Clan McDonald of Sleat. The McKinnons of Strath were a smaller but, as we will see, still significant clan in the history of the Isle ('Isle of Skye', 2024).

Clan MacKinnon

The Gaelic name of Clan MacKinnon was *Mac Fhionghuin or Clan Fingon*. The name MacKinnon is the eighteenth century, Anglicisation of the Gaelic name (MacKinnon, 1899). According to Rev MacKinnon (1899) ancient documents, including one by Tighernac, an Irish Annalist, suggest the Clan originated from the son of the Irish King of Dalriada, *Loarn mac Eirc* in the sixth century. The Clan seat was on the Isle of Mull, and Clan MacKinnon was closely connected with the monastery of Iona, founded by St Columba in the sixth century (MacKinnon, 1899).

It is widely thought that Clan MacKinnon is one of seven clans descended from King Alpin MacEochaid, father of Kenneth MacAlpin (*Cinaed MacAilpin*), the first King of Scotland. When the Norse (Norwegian) invaders began raiding the Western Isles in the ninth century, Kenneth MacAlpin, through a series of bloody and treacherous battles, united the Dalriadic Scots (Gaels) and the various Pictish thrones into one (Skene, 1837).

However, the Norsemen were fierce fighters and they prevailed. In due course, many of the invaders intermarried with the local people and settled on the Isles, including on Skye. Tradition suggests that in the ninth century a Norse Princess married the MacKinnon chief. The Princess built a castle on Skye at the site of *Caisteal Maol,* on the Strait of Kyle Akin, which sits between Skye and the Scottish mainland. According to legend, she stretched a chain across the strait and collected a toll from passing boats. She apparently exempted Norse boats who were allowed to sail past without charge (MacKinnon Gazetteer, 2024).

In the twelfth century, a new system of rule developed under the Norse-Gaelic rulers and their descendants, which was known as the Lordship of the Isles. The MacKinnon chiefs sat on the Council of the Isles under the King, or Lord of the Isles (MacKinnon, 1899). In 1266, the *Treaty of Perth* was agreed, and the Norse King transferred the sovereignty of Skye, the Inner Hebrides and the Isle of Man, to Scotland ('The Treaty of Perth: 109716', 2024).

Only thirty years later, in 1296, the English invaded Scotland, starting the First War of Scottish Independence. The MacKinnon's protected Robert the Bruce, the King of the Scots, when he was escaping the English. In 1314, after Bruce's victory in Bannockburn against King Edward II, he rewarded the MacKinnon clan by increasing their landholdings in the Western Isles, including a new charter of lands at Strathaird (*Strathordil)* on the Isle of Skye (MacKinnon Gazetteer, 2024). The MacKinnons of Strathaird occupied the site of the Iron Age broch, known as *Dun Ringill* on the Strathaird peninsula, for approximately two hundred years ('Iron Age Ruins of Dun Ringill', 2020). Then, in the sixteenth century, the Clan moved their seat to *Caisteal Maol*, where Neill MacKinnon built a three-storey tower. However, *Caisteal Maol* was destroyed by fire in the early seventeenth century (Dunakin/ Caisteal Maol, 2021).

The Act of Union was passed in 1707, to unite England and Scotland into one kingdom. 'Great Britain', as it was known, was officially ruled by an English head of state ('History of Scottish Surnames from the Isle of Skye', 14 January 2016). However, many Scots resisted British rule. Clan MacKinnon of Strath, under their chief Iain Dubh MacKinnon, joined with others in the unsuccessful 1715 'rising' - an attempt to try to resist the union of England and Scotland. Their aim was to restore Scottish sovereignty and the reign of James III of England/James VIII of Scotland (James Edward Francis Stuart) (MacKinnon, 1899).

In 1745 another uprising was instigated by Prince Charles (Charles Edward Stuart, son of James Edward Stuart) who was attempting to restore his father, the Catholic heir to the throne of England and Scotland. The Jacobites managed to get all the way to Derby in England before retreating to Scotland (MacKinnon, 1899). Then, on the 16 April in 1746, the MacKinnon's of Strath supported the Jacobites on the battlefield at Culloden Moor in a final bid to overthrow the Protestant King George II. However, they lost the battle.

Between 150 and 200 soldiers from Clan Mackinnon fought for the Jacobites. They fought with the MacDonald's of Keppoch regiment and were led into battle by the clan chief himself, Iain Dubh Mackinnon, who was well into his sixties. The initial Jacobite charge broke the government line, but they were soon forced back with devastating consequences. It is believed that in less than an hour, about 1250 Jacobite soldiers died or were badly wounded on Culloden battlefield that day ('The Battle of Culloden', 2023).

After the defeat at Culloden, Prince Charles was on the run from the government forces and after many months, the government forces were closing in on him at Uist. So, to help him escape, a young woman called Flora MacDonald took him from Uist over to Skye in a small row boat. He was dressed as one of her maids. The rough crossing from the mainland over to Skye, during a wild storm, is captured in the well-known and beautiful 'Skye Boat Song', originally written by Sir Harold Boulton and Anne Campbelle MacLeod in the 1870s.

Skye Boat Song – (The Original Lyrics)

[Chorus]

Speed Bonnie Boat like a bird on the wing

Onward! the sailor's cry;

Carry the lad that's born to be king

Over the sea to Skye.

———-

Loud the wind howls, loud the waves roar

Thunderclaps rend the air;

Baffled our foes, stand on the shore,

Follow they will not dare.

———-

Many's the lad, fought on that day

Well, the claymore did wield;

When the night came, silently lay

Dead on Culloden's field.

———-

Though the waves leap, soft shall ye sleep,

Oceans a royal bed.

Rocked in the deep, Flora will keep

Watch by your weary head.

———-

Burned are their homes, exile and death

Scatter the loyal men;

Yet ere the sword cool in the sheath

Charlie will come again.

The clan chief, Iain Dubh Mackinnon, and his nephew John then sheltered 'Bonnie Prince Charlie' on Skye. After twelve days Iain, his nephew and several others, rowed the prince over to Borrodale on the mainland so that he could flee to France. As a result of their actions Iain, John and their boatmen were arrested the next day, flogged and imprisoned. Iain MacKinnon spent a year in prison, first in Tilbury Fort and then the Tower of London. He was imprisoned for aiding and abetting Prince Charles' attempt to take the English throne. Flora MacDonald was also imprisoned in the Tower of London for assisting the fugitive prince to escape. Flora MacDonald was then released the following year (MacKinnon, 1899). She died on 5th March 1790, and is buried in Kilmuir cemetery on the Isle of Skye.

Following the battle of Culloden, there was a concerted effort by the government to eradicate the clan system and the traditional way of life in Scotland. As a result, the *Act of Proscription 1746* was enforced. This meant that wearing tartan, playing the bagpipes and teaching Gaelic were all outlawed (Eyre-Todd, 1923). Also, the *Heritable Jurisdictions (Scotland) Act 1746* was passed, which meant that clan chiefs and landowners who didn't submit to English law, lost their land and it was sold to 'outsiders'. 'Bend the knee or surrender your birthright' was the subtext (Stewart, 2017). Culloden marked a turning point in Scottish history, which brought about the fall of the clan-based society.

The MacKinnon clan chief, Iain Dubh MacKinnon, was later freed in 1749, after he petitioned for release saying he was 'old and destitute'. As a result of the enormous outlays to fund the Jacobite rebellion he was unable to pay all the clan's debts. The once strong, wealthy clan was reduced to poverty (MacKenzie, 1881). The southern part of the estate was sold to John MacKenzie of Devlin. Then in 1760 it was sold on to the trustees of the MacDonald Estate, since Lord MacDonald was only a child at the time. The Macalister family from Argyleshire bought the northern part of the estate, including Strathaird, in 1774 (Watson, 1984) leaving the clan landless. In 1792, as the memory of Culloden had faded and the once strong clan system was in ruins, the *Act of Proscription 1746* was finally repealed. Other laws designed by the government to undermine the Highland way of life were also revoked (Highland Clearances, 2018).

The Highland Clearances

Traditionally, most landless people on Skye were subsistence farmers who rented land as joint tenants. Usually about six to eight people, and their families, worked a mix of co-operative and individual, small-scale farming. They used a run-rig method to farm, which was also known as *rig-a-rendal*.

Open arable land was divided into strips or rigs, which were worked by the tenant farmers. The land was worked with hand-tools, or some farmers had a communal horse and plough, which they shared. The rigs were rotated among the farmers, often by drawing lots, so that no one person had continuous use of the best land. The system is thought to date back to late medieval times. Traditional farming also relied on Highland black cattle, and larger areas of less arable land were used for common grazing among the tenants ('The Runrig System of Land Tenure', 2022).

However, the price of wool and mutton began rising in the 1760s in Britain. At the same time, new breeds of sheep, such as the black-faced sheep and later the Cheviot, were being introduced to the Highlands. The new sheep breeds were more hardy than traditional breeds, and made sheep farming increasingly lucrative in the harsh Highland conditions. As the agrarian and economic landscape changed, smaller farms were being consolidated into ever larger estates in order to maximise profits for the estate owners (The Highland Clearances, 2016).

Cash strapped clan chiefs and English landowners saw the economic benefits of sheep farming. Starting in the 1760s up until the late 1860s, tens of thousands of tenant farmers were pushed off their land in the Scottish Highlands to make way for sheep farms. For those tenant farmers that remained, the rents on their farms were raised, often to unsustainable levels. The high rents together with the ever-increasing population, made it very difficult for them to support their families and this led to further evictions. Poor tenants, whose families in some instances had lived in the same house for hundreds of years, were forcibly moved to make way for sheep. This mass scale eviction of tenant farmers from the Highlands became known as the 'Highland Clearances' (Macpherson, 2020).

The historian, Professor Smout (1986, p.64) argues that for many Highlanders on Skye, the occupation of traditional clan land was seen as 'the greatest good that life had to offer'. They believed it was their birth right but, despite this belief, tens of thousands of men, women and children were forced to leave the land on which their families had lived for countless generations. The number of people affected by the Clearances was astounding, estimated to number in the region of 150,000 ('Highland Clearances', 2024). Many people were pushed on to coastal regions with low quality land, while others left their homeland and emigrated to the Americas. Some commentators have likened the Highland Clearances to what we now call 'ethnic cleansing' (Judah, 2015). It also meant that without land of their own, after more than 1000 years in the Hebrides, the MacKinnon's were particularly susceptible to eviction and destitution.

Lord MacDonald's Estates

By 1799, Lord Macdonald was the largest landowner on Skye (MacKenzie, 1881). In 1800 he, like many of the highland estate owners at the time, commissioned a detailed survey of his estate. The objective of the report was to recommend ways of 'improving' the land use and hence increasing his income from the estate. The initial survey, which was conducted by John Blackadder in 1800, recommended radical changes in the way land was used on the estate, including the establishment of large sheep farms and the relocation of people into crofting settlements (Blackadder, 1800).

As mentioned earlier, farming sheep had become the most profitable agricultural endeavour in the Highlands. However, sheep farming was not compatible with traditional small scale, animal husbandry. Hence tenant farmers were being moved on to crofts. A croft is a relatively small area of land, usually just a few acres, which a tenant farmer or crofter rents for food production to sustain their family. The tenant farmer pays rent to the land owner on a year-to-year basis ('About Crofting', 2024). The establishment of crofting settlements was seen by many to be merely a way of removing existing tenants from good grazing land on to poorer land, making way for large, profitable sheep farms.

Also, in the early 1800s, Lord MacDonald made about £7,000 a year from the kelp industry on his estates on Skye. Tenants were needed to work the coastal industry. The establishment of crofting settlements, with high rents, would mean that there was a readily available workforce. The tenants would have no choice but to work for low wages in order to supplement their incomes, as the crofts alone would not sustain their families ('Report on Comparative Kelp Prices', c1805, p.1).

After his initial recommendations (1800), Lord MacDonald commissioned a second report from Blackadder in 1811 (Blackadder, 1811), setting out the preferred division of land on his estate. As a result of Blackadder's work, many crofting settlements were established during the 1810s on Lord MacDonalds Estates. Tenants were moved from farmland they had rented as co-operatives, often for generations, on to crofts. There are two crofting settlements which were laid out in Blackadder's report (1811) for Lord MacDonald, which are of particular interest to this story. The first is a settlement called Tallanantain and the other is a place called Kendram.

Tallanantain

The earliest records available have positioned Catherine's maternal ancestors at Tallanantain. Tallanantain is in Glen Conon (*Gleann Conain*), east of Uig (*Uigg*) in Snizort parish, on the Trotternish (*Trondairnis*) Peninsula, in the north of the Isle of Skye. Tallanantain can be spelt many different ways including, *Tailanthien, Tala nan Taighean, Talnataithen* and literally means 'Land for houses' in Gaelic. The river *Tala nan Taighean* runs through the settlement.

Catherine's maternal great grandfather was Alexander Martin (c1710-). There is a rental record at Armadale Castle on Skye, which houses the MacDonald family archives, showing that for the period from 1769 to 1772 Alexander, together with five other men, rented a farm from Lord MacDonald, at Tallanantain (Tallanantain Rental Table, 1718 -1823). However, he may well have rented the property for a much longer period. Not all of the rental records have survived the test of time. Also, he may have been a subtenant of someone else renting at Tallanantain in other years. The subtenants are not listed on the records.

Alexander Martin's daughter Ann Martin, married Alexander Cameron in the mid 1700's. Alexander Cameron had lost his clan land on the Scottish mainland at Lochaber after the Jacobite uprising in 1745, and moved to Skye (Cameron Family Index, 2021). According to Cameron family history, Alexander Cameron obtained his home from his father-in-law, Alexander Martin (Cameron Family Index, 2021). He was most probably a sub-tenant of Alexander Martin. Ann and Alexander Cameron then had a son called Angus Cameron (1755-1836). Angus was most likely born at Tallanantain, although there are no records to support this.

Angus Cameron became a tailor (Flora MacKinnon, 1870). He and his wife Ann Campbell (1748-1838) had eight children: Flora, Alexander, Ann, Duncan, Malcolm, Ewen, John and Christy. Their eldest child, Flora, was born in about 1781 in Snizort parish (Flora McKinnon, 1861), most likely at Tallanantain. Flora is Catherine McKinnon's mother.

In the latter part of the eighteenth century the land at Tallanantain was administered by the trustees of the MacDonald Estate. When he came of age, at the start of the nineteenth century, the estate was administered by Lord MacDonald himself. So, after Blackadder's recommendations in 1811, Tallanantain became a crofting settlement.

Catherine's grandfather, Angus Cameron and his family rented a croft at Lot 8 Tallanantain. The earliest surviving rental record is from 1823. However, he was most likely one of the original tenants of the crofts. As we discussed earlier, his ancestors had been farming in the area for at least a couple of generations (Tallanantain Rental Table, 1823-1855). His daughter Flora Cameron, Catherine's mother, was married by the time Tallanantain became a crofting settlement and she had moved to Kendram with her husband Ewen McKinnon. We'll talk more about that later.

Angus Cameron (Catherine's grandfather) continued renting Lot 8 until 1836, but he was sharing the croft with his son, Alexander Cameron. Angus most probably died, in or soon after, 1836. Alexander Cameron then became the sole tenant for the next few years until 1839/40 (Tallanantain Rental Table, 1823-1855).

The Cameron family had all left Tallanantain by the 1841 census. Five of Flora's seven siblings immigrated to Prince Edward Island in Canada. In 1829 two of her brothers, Ewen and John, both emigrated on the *Mary Kennedy* together with Ann MacDonald, who was Ewen's wife (Ewen Cameron 1824). John later married his wife Mary in Canada. Flora's brother Alexander and his wife Catherine MacLeod, together with Flora's sister Ann and her husband, John MacPhee all immigrated to Prince Edward Island in 1840. Her brother Duncan emigrated sometime before 1845, and he married his wife Margaret MacQueen in Canada, although she was also originally from Skye (Cameron Family Index, 2021). There were few opportunities left on Tallanantain, or Skye more generally, in the nineteenth century and emigration presented an opportunity for a better life.

Only two of Flora's siblings remained on Skye. Her sister, Christy, married John Matheson from Glasphein in Kilmuir parish (Christy Cameron, 12 March 1828). Flora's remaining brother, Malcolm Cameron, married Ann MacKay. By the time of the 1841 census, they had moved from Tallanantain, just across the glen, to a croft where he had farmed five acres at Balnacnock, (Malcolm Cameron, 1841). Balnacnock was later cleared in 1865 (Notice to remove tenants of Tallanantain, Peinvraid and Balnacnock, 1865) and the Cameron's rented just the cottage at 2 Balnacnock (Malcolm Camron [sic], 1861). After Malcolm died in 1873 his son, Angus Cameron who was Catherine's cousin, took over the cottage. Angus's occupation on the census was given as an unemployed shepherd (Angus Cameron, 1881) Angus was married to Ann Graham whose mother Flora Graham lived next door (see Figure 2). Life was a struggle and it must have been difficult just to survive.

Captain William Fraser

Also in 1841, Lord McDonald went bankrupt and much of his estate was then administered by trustees until it was sold (Smout, 1986). In 1855, Captain William Fraser from Nairnshire, purchased the entire parish of Kilmuir, which included Kendram. He also bought part of Snizort parish

Figure 2. Flora Graham (nee MacQueen) and family, at Balnacnock, c1888. Flora Graham is seated at the spinning wheel. The Graham's were originally from 8 Tallanantain (Photo courtesy of Debbie Little).

from the trustees, which included Tallanantain and Balnacnock ('Kilmuir Estate', 2015). Fraser paid £85,000 for the Estate. Fraser's family had made their fortune from the slave trade in the West Indies. Fraser's grandfather, William Fraser of Culbokie, together with Colin Mackenzie, owned the Union Plantation Estate in Berbice, British Guiana which included 150 slaves. William Fraser succeeded his grandfather, because his own father had died at a young age ('William Fraser of Culbokie', 2023). Significantly, Captain Fraser had no historical connection to the area, or the people living there.

In about 1860, Captain Fraser built a tower in Uig which became known as 'Captain Frasers Folly' (see Figure 3). It still sits on the headland south of Uig harbour, in northern Snizort parish (not far from Tallanantain). The tower is a two-storey circular structure which was built in a Romanesque style. It has five arched windows and two narrow cross-shaped lancets. The tower has no defensive or military function. It is commonly thought that the tower was used by Fraser's factor (manager), Harry MacDonald, as a place to collect rents and taxes from Fraser's tenants. It was built purely as a symbol of power and wealth, designed to intimidate Fraser's tenants. According to Ross (2024) many of the locals today still equate the tower with the Clearances.

Fraser charged the crofters unreasonably high rents and gave them no security of tenure. The way the crofting system was structured meant that the crofters had no incentive to improve their homes. The rent they paid was estimated on the value of the house and land. Any improvements meant rent increases, which they couldn't afford. They could also be evicted at the end of any year and any improvements they had made would go to the landlord. The tenants were in a precarious position, and they had no claim to compensation (Napier Commission, 1883).

Figure 3. Captain Fraser's Folly, 2022 (Photo by Gail Barnes, 3 May 2022, Uig, Isle of Skye, Scotland).

Fraser is notorious for his part in the final stages of the Highland Clearances, when he evicted large numbers of tenants from his estate to make room for sheep grazing. These Clearances included the eviction of the Camerons, who were mentioned above, from the crofting settlements of Tallanantain and Balnacnock (Notice to remove tenants of Tallanantain, Peinvraid and Balnacnock, 1865).

Eventually, there was considerable agitation and pushback by crofters in the 1880's on Skye, which came to be known as the 'Crofters War' (McKenzie, 2013). The government stepped in and held the Napier Commission (1883), which was a *Royal Commission of Inquiry into the Conditions of the Crofters and Cottars in the Highlands and Islands of Scotland*. However, the people grew tired of government inaction and some of the tenants on Captain Fraser's estate held rent strikes in November 1884 during which the crofter's withheld payment of their rents and some of them occupied grazing land. Fraser called in the Royal Navy to try to break the strike, but no resolution ensued and the navy withdrew (Reid, 2013).

This heralded the beginning of change, and a century of land reform legislation ensued. It is beyond the scope of this story to explore any further the changes that followed, but once the crofters had land-security they immediately started to improve their land and build more substantial houses. Needless to say, Fraser was not well regarded by his tenants, or the people of Skye generally. Despite his bad reputation among the local people, in 1885 Captain Fraser was promoted to the rank of Lieutenant-Colonel ('Kilmuir Estate', 2015).

By linking the lives of Catherine's ancestors with the socio-economic and political forces which dominated the era, it is clear to see the destruction these forces exerted on a vulnerable population. The poor tenant farmers and crofters, many of who had no formal education and lived a subsistence existence, experienced great insecurity including potentially life-changing displacement. As individuals and families who had been dispersed and dislocated, the poor crofters didn't hold any sway over the existing landed gentry.

However, once the crofters started to organise themselves into a larger group and hold rental strikes, the establishment began to take notice of their grievances. This was an important moment in the history of land relations on Skye and in Scotland more generally.

Despite the poverty and insecurity, which Catherine's ancestors and many others like them experienced, their lives were based on a rich history which informed their traditions and enriched their day-to-day existence. This history formed the very foundation of their close family ties and afforded them a proud cultural identity, which they passed on to future generations. This is where Catherine's own story begins at Kendram on the Isle of Skye.

Chapter 2
Catherine McKinnon

*Kendram - Catherine's childhood - poverty and famine - Rev Dr
John Dunmore Lang - the Midlothian - Angus McDonald (2)*

Kendram

Kendram (see Figure 4) is sometimes spelt 'Kendrom' or *Ceandrom*. The
name is Gaelic and means 'head of the ridge' ('The Gazetteer for Scotland',
2021). Kendram is on the Trotternish Peninsula in the northern part of Skye
and is in the Parish of Kilmuir. The Kilmaluag (*Cill Moluaig*) River runs
down beside the settlement. There are a number of other crofting settlements
surrounding Kendram including Balmacqueen, Conista, Aird and Solitote

**Figure 4. The remains of St Molaug's and the Kilmalaug cemetery, looking back
towards Kendram, 2022.** Many of Catherine's relatives are buried in unmarked graves in
the cemetery (Photo by Gail Barnes, 3 May 2022, Kilmalaug, Isle of Skye, Scotland).

('The Gazetteer for Scotland', 2021). Like the settlement of Tallanantain, Kendram was also initially part of Lord MacDonald's Estate and became a crofting settlement after Blackadder's (1811) report. Kendram is particularly relevant to Catherine's life, as it is where she was born and spent her formative years living with her parents, siblings and extended family.

Catherine's father Ewen (Hugh) MacKinnon (1774-1861) (Catherine Ballard, 1904), was the child of John MacKinnon and Dorcas MacLeod, and he was born in Kilmuir (Ewen MacKinnon, 1861). Little is known about Catherine's paternal grandparents, or their ancestry. Also, there are no surviving records indicating where Catherine's paternal grandparents were living, so we don't know how long the family were living in the Kendram area. However, there was a Donald MacKinnon renting farmland from the MacDonald Estate in 1778 and 1802 at Kendram before the crofts were established (Kendram Rental Table, 1718-1823). Donald may well be related to Catherine, but it is not certain. As was mentioned earlier, before the crofting system began families and small communities would often work land together in a co-operative system. Only one or two names would go on the rental record and the others would be sub-tenants. This makes it very difficult to trace individuals.

There are rental records which remain from Lord MacDonald's Estate, indicating that Catherine's father paid rent on Lot 1, at Kendram, from at least May 1823 (Kendram Rental Table, 1718-1823). He was most probably there some years earlier as one of the original eleven tenants, when Kendram first became a crofting settlement. The earlier rental records have not survived the test of time.

We know that Catherine was born in 1823 at Kendram (Catherine Ballard, 1904). Her birth is not listed in the Old Parish Registers (OPRs), so the exact date is unknown. The OPR for Kilmuir parish didn't begin until approximately 1823 and, even then, the registration of births, deaths and marriages was limited and haphazard ('Finding your Family', 2024). However, as we will see later in the story, Catherine was registered as thirteen years old on the passenger list for the *Midlothian*, which sailed on the 8th

August 1837. This means her birthday must have been in the later part of the year.

Three of Ewen McKinnon's siblings also settled at Kendram on crofts. Ewen's sister Marion MacKinnon, her husband Murdo Campbell and their children, lived on Lot 8, Kendram (Murdo Campbell, 1841). Ewen's brother, Charles McKinnon (Charles MacKinnon, 1864), lived at Kendram on half of Lot 9 (Kendram Rental Table, 1823-1855). Charles was married to Marion MacIntosh. However, at the time of the 1841 census, Charles was a widower with seven children aged from two to twenty (Charles McKinnon, 1841). Ewen also had another sister living at Kendram. Her name was also Catherine and she was married to John Campbell. They lived on Lot 11 (Jonathan Campbell, 1888).

There were originally eleven lots at Kendram. Later, when times were hard or when children grew up and married, many of the lots were divided in half, or even into thirds. By the 1841 census there were twenty-two lots, making it more and more difficult for each family to make a sustainable living on ever smaller pieces of land.

Catherine's siblings

Catherine was Ewen and Flora McKinnon's fourth child and she had five siblings. The McKinnon children were John, Ann, Dorcas, Catherine, Margaret *(Peigi)* and Angus William ('Catherine McKinnon's Family', n.d.). Her oldest sibling, John, was born in 1808 (John McKinnon, 9 January 1872). Margaret was born on the 1st of June in 1828 and the youngest sibling, Angus William McKinnon, was born on the 5th of May in 1830. The two youngest were both born at Kendram and registered in the OPR (Margaret Mackinnon, 1828, p.4). Three of Catherine's siblings - John, Margaret and Angus - all eventually immigrated to Australia and we will talk more about them later. Only her sisters, Ann and Dorcas, remained on Skye.

According to the 1851 and 1871 census, Catherine's oldest sister Ann McKinnon was born in 1810 in 'Kilmuir' (Ann Macleod, 1861) (although the 1851 census says she was born in Snizort Parish (Ann Macleod, 1851)). Census data has been collected every ten years in Scotland, beginning in 1801. However, little remains of individual datum before the 1841 census (Census Returns, 2023). The 1841 census was four years after Catherine left Skye, so she doesn't appear in that record. However, the census data does include her parents and her two sisters, Ann and Dorcas who remained on Skye.

Catherine's sister Ann, married William MacLeod who was the son of John Macleod and Betsy Matheson (John MacLeod, 5 January 1883). Like the McKinnon family, the MacLeod family were also original tenants of the Kendram crofts (Kendram Rental Table, 1823-1855). They may well have been related to Catherine's paternal grandmother, Dorcas MacLeod. Ann and William both grew up at Kendram. Their first child, Donald MacLeod, was born in Kilmuir parish in about 1833 (Donald MacLeod, 1891). Their children were Donald, John, Betsy, Hugh, Christian, Murdoch, Catherine and Alexander. The 1841 census has Ann, William, their son Donald, and the next two children John and Betsy living at Conista. Conista was the crofting settlement next to Kendram (William MacLeod, 1841). They hadn't moved very far.

Catherine's second oldest sister Dorcas, was born in 1815 at 'Kilmuir by Uig' (Dorcas Ross, 1851). There were two settlements in Skye called Kilmuir. So, sometimes this particular Kilmuir was referred to as the Kilmuir which is near Uig in order to differentiate it from the other one near Dunvegan. Dorcas was known by the Gaelic name *Gormhail,* (Dorcas Gormhail Ross, 18 June 1855(a)). According to Google Translate the word *Gorm* in Gaelic means 'blue'. I assume then, that she had blue eyes.

Dorcas married Ranald Ross in 1838 (Dorcas Ross(b), 18 June 1855). Ranald's parents were John Ross (a tenant farmer) and Margaret (Peigi) MacDonald (Ranald Ross, 1 June 1875). Ranald was known in Gaelic as *Raghnall Buidhe,* which means 'Ranald the yellow-haired' as he had blond hair (Tolmie, 1911(b)). Dorcas and Ranald also settled on a croft at

Kendram (Dorcas Ross, 1851) where he worked their croft with 'industry and intelligent method' (Tolmie, 1911(b). So, Dorcas like Ann, didn't move far from her parents or the known world. Sadly though, Dorcas died when she was in her early forties, leaving her husband Ranald a widower with five children. We will talk more about Dorcas's death later in the story.

Mary Ross

Dorcas and Ranald's second child, Mary Ross *(Mairi Ranuill)* who was born in about 1848, was Catherine's niece, although they never met. Mary was a housemaid for the Skene family in Portree and then for Mrs Margaret Hope Tolmie. She also worked for Mrs Tolmie's daughter, Francis (Fanny) Tolmie, in her home in Oban, and then also in Edinburgh. Francis Tolmie was a well-known Scottish folklorist who collected Gaelic songs (Bassin, 1977). Mary, who was only seven when her mother died, never married (Mary Ross, 1926). According to Ethel Bassin (1977, p.76), Mary Ross was tall, intelligent, witty and an excellent cook. Bassin also suggests that Mary was fluent in Gaelic and had an excellent knowledge of Gaelic culture but her English was 'sketchy' (see Figure 5).

Mary contributed thirty-eight of the one hundred and five songs in Tolmie's collection of Gaelic songs called *One Hundred and Five Songs of Occupation from the Western Isles of Scotland*. The collection was originally published in 1911 in the *Journal of the Folk-Song Society*. Individual songs have since been published in various other sources.

Like Mary, Francis Tolmie never married. She was educated, the daughter of a Tacksman from the MacLeod Estate in Skye (the western side of Skye), and she had a wealthy circle of friends. However, the preface she wrote to the original publication of songs states that the material is 'merely the notes and fire-side memories of two friends [*herself and Mary Ross*], natives of the Hebrides, who are fully aware of many gaps amongst the verses' (Tolmie, 1911(a)). Mary shared many of her childhood memories with Tolmie over these fire-side chats which help to illustrate the nature of life at Kendram.

Figure 5. Mary Ross, n.d. Mary was Catherine's niece (Photo courtesy of Mary Ann Bowdler nee Budge & Amina Hussain).

Mary's father, Ranald Ross, remarried a woman called Anne MacLeod (Ann MacLeod, 25 December 1856). Anne was twenty-three years old and Ranald was forty-five. Mary told Francis Tolmie (1911(b)) that her step mother Anne, who was a weaver, spent many hours working at her loom. As a result, it often fell to Mary to look after her younger siblings. There were many siblings, cousins and friends for the children to play with at Kendram. According to Mary (cited in Tolmie, 1911(b)), the children used to 'run about the hamlet...entering the neighbours' houses', singing and playing games with each other. Mary also said that she sang traditional songs and lullabies from her own childhood, such as 'cradle songs and *"puirt-a-beul"* (vocal tunes for dancing)' to soothe or to entertain the younger children.

Mary also learned many of the songs she passed on to Tolmie while she was sitting 'waulking' with the women at Kendram (Tolmie, 1911(b)). Waulking is a traditional process whereby women full or felt woollen cloth. They would spend many hours singing as they sat around together cleaning and thickening the local homespun wool. The women would rhythmically beat the cloth on a hard wooden table or board, to shrink and soften it, singing as they worked (Historic Britain, 2017).

Usually, one woman would sing a verse and the other women would then join in the chorus. The words were sometimes improvised by the singer leading, or parts of older songs included. As the wool softened, the tempo of the song increased often causing much laughter among the women as they worked. It was considered bad luck to repeat any of the songs, so there were many different songs which came out of waulking and the songs often had many verses. Apparently, it could take a good hour to get a single cloth in the right condition (Purser, 20 July 2020).

Mary Ross described her father Ranald as 'a grave and usually silent man', who would quietly sing rhythmic, solemn chants from ancient Celtic prose in the evening, as he mended the horse harness and fishing nets, or plaited straw, or twisted heather to make ropes (Tolmie, 1911(b)). She also talked about her father Ranald, and her grandfather, sitting around at the Kilmalaug Inn with the other local men. The Kilmalaug Inn was a thatched building, just across the way from Kendram which was 'licensed to sell spirits, Porter and ales.' It also had some accommodation for the occasional traveller caught in a storm (Ordnance Survey Field Notebooks Inverness-shire – Isle of Skye (Kilmuir), 1875).

According to Mary, the menfolk at the Inn would talk and sing as they passed the bottle around. Mary remembered how Alexander MacDonald would sing songs about the sea, or sing of his loyalty to the prince and chief (Clanranald) of the Jacobite uprising. She also recounted Duncan Ban

MacIntyre singing tenderly of his love for the mountains and moor, where the deer had been replaced by sheep (Tolmie, 1911(b)).

Late in her life, Mary Ross returned to Kendram to live with her younger brother Alex Ross and his wife Mary Ann on their family croft at Kendram. Alex was apparently known in Gaelic as *Alasdair Raghnall Buidhe* (Hussain, 9 February 2023,). As was mentioned earlier *buidhe* means yellow-haired so, like his father, he must have also had blond hair. Mary Ross died at Kendram in 1926, at the age of eighty-five (Mary Ross, 11 April 1926).

Like Mary's mother Dorcas, Catherine and her other siblings would have also heard the same songs being sung that Mary refers to and Francis Tolmie published. When she was growing up, Catherine would have also sat for many hours, waulking the cloth with her mother, sisters, aunts and cousins at Kendram, singing and laughing as they worked. In turn, Catherine would have sung these Gaelic folk songs to her own children in Australia, in order to softly sing them to sleep or to entertain them as they played. The songs would have elicited memories of her parents, and her own childhood on Skye. No doubt, the memories were bittersweet for a childhood long gone.

Times were hard

The McKinnon croft where Catherine and her siblings spent their childhood years, had four acres of land (Ewen McKinnon, 1841). The house was described as having 'two rooms with one or more windows' (Flora McKinnon, 1861) (see Figure 6). When Catherine was growing up there were eight members of the family living in the two rooms.

A traditional house on a croft such as theirs was known as a 'blackhouse'. The McKinnon's blackhouse was made with very thick, stone walls for insulation against the harsh weather. Some blackhouses had roofs made from peat. However, the roof on their house was most probably thatched, made from readily available local reeds. Thatch rooves were usually weighted down with stones hanging around the edge. Dried peat was burned in the fire rather than wood, as there were very few trees. According to Johnson (1773), it was common for the farm animals to share one end of a blackhouse with the family. In the long winter evenings, the light was from the blazing peat fire or a '*crusie*' or lamp fed with a wick and home-made fish oil' (Tolmie, 1911(b)). A blackhouse was usually dark, filled with smoke from the fire, and cramped. Also, according to Mclan (1845), many people were barefoot all year, no matter what the season. Most people would have been constantly cold and damp.

Figure 6. Believed to be the remains of the McKinnon house at Kendram, 2022. The original two room, stone walled blackhouse would have had a thatched roof made from local reeds (Photo by Gail Barnes, 3 May 2022, Kendram, Isle of Skye, Scotland).

Catherine's family were poor subsistence crofters who barely eked out a living on the land. The winters were long and cold and the days were short. Snow sometimes covers the ground at Kendram. As a result of the cold winters, crops would only grow in the warmer, summer months. Traditionally, the population had a diet of barley, oats, kale, cheese, milk and occasionally meat or fish. Over a couple of generations, as the Clearances had pushed ever increasing numbers of people to the margins, the potato which grew in poor soil came to provide 80% of their diet. However, the potato is prone to disease particularly in the damp conditions which often prevail on Skye (MacPherson, 2020).

In 1836, after a couple of wet summers and poor crops, a potato blight hit the region. A famine then ravaged the people of Skye, leaving thousands of people starving and many deaths (The Highland Clearances, 2016). Leslie McKinnon (1973) described the 1836 famine. He wrote,

> Half the population of Skye was destitute and starving. Bad weather had destroyed peat stocks. People burned divots from their roofs. Each week the men of some villages met to draw lots to decide whose house should be next taken down for fuel. Destitution had followed eviction, and now famine had made a trinity.

As a result, most of the people on Skye began 1837 with little food to eat and no seeds to plant. Rev Robert MacGregor of Kilmuir wrote in the beginning of 1837, that of the 2,275 people living in Kilmuir parish 'very few would have any food by the end of July' ('Extracts from letters transmitted by Clergymen, Magistrates and others, relative to the present destitution in the Highlands and Islands of Scotland', 1837). Furthermore, a rental record from Lord MacDonald's Estate for 1839, suggests that Catherine's father Ewen, had paid £9.18 for the year in rent. However, he was still in arrears for the 1837/38 year (Rental Ledger, 1837/38/39). Life was hard, and Skye could no longer sustain them all.

In 1837, the Rev Dr John Dunmore Lang initiated a bounty scheme for bringing Scottish emigrants to the NSW colony. On a visit to Britain from NSW where he resided, Rev Lang had convinced Lord Glenelg, a Scotsman who was the Secretary of State for the Colonies, that the Crown land grants fund could be used for an assisted immigration scheme. Under the scheme, Lang recruited Scots and brought them to the colony. Once they were accepted by a Board which was appointed by the Governor of NSW, the new immigrants were issued with a certificate which entitled them to work (Huntsman, 2002).

The NSW Colonial Government bounty scheme had operated to bring immigrants to the colony since 1831 using funds from the Crown land grants. However, the number of Scots travelling to NSW under the scheme had declined to only 134 people in 1834. In the same year, 4954 Scots emigrated to the North American colonies and 2880 went to the United States ('Large Scale Emigration to Australia after 1832', 2023). These destinations were considerably closer to Scotland than NSW, making them more appealing. In comparison, it was a long, and often dangerous, journey to the NSW colony.

'Lang's bounty scheme', as it was known, operated from March 1837 until February 1840. Under Lang's bounty scheme twenty ships sailed direct to NSW from Scottish ports, meaning Scottish emigrants with no resources didn't have to travel far to board ships. Lang's scheme also relaxed the usual criteria associated with assisted migration: older immigrants over thirty-five, families with children and those without skills or trades were accepted ('Large Scale Emigration to Australia after 1832', 2023), although unaccompanied women were not. Women had to be under the protection of a male relative to be eligible for Lang's bounty scheme ('Bounty Immigrants', 3 February 1842, p.2). Lang's scheme made emigration to NSW a desirable proposition for many more people and particularly poor Highlander families.

Rev Lang (Lang, John Dunmore, 1854) assumed credit for the immigration of 4000, mostly destitute, Scottish emigrants from the Highlands and Islands of Scotland after his intervention with Lord Glenelg in 1837. Furthermore, he suggested that;

> hundreds, and even thousands of respectable families and individuals besides, have been induced by my writings, and lectures, and personal intercourse in the Mother Country to leave their native land and to become colonists in Australia.

When he was in Skye, working as an agent of the scheme, Rev Lang was said to be very exuberant and enthusiastically talked up the prospects for the Scottish emigrants if they came to NSW. He had an aspiration for the impoverished Highlanders to make the 'the hills and vales of Australia resound with the wild note of the pibroch and the language of the ancient Gael' (cited in Watson, 1984, p.56). So, it must have seemed a very compelling option for many residents of Skye to migrate to the colony, given there weren't many other choices. Catherine, her brother John and his young family left in search of a better life and a more prosperous future.

The voyage to New South Wales (NSW)

The ship on which Catherine and her kin sailed was called the *Midlothian*. The *Midlothian*, with its 259 passengers, was the third of twenty ships to sail to Australia under Lang's bounty scheme. The ship left the port at Uig, in Loch Snizort on the Isle of Skye, on the 8th of August 1837. They were heading for Sydney. The *Midlothian* had three masts and weighed 414 tons. The ship was under the command of Captain Morrison and the Surgeon Superintendent was Dr Robert Stewart. A Gaelic speaking clergyman, Reverend William McIntyre accompanied the emigrants ("Braemar", 18 February 1939). The emigrants were described as being 'upright Calvinist highlanders' (Dunmore House, n.d.). On the *Midlothian* there were only six unmarried males (this didn't count widowers) and seventeen unmarried females. The rest were families ('Unmarried Male Immigrants', 1837).

Catherine was registered on the passenger list for the ship as thirteen years old and a 'country servant'. She was brought out by 'Her Majesty's Government', and a bounty of £15 Sterling was paid (Catherine McKinnon, 1837). She was travelling with her older brother John McKinnon, and his family, who were also from Kendram. John's wife was Margaret Mathison (Ann McKinnon, 1834) and they had two young children, Ann who was two years old, and one year old John (John McKinnon, 1837).

It must have been difficult for all of the passengers sailing on the *Midlothian* to leave their home, for most of them it was all they had ever known. This is the opening stanza of a very descriptive poem called *An Episode of the Ship Midlothian*. The poem was written by Donald Roderick (Rory) Campbell and published in 1879 in *The Clarence and Richmond Examiner*. Campbell wrote the poem about the voyage on the *Midlothian*, from Skye to Australia, which was the same voyage that Catherine and her kin sailed on.

Around its orb this earth has turned in number forty-two

Since I have bade my native land - my native vale-adieu;

Since in the ship Midlothian we sailed from Isle of Skye

That land where oft my fathers trod, where now their ashes lie,

The sea was calm, the wind was fair, and bright and clear the day

I do remember well. On which we sailed from Snizort Bay;

And as the ship majestically plough'd through the mighty main,

And far behind she left that shore we n'er shall see again.

But while the hills were glimmering still far in the twilight view,

Unto our fatherland we gave a long and last adieu.

But when the darkness cast her mantle o'er each hill and dell,

I laid me down to sleep; but ah my heart did heave and swell,

As well as all that company who left their Highland home

To pioneer Australian wilds where wild men did then roam.

The ship did not stop on the long journey half way around the world. So, it had to carry all of the fresh water, food and other supplies needed to service the 259 passengers (Old Friend, 22 July 1941). There was a lot of sickness on board the ship, including typhus fever and dysentery. Hygiene was poor. Immigrant ships, such as the *Midlothian*, were usually over-crowded and during bad storms passengers in steerage (the lowest deck below the water line), such as Catherine and her kin, would be confined to staying below deck, with little ventilation. Candles and lanterns were a fire risk, so they were often forbidden. Conditions below the deck were dark, cramped and stuffy. They were often perilous ('Journeys to Australia', 2024).

Only five weeks into the voyage off the Cape de Verde Islands, twenty-four of the passengers died, including eighteen children and six women. No adult men died ('The Mid-Lothian', 18 December 1837, p.2). Sadly, Catherine's sister-in-law, Margaret was one of the women who succumbed to disease early on in the voyage (John McKinnon, 1837).

Apparently, after the deaths of the twenty-four passengers, Dr Stewart - the ships doctor - ordered changes to the passengers' food rations. He doubled the oatmeal rations for each passenger, gave everyone extra sugar and banned the use of all animal products in the meals in order to improve the health of the passengers and curb the disease. These measures were successful and no more passengers died on the long journey to the shores of NSW ('The Mid-Lothian', 18 December 1837, p.2).

Dr Stewart later reported to J Denham Pinnock (Denham Pinnock, 1838), who was the first Colonial Agent for Immigration, that once the ship left the tropics the passengers on the *Midlothian* settled into life onboard and they became 'reconciled' with the conditions. He said that a school was run for the children, 'Divine Service' was held every Sunday and the passengers also started to play music and dance in the evenings.

Angus McDonald (2)

Angus McDonald (2), who was to become Catherine's first husband, also came out from Skye to Australia on the same voyage on the *Midlothian*. He travelled with his parents, his six siblings and three children. Angus's (2) mother, Flora McDonald (nee Stewart) was registered on the *Midlothian* passenger list as a 'midwife' who was 'in fair but weak health'. Angus McDonald (1), his father, was listed as a 'cattle doctor' who, upon arrival, was said to be 'confined with pain in his limbs' but was recovering (Angus McDonald, 1837). He could have been suffering from the effects of scurvy which caused aching limbs. Apparently, scurvy was most common in those who had been weakened by dysentery earlier in the voyage ('The Mid-Lothian', 18 December 1837, p.2). It appears that neither of Angus's (2) parents were very well on the journey out from Scotland and they both died in Maitland within a few years of arriving at their new home in NSW ('Generation No.1', n.d.).

Catherine's future husband, Angus (2) and his family were from Skeabost (*Sgeitheabost*) in Snizort parish on the southern tip of Loch Snizort

(*Sniosort*) on the Trotternish Penninsula on the Isle of Skye (Angus McDonald, 1837). Angus (2) had been married on Skye before he left for Australia. His first wife was Flora Ross. It is recorded in the OPR (Angus MacDonald, 1837 p.132) that they were married on the 3 August 1837, which was only five days before Angus (2) left for Australia. However, Flora doesn't appear on the *Midlothian* passenger register. It is possible that Flora Ross, Angus's (2) first wife, died just before the *Midlothian* left Scotland.

Angus (2) and Flora Ross had one child together. Her name was Catherine McDonald. Angus (2) and Flora's baby Catherine, was only nine months old when she set sail on the *Midlothian* with her father. According to the passenger list, she was 'in delicate health' (Catherine McDonald, 1837). Flora also had two other children from a previous marriage: Flora Graham, who was twelve years old and Murdoch Graham, who was nine years old. Both of these children also travelled with their step father, Angus McDonald (2) to Australia.

Angus (2) is registered on the *Midlothian* passenger list as a twenty-seven years old widower, travelling with three children. The Graham children are listed as 'Flora Graham McDonald' and 'Murdoch Graham McDonald' (Angus McDonald, 1837, p.2). So, they were using his last name, at least on the voyage. His marriage to Flora may have been a deathbed marriage so that he could legitimately take the children to NSW. Flora Graham was only a year younger than Catherine McKinnon (her soon to be step-mother), when they set out from Scotland. So, it is also probable that the girls became friends on the voyage.

It is fair to assume that once she left Skye, Catherine never saw her parents again. There is no record of her ever returning to Scotland and her parents remained at Kendram all of their lives. It is impossible to know how she felt about leaving. It is unknown if it was her own choice to leave and seek a better life, or if she forced to leave as there was simply no alternative. She was still very young. However, as well as leaving her parents behind, she also left her childhood on Skye. She was propelled into life as an adult, a life with responsibilities and people who depended on her. We don't know what her expectations and dreams were for her new life, but we do know she had no idea what was ahead.

Thousands of mostly destitute people left Scotland as a result of the Highland Clearances. Each of those who left had a story. Each of them was hoping to forge a more prosperous future for themselves, their families and for future generations. The mass exodus of people from the Highlands was a tragedy, but for those who left it gave them the prospect of a new life. Hope was all but lost for many of the people who remained.

Chapter 3
The Colony of NSW

*The penal colony of NSW - the dispossession of First Nations people
- Aboriginal women as sex slaves - arriving in the colony of NSW
- Catherine is pregnant - heading to Dunmore Estate - the end of
Lang's Bounty Scheme*

The transportation of convicts

The British colony of NSW began in 1788 after the arrival of the First Fleet in Sydney. The year before the First Fleet arrived, the initial boundary of NSW was set in London by drawing a line through the centre of a map of Australia at east of 135 degrees longitude. This meant that when it was first colonised, NSW comprised of the whole of the eastern half of Australia and included what are now Queensland, Victoria, South Australia and Tasmania. It also included New Zealand ('Documenting a Democracy', 2011).

In 1828, the boundary of NSW was moved west to 129 degrees longitude. The western part then became Western Australia. Van Diemen's Land (Tasmania) gained *defacto* independence from NSW in 1824 and full independence in 1856. South Australia was declared an independent colony in 1836, and New Zealand became a separate colony in 1841. Then Victoria separated from NSW in 1851. Queensland was not formally proclaimed a separate colony from NSW until 1859 (Brown, 2024).

Initially, the governing of the colony was overseen by a series of British appointed Governors, beginning with Captain Arthur Phillip from the First Fleet ('History of Democracy in NSW', 2023). NSW began as a penal colony. From the arrival of the First Fleet convicts were sent from Britain by the shipload. Over 160,000 convicts landed on Australian shores from Britain in the eighty years of convict transportation (NSW Migration Heritage Centre, 2010). About 80,000 of those were sent to NSW.

Approximately eighty-five percent of the convicts who were transported to NSW were men, and only fifteen percent were women. About two thirds were English and a third were Irish. There were a small number of Scots and Welsh convicts. Most were given sentences of seven years, fourteen years or were imprisoned for 'the term of their natural lives' ('Convicts Guide', 2024).

Convicts had no rights and were considered government property. They were a source of labour to build roads, buildings and infrastructure. They often worked on chain gangs where they were shackled together. The cat-o-nine tails, was used to enforce discipline. The more educated convicts sometimes worked in government administration roles. Once they had served their sentence or were granted a pardon, they could get jobs or apply for land grants from the Colonial Government (The Convict Experience, 2021).

First Nations people

Australia wasn't an empty land before colonisation. Based on the latest evidence, it is thought that First Nations people had lived on the Australian landscape for 65,000 years prior to European colonisation (Clarkson, Jacobs & Marwick, 2017). There are hundreds of distinct clans and language groups, each with their own traditions, practices and intimate relationships to particular sites. First Nations people were deeply connected to Country and their worldview was embedded in the Dreaming and spiritual law (Lake, 2020, p.51).

Despite the obvious presence of First Nations people, the English colonisers claimed the land was 'uninhabited' and therefore theirs for the taking. There was a general understanding by the English that for land to be 'owned' it needed to be 'improved', and the colonisers did not recognise Aboriginal people as 'improving', or therefore as owning, the land. This notion was based on the idea of the English philosopher, John Locke, who suggested in the late seventeenth century that God had given the world to all, but he required man to work the land. According to Locke, whoever 'in obedience to this command of God, subdued, tilled and sowed' the land 'transformed nature into their own private property' (Lake, 2020, p.104).

One commentator in *The Sydney Herald* ('Crown Lands', 7 November 1838, p.2) suggested 'this country was to them *[the Aborigines]* a common - they bestowed no labour upon the land and that - and that only - it is which gives a right of property in it'. However, pre-colonisation, First Nations people were living with a light footprint, which encompassed a deep and complex understanding of the ecosystem (Sutton & Walshe, 2021). As we have only come to realise in more recent times, as colonisers we were blind to seeing the rich, complex relationship that First Nations people had with the land and the ways in which they 'used' it sustainably. For example, Eric Rolls (1981, p.37) notes that early settlers and explorers of the Hunter Region, frequently observed that 'the hills have a look of a park and grounds laid out'. By the controlled use of fire, Aboriginal people altered the landscape in ways that were sustainable and brought new life to the land.

In order to ensure that First Nations people had no claim to land in the colony the NSW Governor at the time, Major-General Sir Richard Bourke, made an official proclamation on the 10th of October 1835. He asserted *Terra nullius*, declaring that no person could own, sell, buy or assign any land other than through the Crown (Governor Bourke's Proclamation 1835 (UK)). *Terra Nullius* is a Latin expression and means 'nobody's land' (Justice Jagot, 20 October 2017). The proclamation indicated that Australia was empty and nobody had lived there before the British arrived. The proclamation made sure that First Nations people had no rights to land under the law. This didn't change until the 1992 Mabo decision in the High Court of Australia. Governor Bourke's proclamation was made only two years before Catherine arrived in Australia.

Australia was a land undergoing enormous upheaval. In many instances, First Nations people resisted the European invasion and frontier wars broke out. Aboriginal people, resisting invasion of their land, usually attacked settlers in small, agile groups of guerilla resistance. They understood the landscape, and they were adept hunters (Reynolds, 2013). They killed European livestock to eat but also, in the words of William Wiseman (1855 cited in Reynolds, 2013, p.80), NSW Land Commissioner, 'to check the progress of the white men by spearing their sheep and murdering the shepherds' in an attempt to 'drive out the white man' from the 'occupation of their country'. The first Australians never ceded their land, but eventually they did have to accommodate the invaders as they weren't able to fend off men with guns and horses indefinitely.

In some instances, First Nations people worked with the colonisers. They made friends with new settler families and learned to speak English as they worked on farms, often doing menial tasks. Over-time many Aboriginal workers became highly skilled with horses and livestock. At the same time, they attended corroborees, initiation ceremonies, made art and held on to their culture and Country as long as they could before they lost access to traditional land and sacred sites (Karskens, 2020, p.11).

Aboriginal women as sex slaves

Appallingly, to add to the demise of First Nations people at the hands of the white settlers, many white men took Aboriginal women as sex slaves. This violation of women often resulted in sexually transmitted diseases, such as syphilis, becoming rampant in Aboriginal communities. Syphilis in turn could lead to infertility, adding further to the decline of the Aboriginal population (History in the Williams River Valley, n.d.). On the 20th September 1837, in order to try and quash some of the unrest between the Aboriginal people and the new settlers, the NSW Governor, Major General Sir Richard Bourke ('Colonial Secretary's Office', 20 September 1837 p.652) decreed that 'persons in remote districts'...

> ...are not unfrequently guilty of detaining by force in their Huts, and as their companions abroad, black women of the Native Tribes resorting to their neighbourhood, an offence not only in itself of a most heinous and revolting character but in its consequences leading to bloodshed and murder.

The Governor went on to say that all 'persons' participating in this 'abominable and unchristian' behaviour would have their land licenses cancelled and they would then be prosecuted as 'illegal occupiers of the land' ('Colonial Secretary's Office', 20 September 1837 p.652).

However, one example of the inadequacy of the decree took place only a few months later, at a property called Underbank, which was near Dungog in NSW. Underbank was owned by John Lord at the time, but Underbank is a place which will become central to Catherine's life. This incident involved a man called Mr Flitt. Mr Flitt worked for John Lord, as a manager on his Underbank property. Mr Flitt held five Aboriginal women against their will and, after a 'formal complaint by a respectable (white) person' was made on behalf of five Aboriginal men who were the husbands of the women, the Dungog Police Magistrate, Thomas Cook interviewed the Aboriginal men. He described them as 'most intelligent fellows' and said that one of them, Fullam Derby 'is a king and speaks English well'. Cook then sent a note to Mr Flitt about the accusation, which he apparently tore to pieces upon receiving it. Cook then wrote to the Colonial Secretary for advice on how to proceed saying that 'he feared ill blood and foul murder may result' (Cook to Thomson, 14 December 1837). As Williams (2012, p.23) argues, because Mr Flitt did not hold a land licence, the threat of cancellation by the governor was meaningless. The Aboriginal men had tried to engage English law without any success.

It is not known what the outcome of this case was, but it is unlikely that Mr Flitt was arrested. The kidnapping and rape of Aboriginal women often led to retribution or murder of the offenders, by the woman's family. In turn, the Aboriginal people who carried out Traditional Law were then punished which more often than not ended in their own death. The Governor's decree was a good start but it didn't put an end to the kidnap and rape of Aboriginal women. Men on remote properties often felt like they were beyond the reach of the laws that were enacted in Sydney. The NSW colony was a violent place.

Arriving in NSW

Before 1830, not many people arrived in Australia as free-settlers. Those free settlers who came before 1830 were mostly either paupers or outcasts who had been sent to the colonies by their families. The other group of free settlers were wealthy pastoralists who made a lot of money farming using free convict labour (McDonald, 1972). By 1830, there were only 15,700 free settlers and 61,000 convicts living in the colony. However, over the next twenty years, 191,000 free immigrants arrived. The majority of these were given assisted passage through various government assisted immigration schemes (Huntsman, 2002, p.801). In 1837, as part of Lang's Bounty Scheme, Catherine and her kin entered the Australian landscape as free immigrants full of hope for a better future.

After the long journey from Scotland, which took about eighteen weeks, the passengers on the *Midlothian* encountered bad weather as they sailed up the east coast of Australia. So, their ship pulled into Jervis Bay in NSW south of Sydney to take shelter. The next morning, according to Donald MacLeod ('Emigration – New South Wales', 14 July 1838, p.2) who was a passenger on the ship, a 'black man' in a five foot long, bark canoe rowed up to the side of the boat. The man was rowing with two little wooden boards rather than oars and he was sitting on his knees. The man said 'I am not a war man; I am a man of peace'. The passengers gave him biscuits and later that day he returned with his canoe full of fresh fish for them to eat. For the passengers on the *Midlothian*, it was their first encounter with an Aboriginal person, a traditional owner of the land they were going to call home.

Once the weather had cleared, the *Midlothian* sailed into Sydney Harbour, arriving on the 13th December 1837. The newly arrived immigrants disembarked at Port Jackson and spent their first weeks at the immigrant buildings in Bent Street in Sydney ('Braemar', 18 February 1939). The *Midlothian* had been commissioned to return to London with a cargo of wool and was heading to Newcastle three weeks later to load the shipment ('Ship News', 19 December 1837 p.2).

Catherine's life was changing, in many ways. When she arrived in Sydney, she was pregnant. She must have fallen pregnant in the early part of the voyage from Scotland to Australia. Catherine was said to be in 'very good health' at the time of her arrival in Sydney (Catherine McKinnon, 1837). However, she was only thirteen years old and without her parents for support. Catherine was a young girl, and she must have felt very vulnerable on the voyage, particularly once her sister-in-law had died.

It is impossible to know for sure who was the father of her child. It is most likely that Angus McDonald (2) was the father as he later claimed the child as his own. However, it is also possible that another man on the ship had consensual or non-consensual sex with Catherine, during the voyage. Then, Angus (2) may have stepped up and claimed the child in order to help Catherine and himself. Angus (2), was a twenty-seven years old widow when he arrived in NSW and he already had two children and a young baby in his care. It certainly would have been convenient for him to find a healthy, young woman to help him with the children, already in his care. Also, Catherine's youth and the age gap between her and Angus (2) was not unheard of at the time.

Whatever the circumstances of her pregnancy, Catherine arrived in NSW pregnant and unmarried. The bounty was only paid by the Government if an immigrant was given an Entitlement Certificate by the Immigration Board upon arrival. One of the stipulations for receiving an Entitlement Certificate was for the immigrant to be deemed to be of good character. According to Shultz (21 December 1971), single women who arrived in Sydney pregnant were considered to be of immoral character and therefore undesirable for immigration. Given her age, Catherine herself may not have even been aware that she was pregnant on her arrival. Whether she realised it or not, the bounty was paid for her, meaning the Immigration Board were unaware of her condition and she remained under the supervision of her brother John, for the time being at least (Catherine McKinnon, 1837).

On the 17th of December 1837, the first Sunday after the boat load of Scottish immigrants had arrived in Australia, the passengers attended the first Gaelic church service to be held in Australia, and probably the southern hemisphere. The service was held at Scots Church in Sydney where 'prayers and praise were offered up to the Almighty for bringing them safely to their new home' ('Braemar', 18 February 1939). Rev MacIntyre, who had journeyed from Skye with the passengers on the *Midlothian*, told the new arrivals in a rousing sermon 'that they were going forth to extend, not the domain and the customs of the Celt, but the kingdom of Zion' (Watson, 1984, p.57). According to *The Sydney Gazette* ('Ship News', 19 December 1837, p.2), the 'scene was indescribably affecting'.

On their arrival in Australia, the Scottish immigrants from the *Midlothian* claimed to government officials in Sydney that they had been told before they left Scotland that they would be resettled as one community. They argued that as most of the group only spoke Gaelic, they needed to stay together with their own Gaelic speaking minister. This request was initially denied by the government. However, upon an application to the governing NSW Legislative Council, it was decided that they would be located together as a group ('Application from the Emigrants per Ship Midlothian to be Located in One District', 29 December 1837).

Initially, John Eales an extensive landholder in the colony, was engaged to settle the group on his estate on the junction of the Williams and Hunter rivers. The arrangement was for five years at low rent, after which time the rent would increase. Eales offered to advance them twelve months rations and assist in the building of a school and a church. This so called 'experiment' was to be the first of its kind in the colony ('Domestic Intelligence', 13 January 1838). However, a deputation from the Highlanders went to inspect Eales' property and decided to decline his offer ('The Emigrants, Residents in the Government Domain', 26 February 1838). The land was flood prone, was heavily timbered and had no elevation for house sites. Also, there was no fresh water. All in all, it was thought to be unsuitable for settlement (Dunmore Lang, 1841, p.2). Seemingly, Eales was known as 'unscrupulous' and a 'rogue' (Walsh, 2020, p.1), so it was probably for the best.

A better offer

Rev Lang's brother, Andrew Lang, then offered to settle the families on his land at Dunmore Estate, near Paterson in the Hunter Valley. Andrew Lang offered the Highlanders fifteen to twenty acres per family which would be rent free for the first four years-as long as they agreed to clear the land. After that, the rent would be twenty-five shillings per acre. On the 19 January 1838, Donald Gillies and Donald McMillan accepted Lang's offer on behalf of the group ('Memorandum of Agreement between Mr Andrew Lang and Donald Gillis and Donald McMillan', 19 January 1838).

Due to the long wait for the matter to be decided, many of the group of Scots had already found work elsewhere. Less than half of the original number of *Midlothian* families, including thirty-two males, twenty-five females and forty-four children under the age of ten, were to settle at Dunmore. The families who accepted the offer included the Beaton, Gillies, McCauley, McKay, McLeod, McMillan, McWilliam, McLennan, McRae, McIntosh, McSwan, McQueen and of course the McDonald and McKinnon families.

However, there was some controversy as to whether the whole thing had been orchestrated by Rev Lang from the start, to enable his brother Andrew to settle the tenant farmers on his land at government expense (Dunmore House, 2018). There was a labour shortage in the colony at the time and the Highlanders provided a ready workforce. By settling the tenant farmers on his land, Andrew Lang was able to get more of his extensive estate cleared and under cultivation without having to pay for the labour.

This suspicion was expressed in a letter which Governor George Gipps wrote in a despatch on the 20th of July 1838 (cited in Dunmore House, 2018) to Lord Glenelg, the Secretary of State for the Colonies back in Britain. He wrote that...

> ...considerable dissatisfaction has been expressed in this Colony at the manner in which a number of Emigrants [from] the ship "Midlothian" were disposed of, they having been settled as a Body and thus become occupiers of land on their own account, instead of being forced to work for wages as farm labourers. One suspects the "considerable dissatisfaction" was felt by other landed gentry

deprived of the opportunity to exploit these new migrants and jealous of Andrew Lang's windfall.

Despite the controversy, the new settlers left Sydney for Dunmore Estate. Catherine's brother John McKinnon, was one of the Scottish immigrants who was enlisted to work at Dunmore Estate as a tenant farmer - and this included his sister Catherine (Correspondence from The Honourable Colonial Secretary to the Immigration Office, Sydney, 8 February 1838). The Highlanders had found their new home.

The group set off on the steam boats, the *Tamar* and the *Sophia Jane*, first traversing the coast to Newcastle and then up the Hunter River to Morpeth. Morpeth was within two miles of Dunmore Estate where they were to settle ('Braemar', 18 February 1939). Each family was given two months of rations (meat, bread, tea and sugar) by the government and transported to their new home at the governments expense ('Correspondence from The Honourable Colonial Secretary to the Immigration Office', Sydney, 8 February 1838).

As the number of families who were going to stay at Dunmore had dwindled to such an extent, the Rev MacIntyre did not join them. He stayed in Sydney where there was a much larger congregation of Gaelic speaking Scots who needed his ministrations. It was decided that Dunmore Estate would be attended weekly by the presbyterian minister, Rev Robert Blain of Maitland. However, Rev Blain only spoke English, so it was agreed that Rev MacIntyre would also journey to Dunmore once a quarter to give a sermon in Gaelic ('Domestic Intelligence', 7 March 1838, p.2).

The end of Lang's bounty scheme

Not everyone agreed with Lang's approach to the selection of immigrants for his bounty scheme to NSW. Some people, such as J Denham Pinnock, the Colonial Agent for Immigration, were not in favour of importing families accompanied by older adults who had very little labour left in them, and young dependent children. Pinnock argued that immigrant families with only one wage earner, and so many unproductive mouths to feed, were a burden on colonial society ('Immigration', 4 July 1839, p.3). He suggested that government bounty schemes were importing immigrants who, had they arrived on private ships, would not have satisfied the requirements for the payment of a bounty (Denham Pinnock, 3 July 1839, p.2).

Pinnock (Denham Pinnock, 1838) remarked in a report to the Immigration Office that the immigrants on the *Midlothian* had too many young children 'attached' to them. He argued that, as a consequence of being in large family groups, they refused low paid positions and some of them had to be 'compelled to leave the *[government]* barracks'. Others, he noted, such as the immigrants who went to Dunmore Estate, remained in the barracks at the government's expense, well beyond the usual one month, waiting for the best job offer.

Pinnock believed that government assisted immigrants should only be young adults without children who, he suggested, could more easily turn their hand to new kinds of work and would be most valuable to the colony for as long as possible. Even so, Pinnock conceded in an 1838 report to Governor Gipps, that all of the immigrants who had arrived that year had found suitable positions around the colony (Denham Pinnock, 3 July 1839, p.2).

From 1840, immigration to the colony became centralised under the Colonial Land and Emigration Board (CLEC). Once the CLEC was established, the British government controlled and monitored the suitability of potential immigrants. In 1841, the last year of full-scale bounty immigration to NSW, ninety-nine ships arrived in Sydney and Port Phillip Bay. Overall, these ships carried 19,523 bounty immigrants and 3,677 unassisted immigrants. The bounty immigrants, including children, were comprised of 4,563 natives of England, 1,616 natives of Scotland and 13,344 Irish passengers. 10,009 of these immigrants were Protestants, 9,476 were Roman Catholic, 37 were Jews and one person was a member of no religion ('Mr. Merewether's Immigration Report for 1841', 4 June 1842, p.2).

The Government Bounty schemes ceased at the end of 1841, with the last ship arriving in early 1842. This was due in large part to the beginning of an economic recession in the colony. However, there were also sectarian qualms about the number of Roman Catholics arriving in the colony. The wave of Catholic bounty immigrants from the south and west of Ireland in 1841, who were sent out by the CLEC, had spurred suspicions that Australia was being inundated by a 'swarm' of lowly, depraved Irish Catholics.

This fear of 'Catholic ascendancy' was based on a general disparagement of Irish Catholics by the mostly wealthy, British Protestant landholders in the colony who were supported in their views by Rev Lang. These men were against accepting Irish Catholic immigrants and argued that their importation in such numbers had to stop ('Colonial Politics', 9 December 1841, p.1). A variety of private and mixed assisted schemes started again in the late 1840s, but they didn't return to the levels previously seen in the colony.

The ability to attract British emigrants to the colony varied at different times depending on the prevailing economic conditions, and the perceived desirability of travelling to the NSW colony. Assisted immigration schemes, such as Lang's, were based on the idea that Britain was over-populated and could not sustain the population it had, yet alone any increase. At the same time Lang, and others like him, believed that respectable Protestant working-class families were needed to fill labour shortages on farms and businesses in the colony. In this way, Catherine and the other passengers from the *Midlothian* who headed to Andrew Lang's property at Dunmore Estate, had found a new home. Andrew Lang had also found the labour he needed to work his land in a time of labour shortages.

By allowing children and older adults to travel, Lang was able to entice the Scots, including those with large extended families, to make the long journey to NSW. Family and community ties were strong, particularly among the Scots. As we will see with Catherine's family, once immigrants successfully settled in Australia, other family members soon followed. As time went on, many of these respectable, working-class immigrants, like Catherine and her kin, participated in the growth of the colony. However, the *Midlothian* 'experiment' of settling a large group of passengers together in one location, didn't continue. Catherine's experience of settling with a ready-made community of people from her homeland on Dunmore Estate was unusual, certainly not the rule. Nevertheless, her emigration to the colony was part of a broader process where immigration was seen as essential to the development of NSW.

Chapter 4
Catherine McDonald

A new life - the Wonnarua Nation and traditional food sources - bushrangers - the end of transportation - marriage - child mortality - more children

Life on Dunmore Estate

Dunmore Estate was originally owned by George Lang, the brother of Andrew and Rev Lang. George was granted 1000 acres of land in 1821 on the banks of the Yimmang, or Paterson River. However, George died only a few years later in 1824 and his grant passed to his brother, Andrew Lang. Later the same year, Andrew Lang was also given a grant of 1,280 acres which he selected on land about thirty miles further up the river from George's existing grant. Very little happened on either property until 1827, when Andrew Lang decided to settle on his brother's grant (Lang, 1834, p.117). George Lang had originally named the grant 'Dunmore' after his mother, Mary Lang (nee Dunmore), and Andrew Lang kept the name (Dunmore House, 2018).

Around 1830-33, Andrew Lang and his father William Lang built the main house on the estate, mostly using convict labour. The two-storey, Georgian style stone house was positioned prominently on a hill between Maitland and the Paterson River overlooking a lagoon. It was constructed around an internal courtyard with partly enclosed flagged verandas on all four of the exterior sides (see Figure 7). The Lang's named their new home, Dunmore House (Dunmore House, 2018).

In 1834, Andrew Lang added to the estate. He purchased land which had belonged to Standish Lawrence Harris. Harris had arrived in the colony in 1823 and was engaged as a Civil Architect by the Colonial Secretary, Major Goulburn ('Law Intelligence', 1 July 1833, p.3). Harris was given a Crown land grant of 2000 acres in 1823, which he called Goulburn Grove Estate. Ten years later Harris became insolvent. As a result, Andrew Lang was able to buy an additional 1400 acres of land at Goulburn Grove from Harris which bordered on Dunmore Estate. The additional land meant Andrew Lang's estate had five miles of river frontage, making it a very lucrative property. However, the new acquisition of land needed clearing. It was covered in thick bush and parts of it was heavily forested with large trees (Dunmore House, 2018). A few years later, when Catherine and the remaining passengers from the *Midlothian* arrived, they were settled on this part of Dunmore Estate as tenant farmers. It is an area which is now known as 'Largs'.

Figure 7. Residence of And'w [ie Andrew] Lang Esqr., Paterson's River, New South Wales, c1837 (Robert Russell, circa1837, Residence of And'w [ie Andrew] Lang Esqr., Paterson's River, New South Wales, *National Library of Australia*, PIC Drawer 62, R7211, No. 2448951).

Not long after they had arrived in NSW Catherine's brother, John McKinnon, had successfully applied to the Female Orphan School near Parramatta to take his daughter, Ann (John MacKinnon, 1839). Ann was two and a half and she was described as 'a very delicate child'. John was unable to care for her adequately at the same time as make a success of farming (Correspondence to the Board of the Orphan Schools, December 1837).

The Female Orphan School at Parramatta was opened in 1818, and it was the first state welfare institution in NSW. The mission of the school was 'to train 'orphaned' girls with the skills they would need to work as domestic servants and escape the life of poverty, idleness, immorality and prostitution that would otherwise befall them' ('Female Orphan School', 2017, p.3). Even though it was called an 'Orphan School', two-thirds of the girls had at least one living parent. There were many reasons girls were admitted to the school which included the children of widowed or single parents whose parents were unable to care for them, as in young Ann's case. The daughters of convicts and itinerant workers and some Aboriginal girls were also admitted on the recommendation of a member of the clergy (Bubacz, 2007).

John also tried to have his young son John, who was about twelve months old, admitted to the Male Orphan School, but was told he would be 'required to provide for him himself' (Correspondence to the Board of the Orphan Schools, December 1837). The Male Orphan School, which was located in Liverpool, usually only took boys who were between the age of seven and ten. They were providing the boys with training, so they could be apprenticed out to work ('Male Orphan School', 2012). As a result, they probably didn't have the facilities to care for such a young child and he must have kept John with him at Dunmore Estate.

Angus McDonald (2), Catherine's future husband, was also one of the *Midlothian* passengers engaged by Andrew Lang to work as a tenant farmer on Dunmore Estate (Correspondence from The Honourable Colonial Secretary to the Immigration Office, Sydney, 8 February 1838). Angus (2) had baby Catherine in his care when he arrived in the colony. He also tried to have her placed in the Female Orphan School. However, as was the case with young John, he was told by the Board of the Orphan School that he would be 'required to provide for her himself' (Correspondence to the Board of the Orphan Schools, December 1837).

In 1821 there were sixty girls at the Female Orphan School, but by 1834 there were over 170 girls. Most of the girls admitted were aged between three and thirteen (Bubacz, 2007). Due to the high demand for places, many applications - such as the one from Angus (2) - were denied.

In another written correspondence, from the Colonial Secretary to the Immigration Office, it was said that Angus (2) had an adult male residing with him. As children were only counted by the colonial authorities, as those under ten years of age, this would have most likely been his stepson, Murdoch Graham. There is no indication in the correspondence of his stepdaughter Flora, who would have been two years older (Correspondence from The Honourable Colonial Secretary to the Immigration Office, Sydney, 8 February 1838) and therefore considered an adult by the authorities.

Perhaps Catherine looked after young John and baby Catherine while the men cleared the land and planted wheat. As her young body changed, Catherine's pregnancy would have been visible by the time they settled at Dunmore. The child growing inside her could no longer be ignored. So presumably Catherine moved in with Angus (2) at this time and they set about establishing themselves in their new home.

The following is a description of life for the Scottish immigrants, once they had settled at Dunmore. The description was given by Rev Lang in a letter to Mr John Bowie in Edinburgh. The letter was later published in *The Sydney Herald* (Dunmore Lang, 1 March 1842, p.4).

According to Rev Lang,

> My brother's estate... consists of about 2,500 acres of land, of which about 1,500 are alluvial land, formed by successive depositions from the river, of the first quality, and of the utmost fertility; and the portion of it on which the Highlanders are settled is within two miles of the village of Morpeth or Greenhills, from which there is a daily communication by steam-boats with the town of Sydney, which, of course, affords an eligible market for farm produce of every description. Alluvial land, when clear of timber, in that neighbourhood, has been let at as high a rental as 30s per acre; but the terms on which the Highlanders were settled were as follows;

Small farms, of from twelve to thirty acres, were measured off to each family – partly clear land, and partly wooded. Leases of these farms were granted them for seven years, at a rate of 1 pound per acre of yearly rental for the clear land – the wooded land being rent free for four years. Rations or provisions, with implements of agricultural labour were also advanced to them on credit, till they should be enabled to pay for them from the produce of their land. The Highland settlement, which was known in the neighbourhood by the name of Skye, was formed in the month of January, 1838; some of the Highlanders preferring to have their land all wooded, that they might sit rent free for four years, and others to have it all clear, that they might have it immediately under cultivation. Houses, tolerably comfortable in some instances, were easily erected by means of saplings found in the neighbourhood – the roof consisting of reeds or bark.

Three or four months after they had arrived at Dunmore, Catherine gave birth to her first child, a son, who she named Angus McDonald (3). The exact date of his birth is unknown, but baby Angus (3) was baptised on the 27th of May 1838 by the Presbyterian Minister, Rev Blain who regularly attended Dunmore ('Catherine McKinnon's Family', n.d.). Also, sometime in 1838, baby Catherine - the child of Angus (2) and his first wife - died ('Generation No.2', n.d.). As mentioned earlier, she was very young when they left Scotland and she was described as being 'in delicate health' on the voyage. There is no record of her death.

The *Act* requiring the registration of births, deaths and marriages in the NSW colony wasn't passed until late 1855. The requirement to register these life events commenced on 1 March 1856 ('*Registration Act 1855 No34a*', 30 December 1855). Therefore, before this date many births, deaths and marriages were not registered and baby Catherine's death may never have been officially recorded.

Despite their loss, Catherine and Angus (2) settled into life as tenant farmers with their young son. It turned out that 1838 was a good year for the wheat crop at Dunmore, and it gave the new settlers a decent start (Dunmore Lang, 7 September 1841, p.2). The new settlers had to work hard to make the most of their new home and they faced many challenges, but also many opportunities.

Rev Lang (Dunmore Lang, 1 March 1842, p.4), states that once their crops were in,

> ...those of them who were inclined to be industrious obtained employment at remunerating wages – either on my brother's property or on others in the neighbourhood. By this means, most of them acquired a little money for the purchase of pigs and poultry, and, in some instances, even of cows.

Rev Blain preached at Dunmore Estate on a weekly basis to upwards of eighty people. Initially, there wasn't a church building at Dunmore, so he preached outdoors. According to one observer,

> His place of worship being a place cleared partly by nature and partly by art, in the middle of the thick bush, the lofty trees of the of the primaeval forest being the pillars of his temple, and its vaulted ceiling the blue skies ('Domestic Intelligence', 7 March 1838, p.2).

Then, later that year, Andrew Lang built a brick school-house in a central location on Dunmore Estate for the settler's children to attend. Once the school was built it also served as a temporary chapel on Sundays (Dunmore Lang, 1 March 1842). Lang's church at Dunmore was known as 'Church Hill' ('Domestic Intelligence', 24 November 1838, p.2). Catherine and her family would have regularly attended the Sunday service.

When Dunmore School opened, it had almost sixty students enrolled by December of its first year. The school was originally established as a private Presbyterian church school. Mr John Whitelaw, from Glasgow, was the teacher employed by Andrew Lang and a salary of £75 per year was paid to him by the Colonial Government (Dunmore Lang, 1 March 1842). The children must have been taught in Gaelic as most of the parents and, therefore most of the children, only spoke Gaelic at home. Ten years later, in 1848, Andrew Lang (Andrew Lang, 19 Jany [sic] 1848) wrote to the government to request that the school be put under the 'general system', saying there were between fifty and eighty children attending. The school was then registered as Dunmore Public School in 1849 (Parkinson, 2013).

Wheat and maize were grown and milled onsite at Dunmore. Dairy products such as milk, butter and cheese were also produced on the estate. Tobacco and various fruits were grown. Wine was also made from the grapes grown at Dunmore. The produce from the estate was either sold in Maitland, or sent by steamer to the Sydney markets (Dunmore, 2018). Over time, more Scottish immigrants who had arrived in NSW joined the tenant farmers from the *Midlothian* who worked the land at Dunmore Estate. The alluvial soil was very fertile and, at one point, the estate supported 300 people including convict workers, tenant farmers and free German immigrants who worked as vinedressers and wine makers. This density of population was rare in NSW at the time (Turner & Sullivan, 1979).

Dunmore Estate presented Catherine and her family with a place to establish their life in NSW with the support of a large Scots community who spoke their native language and shared their culture. The Scots community at Dunmore also understood their history and shared their dreams for the future. As Watson (1984, p.xv) so aptly framed it, the Scots Presbyterian settlers had 'dreams of cow yards and cream cans and paddocks full of rustling maize, and with God on their side their hearts were unstoppable'.

The Wonnarua Nation

The opportunities for a better life for the immigrants, and the new settlers in the area around Dunmore came at the expense of First Nations people who had lived on the land for tens of thousands of years. The traditional custodians of the land in the Maitland area are the people of the Wonnarua Nation. The people of the Wonnarua Nation occupied most of the Hunter Valley before European settlement, including Dunmore Estate. The Wonnarua Nation includes various tribal and clan territories ('Boundaries of the Hunter Valley Aboriginal People', 2021).

Early European settlement in the area saw the land with the best river frontage granted to wealthy pastoralists. As many of these settlers claimed ownership of the country for themselves, they denied First Nations people access to the land where they had sourced food for thousands of years (Bennett, 1964). The Wonnarua initially fought back against European settlement in the area by destroying crops and livestock. As Karskens (2020) points out, payback happened on both sides. However, she argues that retribution by the white settlers was often disproportionate and included killing many unrelated and innocent Aboriginal people, leading to more retribution. Inevitably, there was violence and resistance, and the Wonnarua were soon overwhelmed.

Some of the early English pastoralists had recorded their observations of the traditional owners living in harmony with the environment. However, most of the new settlers didn't value the sustainable methods of sourcing food that First Nations people used. For example, yam daisy or murnong tubers (*Microseris Lanceolata*) had been a staple food source for the local people in the area for thousands of years (see Figure 8). According to Bruce Pascoe (2018), the tubers are eight times more nutritious than a potato and taste as sweet as coconut. Pascoe (2018) also points to evidence of the storage and use of grains by Aboriginal people from native grasses such as Curly Mitchell grass (*Astraleba Lappacea)* and Native Oatgrass (*Themeda Avanacea)*. He suggests that the grains were ground and then baked to make bread.

Figure 8. Aboriginal women dig for murnong (yam daisy) roots at Indented Head, 1835 (John Helder Wedge, 1835, The Todd Journal: Andrew alias William Todd (John Batman's recorder) and his Indented Head Journal, p.70, Courtesy of *Geelong Historical Society,* Victoria).

However, instead of learning from the ancient and sustainable practices used by First Nations people, the new settlers went about imposing their own European methods of farming on the Australian landscape. The new settlers often ploughed up areas containing indigenous food in order to plant their own imported European crops, such as wheat and corn. There was also the widespread introduction of sheep, cattle and other imported livestock, which resulted in the further destruction of indigenous food sources and the compacting of once fertile soils, leaving many First Nations people to starve (Pascoe, 2018).

Dunmore Estate was no exception. After an initial good start for the tenant farmers at Dunmore, the years between 1838 and 1840 brought drought (Dunmore Lang, 7 September 1841, p.2). The low rainfall, together with colonial farming practices such as land clearing and the introduction of European livestock, brought environmental changes to the landscape. These changes inevitably led to a scarcity in traditional food sources for First Nations people.

It is impossible to know if the new immigrants saw the connection between their own exclusion from their cultural heritage and way of life back on the Isle of Skye, and the plight of First Nations people of Australia. Under the Highland Clearances, which were imposed on the Scottish tenant farmers, they were pushed on to marginal land and they faced famine. In turn, Aboriginal people in the colony of NSW were being pushed to the margins of their own land by the British immigrants. Increasingly, they were unable to access their traditional sources of food, which they had relied on for tens of thousands of years.

Catherine was still very young. She was illiterate and Gaelic was her only language. She may have started to learn some English, but as a young mother and wife she probably mainly conversed with other Gaelic speaking women in the Dunmore community. It might have taken quite some time for her to learn to speak English comfortably. It is unlikely that she was even aware at this stage in her life of the socio-political situation in the new colony regarding First Nations people, or the irony of their dispossession by immigrants, who themselves were dispossessed. Her focus would have been on survival, and working hard to care for her growing family.

Bushrangers

There were bushrangers carrying out crimes in the area around where Catherine and her family were living at Dunmore Estate. The NSW legislative Council had introduced what was known as the *Bushranging Act* in 1830 in reaction to the large number of bushrangers operating at the time. The new *Act* gave police and free men the power to detain any person they suspected of being an escaped convict, and take them before a Justice of the Peace. Also, any police officer or free man, could search for suspected stolen goods and detain any person thought to be harbouring an escaped convict ('Bushrangers' Act', 21 June 1834, p.2).

Furthermore, the *Act* placed the onus of proof on the person detained, meaning that anyone detained under the *Act* had to prove to the Justice that they were innocent. As a result, innocent people were often handcuffed and detained for days or even weeks. The *Act* came to be resented and ordinary, working-class people railed against it ('Bushrangers' Act', 21 June 1834, p.2). Even Governor Bourke challenged the legality of the Act and stated that it was 'contrary to the spirit of English law'. Despite these feelings, the *Act* continued in various forms until 1853 (Seal, 1996). According to Seal (1996), the heavy-handed policing under the *Bushranging Act* 'contributed to a strong current of resentment against the state and its protectors that is still evident in Australian society today' (Seal, 1996, p.125).

The so called 'Jew Boy Gang' was one group of bushrangers who were operating in the area around Dunmore. The Jew Boys were known to terrorise the Hunter Valley - 'except on Saturdays', the Jewish Sabbath ('Dungog, NSW', 2020). Edward Davis, a Jewish escaped convict, was the leader of the gang. Apparently, the Jew Boys were polite and 'had the appearance of gentlemen'. Davis and his crew were also known to wear broad-rim manilla hats with coloured ribbons ('Criminal Sittings', 25 February 1841, p.2). Karskens (2009, p.305) cites the work of Byrne (1993) to suggest that this finery, as well as being enjoyable to wear, 'mocked the trappings of wealth and status' and was an emblematic gesture of defiance. Davis, together with his five companions, even robbed Dunmore House in 1840. It was said that they held 'up the Langs in their elegant dining room' (Turner & Sullivan, 1979 p.50).

In 1840, bushrangers attacked another estate which was known as 'Underbank'. Underbank Estate was about seventy kilometres (forty-four miles) from Dunmore. As was mentioned earlier, Underbank is a property which will become important later in Catherine's life. However, at the time of the raid, Underbank was owned by John Lord. Apparently, a posse of 'freebooters' bailed up the servants, together with Mrs Lord and Mr Craig. Then 'after dining comfortably', they carried away all of the ammunition and rifles on the property. The robbers also took tea, sugar, flour, butter, £8-£10 in cash and a horse. When they were finished, the bushrangers took off over the mountains towards Paterson ('Bushranging on the Williams', 10 December 1840, p.2). At the time, horses were expensive and hard to come by in the NSW colony, making them a valuable asset particularly to bushrangers (West, 2005).

Attacks by bushrangers in the area were increasing to the point that the Governor, Sir George Gipps, proposed a 'free pardon and a passage to England' for any Prisoner of the Crown who provided confidential information which led to the capture of the following bushrangers: James Everett, John Marshall, John Shea and Edward Davis ('Advertising', 26 December 1840(b), p.4). Not long afterwards, Edward Davis and his gang were captured. They were all hung on the 16th March 1841 at the back of the old Sydney jail ('Supreme Court', 18 March 1841, p.3). Seemingly, when Davis was hung, 'the soldiers had to hold back a vast, emotional crowd of his supporters' (Karskens, 2009, p.308).

The end of transportation

There was growing concern in the NSW colony about the amount of crime, as well as the increasing costs of maintaining the judicial system, the police force and the jails. Most of the bushrangers active in the colony at the time, were escaped convicts who had been transported to Australia from Britain (Ward, 1958). As a consequence, it was widely believed that ending the transportation of convicts to the colony from Britain would put an end to the high crime rate, including the increasing number of bushrangers ('The Anti-transportation Movement', 15 January 1851, p.3).

There were also claims of rampant sexual 'depravity' in the colony. The huge gender imbalance brought about by transportation led many commentators to see the colony as 'depraved'. These accusations were expressed in the Molesworth Report (1838) which was commissioned by the British Government to investigate transportation to NSW and Van Dieman's Land (Tasmania). The Molesworth Report was widely believed to be politically motivated to end transportation ('The Transportation Committee [?]', 7 March 1839, p.2). Nevertheless, it certainly wasn't the first time these accusations were made, and they left a persistent stain on the reputation of the colony.

Many female convicts and unaccompanied immigrant women married and lived 'respectable' lives. However, there were few economic options available to women in the colony who were without the 'protection' of a man, other than prostitution or concubinage (Summers, 2016). Anti-Irish Catholic racism meant that many single Irish women found it particularly difficult to find employment. 'No Irish need apply' (or NINA) was often included in job advertisements. For example, Mrs Robert Stark's advertisement in *The Sydney Morning Herald* clearly stated that 'no Irish need apply' for the position she was seeking to fill for a female servant ('Advertising', 26 August 1854, p.1). Another advertisement placed by a Mr Lewis, who was looking for a general servant who could 'wash and iron well', also stated that 'no Irish need apply' ('Advertising', 30 December 1856, p.8). Prostitution offered flexible hours for single women with children. It also gave many women financial independence, and a degree of autonomy, in a patriarchal society where most women lacked both.

Despite the moral outrage which was regularly expressed in newspapers, prostitution wasn't technically illegal. Although, sex workers could be apprehended for disorderly conduct, such as two prostitutes who were given twenty-one days in prison by the Sydney courts in 1851 ('Advertising', 29 October 1851, p.3). The *Vagrancy Act 1835* was introduced 'for the prevention of Vagrancy, and for the punishment of Idle and Disorderly persons, Rogues and Vagabonds, and Incorrigible Rogues, in the colony of NSW' ('*Vagrancy Act 1835,* No11a', 25 August 1835). The *Act* was used to imprison sex workers, the unemployed, drunks and whites who consorted with First Nations people (Gregoire & Nedim, 9 March 2021). However, large profits were made by those who had businesses that relied on the trade, such as landlords who charged inflated rents, businesses who hired furniture, cooks, housekeepers, laundry services, and those in the liquor trade. Also, many wealthy powerful men, as well as police officers, availed themselves of their services. As a result, prostitution was seen by many in the colony to be a necessary evil and, more often than not, a blind eye was turned.

Some women formed intimate relationships with other women, but there was little focus on relationships between women. Lesbianism was not deemed to be illegal in the colony and as such there are no records available, only anecdotal reports which have come mostly from female corrective institutions. These reports usually referred to women who dressed as men, and took the role of 'husbands' with other female inmates ('The Female Factory', 18 May 1841, p.2). The indifference to lesbian behaviour is not surprising given the patriarchal nature of colonial society. There was no perceived threat from lesbian women - if they were recognised at all. Many lesbian women were hidden in plain sight and did not attract the homophobic gaze of phallocentric colonial society.

Homosexuality, on the other hand, which was relatively common in the convict population, was a crime which was punishable by death under British law. Under the *Offences Against the Person Act 1828,* the difficult requirement to prove ejaculation was removed from the existing legislation. As a result, there was a notable rise in the number of men charged with what was referred to as 'buggery' in NSW during the 1830s. The death penalty was widely believed to perform a vital role in the 'preservation of social order' in both Britain and the colony, even though the sentence for those charged with buggery was often commuted to life in prison. During the 1830s, buggery came to represent the 'unnaturalness' of convict transportation. Male homosexuality was seen as a threat to 'civilised' British values and the respectable working-class family (Taylor, March 2020).

Certainly, the transportation of convicts to NSW did not sit well with Rev Lang's vision of the colony, and he vehemently opposed it. Lang saw the convict transportation system as a failure, and he believed that immigration was the answer to the moral woes of the colony ('Dr Lang's Immigration Lecture', 9 November 1850, p.2). Also, most of the free settlers, like Catherine and the tenant farmers at Dunmore Estate, would not have supported the continuation of transportation of convicts from England. Most people, apart from the large pastoralists, believed like Lang that convict labour was no longer needed in the colony and that respectable British immigration was the answer.

Due to the growing sentiment opposing transportation, an order was issued in London on the 22nd of May 1840 which stated that the transportation of convicts to the NSW colony was to cease. NSW officially stopped being a penal colony and was defined as a 'free colony' from 1 August 1840 ('Order-in-Council Ending Transportation of Convicts', 22 May 1840 (UK)). Despite the official declaration, there were another 1400 convicts who were transported by the English parliament to NSW against the will of the majority of those living in the colony, before it finally stopped (Turnbull, 2008). The transportation of convicts to NSW continued to be debated for many years. At times, there were concerns that transportation might even be reinstated ('The Anti-transportation Movement', 15 January 1851, p.3), but it didn't eventuate.

Catherine McDonald

In January of 1841 Catherine's second child, (another son), was born at Dunmore Estate. Catherine named the baby Ewen (Hugh) McDonald, after her own father. Also, according to Catherine's death certificate (Catherine Ballard, 16 May 1904), she and Angus were married at Dunmore sometime in 1841. Catherine was seventeen at the time and Angus (2) would have been thirty. However, there is no official record of their marriage. As stated earlier, it was not a requirement to register a birth, death or marriage in NSW before 1856. Many years later, when Catherine married for a second time, her name was given as Catherine MacDonald, having taken Angus's (2) name.

The minimum age that people could marry in the colony at the time with parental consent was twelve for a girl and fourteen for a boy (Preston, 2014). Twenty-one was the minimum age which a marriage could be conducted without parental consent in the NSW colony. Legislation had come into effect on the 5th August 1836, which was based on the English *Marriage Act* to prevent so called 'clandestine marriages' by minors. The *Act* stipulated that for people under twenty-one parental consent was needed from the father and, if he was deceased, the mother. If both parents were deceased a guardian could consent ('*Clandestine Marriages Act 1836 No10a*', 5 August 1836).

The *Act* was not without its critics. An article in *The Sydney Gazette and NSW Advertiser* ('New Enactments', 4 August 1836, p.2) in relation to the applicability of the *Marriage Act* to the NSW colony, argued that twenty-one was too old to require parental consent to marry. The commentator's argument was based on the notion that 'both sexes attain maturity much earlier in this colony than under Northern European climates of the British Isles'.

Despite this argument, because of her age, Catherine's father, Ewen McKinnon, living back at Kendram on Skye in Scotland, would have needed to consent to the marriage if there was one between Catherine and Angus (2). However, because Catherine and her parents were all illiterate, as well as the difficulties of even sending letters between Dunmore and Kendram, it is unlikely that parental consent was ever obtained.

The marriage between Catherine and Angus (2) may well have been what was known colloquially as a 'Scotch marriage'. In Scotland, it was not uncommon for so-called 'irregular marriages' to take place. These irregular marriages involved an exchange of consent to the marriage to be made by both parties, either privately or in front of witnesses. This exchange was a mainstay of the legal status of irregular marriages in Scotland up until the *Marriage (Scotland) Act 1939,* when they were abolished ('Church Registers', 2022).

There was rarely any registration of these so called 'Scotch marriages' in NSW. So, it is possible that Catherine and Angus (2), in the absence of parental consent, exchanged vows or in some way formalised their union, without officially registering it. By now they had two children together, Angus (3) and the newborn Ewen, and they were living together as husband and wife.

There was also another wedding that year at Dunmore Estate to celebrate. Catherine's widowed brother John McKinnon, who was living at Dunmore, remarried. John married Christina Cameron (John McKinnon, 1872), who was also a bounty immigrant from Scotland. He had taken his daughter Ann back from the Orphan School, two years previously, in March 1839.

John had commissioned someone to write a letter, on his behalf, to the Colonial Secretary. Even though most of the admissions to the Orphan School were voluntary, parents who requested to have their children back had to demonstrate they were capable of providing for them. Some applications were not accepted and the children were not returned ('Female Orphan School', 2017). John's letter stated that he 'had a good crop of wheat' and was 'desirous' of taking his daughter back into his care.

The letter also said that Ann's health had not been good since entering the orphanage (John MacKinnon, 21 March 1839). The conditions were cramped at the Orphan School and there was only limited understanding of hygiene. There were outbreaks of scarlet fever and measles and, in 1839, a third of the girls were reported to be sick. Deaths from these outbreaks were common ('Female Orphan School', 2017). John had his daughter returned to him, but it is no wonder young Ann didn't thrive.

It is unknown what became of either of John McKinnon's children. There isn't a death certificate or any other information available for either young John or his sister Ann. It is most probable, that like many others in the nineteenth century, neither of them survived their childhood.

Catherine's sons

Sadly, the following year in 1842, Catherine's first child Angus (3), who was conceived on the *Midlothian*, died when he was just four years old ('Catherine McKinnon's Family', n.d.). Catherine's second son, Ewen, would have been one year old when his brother Angus (3) died. It must have been a terrible loss, particularly on top of losing baby Catherine. However, like baby Catherine and John McKinnon's children, Ann and young John, there wasn't any official registration of his death. Therefore, the cause of his death is unknown.

There were very few European families and young children living in the NSW colony before the late 1830s. As such, there weren't any of the common childhood infections which were prevalent in Britain. However, with the increase in the number of young families arriving, and the high local birth rate, the extent of childhood illnesses increased. There were outbreaks of whooping cough and measles in 1838-39, as well as local influenza epidemics that infected communities. Many infant deaths were also caused by intestinal infections (Lewis, 7 July 2014).

In fact, there was so much sickness in Sydney in 1841, that Governor Gipps wrote to the NSW Medical Board asking if anything could be done by the government to curb the extent of illness. The Board replied in a report on 10 May 1841, which was published in the *Sydney Herald* ('Prevalence of Sickness in the Town of Sydney', 15 May 1841, p.2). The Board advised that there was 'an unusual amount both of sickness and mortality' in Sydney at the time. They said that scarlatina (scarlet fever) was a highly contagious disease which had first appeared in the colony earlier that year. The disease had started in north-western Sydney, but had now spread outwards to many parts of the colony.

The Medical Board's report ('Prevalence of Sickness in the Town of Sydney', 15 May 1841, p.2) suggested that contagious diseases are always more fatal in populations when they are first exposed to them. The Board had no recommendations for how to alleviate the spread of the disease, other than strict quarantining of patients. They suggested that all classes of the population were being equally affected by the disease, thereby arguing it was not due to poverty, or poor living conditions.

Catherine's first child, baby Angus (3), may well have died from scarlatina. Young children were particularly vulnerable to infectious disease and child mortality rates in the colony were high. The following year, in December of 1843, Catherine and her husband Angus (2), had another son and they also called him Angus (4) (1843-1927). Young Ewen and the surviving son, Angus (4), were soon followed by Malcolm in late October 1844 and then John McDonald in March 1847.

The names of Catherine's children follow a traditional Scottish naming pattern. The first son was named after the father's father (paternal grandfather), the second son was named after the mother's father (maternal grandfather) and the third son was named after the father. The same applied for female children who were named after their grandmothers, then their mothers. Needless to say, if the parent was named after their own parent (the grandparent), this could result in multiple children in one family with the same name. Also, when a child died the name was often reused with the next child ('Forenames', 2021). This is why, in this story alone, we have four different males, all called Angus McDonald. Not surprisingly, the traditional Scottish naming patterns gradually went out of favour over the nineteenth century.

Population growth was an essential part of the projected economic prosperity of NSW. Aside from the families who emigrated to NSW with children, many of the single women, like Catherine, married and had large families of their own. These children were crucial to produce the next generation of Australian labourers, apprentices and servants. Women's reproductive labour became an integral part of the economic future of the colony, particularly once the transportation of convicts from Britain ceased.

Like most of the bounty immigrants who travelled under Rev Lang's scheme, the Scottish immigrants who settled at Dunmore Estate took up positions requiring low paid labour, and they raised large families. Women's unpaid domestic labour in the home, on the farms and in the community also came to uphold a family-based economy. Over time, the family unit transformed what Lang considered to be the 'moral woes' of colonial society, effectively fulfilling the intention of his scheme. As such, the economic and social importance of women's unpaid reproductive and domestic labour to the success of the colony should not be underestimated.

Summers (2016, p.428), suggests it is not surprising that the 'social engineers' of the colony such as Rev Lang, looked to import working class British emigrants for the values they wanted to imbed in colonial society. She argues these working-class immigrants wanted to emulate the social and economic systems of Britain. At the same time, they hoped these systems would work more to their advantage than they had back at home.

Chapter 5
A Spin of the Wheel

The squattocracy - the importation of Indian and Chinese indentured labour - steps towards democracy - the growing power of the squattocracy - economic depression - the first Australian lottery - first prize - a fatal accident - a new home - the Gringai - Dungog - siblings reunited - the gold rush

The Squattocracy

The administration of land in the colony was managed by the colonial government. In the early days of settlement land grants were given by the Governor. In 1825 the sale of land by private tender also began. Then, in 1826, the so-called 'limits of location' were created, to define the boundaries of land settlement around Sydney. These limits were then extended in 1829 to include a further nineteen counties surrounding the Sydney area. The limits were imposed to prevent the population spreading too far from Sydney too quickly. The boundaries also gave the government surveyors time to keep up with the administration of land ownership ('Government Order', 17 October 1829, p.1). However, in reality the limits posed no real restriction and they were often ignored. There were no free land grants given after 1831 ('Government Order', 8 August 1831, p.1).

According to Sykes (1998, p.24-25), the 1830s saw a boom in the colony's fortunes. The whaling (and sealing) industry, which accounted for about half of NSWs exports to Britain, had seen a series of good years. The wool industry was also expanding at a rapid rate. 'Between 1830 and 1835 wool exports quadrupled' (Sykes, 1998, p.24). This meant there was considerable money to be made from wool. As a result, eager pastoralists pushed further into uncharted land beyond Sydney and took up land, without legal tenure, to run sheep and cattle. By the mid-1830s, the practice of squatting on land had become so widespread that Governor Burke began to regulate the practice, and so legitimise it. For £10 a year, squatters were given a licence to graze livestock on sizable tracts of crown land outside the 'limits of location' ('Squattocracy', 2023).

The squatters had relied on the use of convict labour to clear land and tend to the livestock on their often remote runs. However, there was a growing demand for cheap labourers in the colony. First Nations people worked stripping bark for buildings and doing other odd jobs, but Davidson (1994, p.90) asserts they were reluctant to herd sheep. Also, in the early decades of the nineteenth century, they were not generally employed as shepherds as they were apt to leave the flock although, as we will see, farmers later came to rely on the skill of the Aboriginal workforce. The thousands of people who migrated to the colony of NSW in the 1830s as free immigrants were also mostly not prepared to work as shepherds or labourers in remote bushland. Molony (2000, p.161) argues that most of them had come from urban centres and 'had no desire whatever to go forth into untracked bush where even the minimal advantages of city-based civilisation were lacking'.

Therefore, to fill the labour shortage in the colony, the powerful squatters began importing men from India and China to work as indentured shepherds and farm hands. These low paid immigrants were known colloquially as 'coolies'. John Mackay organised the first importation of forty-two men from India to NSW. The first sizeable group arrived in December 1837. Nineteen of them were 'leased out' as shepherds to work at Underbank, which was owned by John Lord at the time. The Indian workers were indentured for five-year terms. They were supposed to be given food, clothing, shelter and pay. However, they were mostly paid very low wages, if anything, often not fed or given shelter ('The Indian "Hill Coolies"', 28 February 1838, p.2).

As they were generally the first Europeans in an area, squatters were able to select and occupy the best, most fertile land. The squatters made large sums of money from their livestock for very little outlay. Many of them had started as agents for 'men of substance' but with the right connections and ambition, they were able to amass their own fortunes. By 1840, many of the 'Squattocracy' - as these pastoralists were known - were men of high social standing and power, wielding considerable influence within the NSW colony ('Squattocracy', 2023).

A fledgling democracy

In 1823, a Legislative Council was formed by the British Government. It consisted of five men who would assist the NSW Governor to enact legislation. However, only the Governor could propose legislation, and the British parliament could override anything they didn't agree with and enact their own laws ('History of Democracy in NSW', 2023).

Then in 1843, the first elections to be held in Australia took place in NSW. Twenty-four of the thirty-six members of the Legislative Council were elected that year with the other twelve appointed by the crown. The only inhabitants of the colony allowed to vote were men over twenty-one who were a 'subject of her Majesty' and who had either freehold or leasehold property in the district in which they were to vote ('Towards Responsible Government-1843 to 1855', 2023). This, of course, included those men who were part of the squattocracy and further entrenched their power and influence in the colony.

This gender, race and class bias meant that women, First Nations people, Chinese people, the working class, and non-landed people were all excluded from voting. These people held no political sway, or power to influence the direction of the colony. It meant that Catherine was excluded from taking part in this first democratic election because she was only twenty and also because she was a woman. Her husband Angus (2) and her brother John, were also excluded from the process because they didn't own land. In fact, most of the people they knew, including their family and friends, were excluded from voting.

Despite NSW attaining a partially elected government, the Governor was still able to override legislation and refer it to the British parliament. The British parliament could still enact legislation on behalf of NSW ('Towards

Responsible Government-1843 to 1855', 2023). These were just the first steps towards democracy in NSW. As we will see, over time the power of the legislature expanded, as did voting rights, eventually leading to a fully-fledged democracy.

Only a couple of years after the first NSW elections, the squattocracy demonstrated their growing power and influence with the British government. They joined together and claimed that they needed more security of tenure on the land where they were grazing livestock. After having no success with the then Governor Sir George Gipps, they sent the Cambridge educated barrister, Archibald Boyd, to London to argue their case ('Mr. Archibald Boyd and the Squatocracy [*sic*]', 7 May 1845, p.2).

As a result of Boyd's solicitations, the British government enacted legislation which was against the wishes of the majority of the colony. The legislation was an amendment to the existing *Act for Regulating the Sale of Wasteland Belonging to the Crown in the Australian Colonies* (*Waste Lands, Australia Act 1846 9 & 10 Vict, c104*, 28 August 1846). The Act, which became known colloquially as the *Squatters Act,* gave the squatters either eight or fourteen-year leases on their runs at £10 a year for 4,000 sheep, or a proportionate number of cattle. They were also able to purchase land for £1 an acre to build a homestead giving them the security they were seeking ('New Squatting Regulations', 9 January 1847, p.1). There was much indignation within the population of the colony about the new *Act*.

Rev Lang was one of those in NSW who was vehemently opposed to it ('Dr Lang on Squatting', 13 January 1849, p.5). He claimed that the so-called squatters took the most fertile land without any cultivation or improvement. Furthermore, Lang suggested that the sale of the land would have put funds into the finances of the colonial government. He argued that the money could have then been used to support the 'humbler classes' to farm crops and produce. *The Citizen* newspaper also asserted that the 'small capitalist' was prevented from acquiring access to land which could be viably farmed. According to *The Citizen*, there were about 1000 squatters in all, with eighteen individuals holding about twelve million acres between them ('New Squatting Regulations', 9 January 1847, p.1).

The *Act* was seen to be very favourable to the squattocracy and at the same time it blocked the chances of ordinary, hardworking people like Catherine and Angus (2) who, without finance, were unable to purchase land of their own. For Catherine and Angus (2), the realisation that under these conditions they would never be able to buy their own place, must have been disheartening. It may have even spurred Angus (2) on to consider other options for acquiring their own land.

A spin of the wheel

The boom of the 1830s had seen rapid growth in the colony which had led to over-speculation, particularly in the property market. According to a Select Committee on Monetary Confusion ('Minutes of Evidence Taken Before the Select Committee on Monetary Confusion', 21 November 1843, p.4), the banks aided this over-speculation by their liberality in advancing money to speculators. However, by 1840 the economy had taken a considerable downturn.

Fitz-Gibbon and Gizycki (October 2001) suggest this was due to a number of factors including: the effects of a severe drought, which led to wheat having to be imported to the colony; a decline in land sales; the British financial crises of 1839, which reduced the flow of capital to the colony; reduced profits from the whaling industry, which had passed its peak; and the slowing expansion of the wool industry. Labour shortages were also an ongoing issue (Butlin, 1968). All of these factors combined to send the colony's economy into an economic depression. The downturn resulted in an increase in the number of bankruptcies and insolvencies among land owners and pastoralists, weakening the position of the banks. The result was the first wave of mostly small bank failures (Fitz-Gibbon & Gizycki, October 2001).

In order to try and alleviate the effects of the depression, the Legislative Council passed the *Insolvency Act 1841* ('*Insolvency Act 1841 No17a*', 29

December 1841). The *Act* enabled debtors to keep control of their estates as long as they were able to convince the court they had a plan to repay creditors an 'equitable return'. Upon the receipt of a Certificate of Insolvency, the insolvent could continue profiting from the estate (Greig, 2023). According to Greig (2023), the *Act* was seen by some observers as providing necessary relief in desperate times, while others saw it as benefitting the wealthy. Apparently, some affluent men took the opportunity to voluntarily declare insolvency, but continued to trade whilst avoiding paying their creditors.

In March 1843, the Bank of Australia was the largest bank to fail ('The Bank of Australia', 2 March 1843, p.2). Three quarters of the Bank's assets were tied up in just seven accounts (Butlin, 1968). One firm in particular, the Sydney merchant and real estate firm Hughes & Hoskings, accounted for nearly forty percent of the Banks total assets. As a result, the Bank was substantially exposed when Hughes & Hosking went into insolvency. The Bank had provided the firm with extensive loans, under questionable circumstances, which they were unable to repay (Butlin, 1968).

Two of the other major debtors were the Bank's own Directors, Edye Manning and Alexander Brodie Sparks. *The Sydney Morning Herald* ('Bank of Australia', 8 September 1843, p.3) reported that after a meeting of the Board of Directors of the Bank, Mr Manning and Mr Sparks stayed behind and approved each other's loans. In a judgement made in the Supreme Court, their behaviour was not deemed to have been an offence against the law, but rather an unethical violation of their responsibilities as Directors ('Domestic Intelligence', 26 April 1844, p.2).

The 180 or so shareholders of the Bank suffered big losses from the Banks failure and they faced personal liability for the Bank's debts (Sykes, 1998). Due to persistent bad management, the failed Bank of Australia had only limited cash reserves. It held considerable land assets from customers who had become insolvent, although many of these assets were virtually worthless ('Minutes of Evidence Taken Before the Select Committee on Monetary Confusion', 21 November 1843). This presented a quandary for the Bank as to what to do with the land it held given the poor state of the property market in the colony at the time.

The politician William Charles Wentworth, who was himself a major shareholder in the Bank of Australia, introduced a Bill into the NSW Legislative Council to allow a one-off lottery. The idea was that the lottery would enable the Bank to recover some money by selling tickets, with the prizes being the land assets held by the Bank. The Bill passed the Legislative Council ('Legislative Council', 24 December 1844). However, the Governor at the time, Sir George Gipps, did not endorse the lottery and Royal Assent to the Bill was declined by the Queen in Britain ('Lord Stanley Despatch to Sir George Gipps', 17 May 1845, pp.350-51).

It was noted in the dispatch from Lord Stanley to Governor Gipps that lotteries were held in 'the highest disfavour by Parliament', and that 'the temporary advantage is gained at the expense of the morality and the permanent interests of Society at large'. He also noted that two of the members of the Legislature who instigated the Bill were shareholders in the Bank (one of who was Wentworth) and stood to gain personally from the lottery, suggesting the potential for a lack of 'vigilance and circumspection' on their part ('Lord Stanley Despatch to Sir George Gipps', 17 May 1845, pp.350-51).

Nevertheless, a few years later a new Governor, Sir Charles Fitzroy, appears to have taken a more tolerant view towards the idea of the lottery. Many people believed that the resolution of the Bank's problems would relieve the economic depression gripping the colony and avert total economic collapse. It was argued by supporters of the lottery that there was no law on the NSW legislature which strictly prohibited a lottery. However, the provisions under which the colony of NSW was governed allowed,

> that all laws and statutes in force within the realm of England at the time of the passing of this Act, (not being inconsistent therewith, or with any charter, or letters patent, or under in Council, which may be issued in pursuant thereof)
>
> shall be applied within the said colonies [9th Geo. IV, ch.83, sec.24] ('Our Third, Upon Mr. Wentworth's Last', 15 February 1849, p.2).

At the time there was a British law which had been in force since 1826, the *Lottery Act*, which prohibited the running of lotteries ('Original

Correspondence', 19 February 1849, p.3). Even though the lottery itself wasn't technically legal, the authorities in NSW turned a blind eye so that it could proceed. Rather than calling the event a 'lottery', it was generally referred to in advertisements, and on the actual tickets, as the 'Plan of Partition' or similar (see Figure 9). Presumably this was to distance the event from any potential claims of illegality. As you can imagine, the lottery generated considerable interest, as well as controversy, in the NSW colony.

Figure 9. Bank of Australia lottery ticket, no.10,140, 1848 (Bank of Australia, 1848, Bank of Australia lottery ticket number 10,140, issued to Duncan MacKellar, dated 19 October 1848. Endorsed on back for £4, *National Library Australia*, https://nla.gov.au/nla.obj-260007374/view).

By late 1848, when the lottery was finally underway, 11,248 tickets were printed and issued to the shareholders, in proportion to their paid-up capital investment with the Bank. The tickets were valued at £4 each and every ticket won a prize. Any shareholder who didn't want to keep their tickets could sell them on, so some shareholders preferred to have the cash, and sold their tickets ('Something New', 19 October 1848, p.2). One hundred tickets were even offered for sale by Messrs Lowes and Macmichael as far away as Tasmania ('No Title', 14 November 1848, p.2).

A catalogue containing a couple of hundred of the most valuable prizes was published just prior to the tickets going on sale ('Original Correspondence', 19 February 1849, p.3). Although every ticket won a prize, it turned out that 10,822 properties had no real value. Most of them were small, remote parcels of land which were inadequately identified and worth less than the value of the £4 ticket ('Bank of Australia Lottery [?]', 23 January 1849, p.2). This information wasn't made public until just a day or two before the draw, when a complete catalogue containing all of the properties was made available ('Original Correspondence', 19 February 1849, p.3). Most people would have purchased tickets believing they had an unrealistically good chance of winning something valuable.

Catherine and Angus (2) had been living as tenant farmers on Dunmore Estate for ten years with their four sons. Dunmore was a strong community, but they must have longed to have a place of their own. So, Catherine's husband Angus (2) decided to try his luck by buying a ticket in what was to be the first Australian lottery. Angus (2) bought his lottery ticket from George D. Craig, of East Maitland, who was a storekeeper and a shareholder in the bank. Craig must have preferred to have the cash and sold his ticket to Angus (2). Angus (2) paid £4 to buy the ticket from Craig, which would have been a lot of money and quite a gamble with many mouths to feed at home. To give the reader an idea of the value of £4 at the time, the Dungog Magistrate Mr Thomas Cook suggested that the average annual wage in the Dungog district in 1844 was £20 ('Evidence on Immigration', 5 March 1844).

Angus (2) was feeling lucky when he purchased his ticket, but then he got cold feet at the last minute and tried to sell half of his ticket to a neighbour for £2 just before the draw. Perhaps Angus (2) had found out that most of the prizes were in fact worthless. To Angus's (2) good fortune, his neighbour wasn't interested in the ticket ('Partition of the Bank of Australia', 6 January 1849, p.2).

The drawing of the lottery prizes commenced on the 1st of January 1849 at the City Theatre in Market Street in Sydney amid great excitement. It took three days to finalise. There were two wheels used in the draw. The first wheel, which was known as the 'Ticket Wheel', allocated a ticket number; and the second or 'Lot Wheel' allocated the prize (Bank of Australia, 1848). For those who couldn't make it to the City Theatre in person, the results were published in *The Sydney Morning Herald* across two days, on the 6th and 7th of January 1849 ('Bank of Australia Result of the Drawing of the Lots', 6 January 1849, p.3). The winning ticket was number 3374 ('Bank of Australia Result of the Drawing of the Lots', 7 January 1849, p.3). Incredibly, Angus (2), Catherine's husband, was the owner of ticket number 3374 and he had won the first prize.

Winners and losers

The first prize included an estate called Underbank and a pastoral run known as Cryon Station. The total value of the prize was £6000 ('Partition of the Bank of Australia', 6 January 1849, p.2). Underbank Estate, the most desirable of the two properties, was on the Upper Williams River in the Dungog-Barrington tops district, north of Newcastle in NSW. Twin brothers, Archibald and George Mosman, who were general merchants, graziers and whalers, had originally been granted two blocks of land, by Governor Darling on the 6 February, in 1829. However, the Mosman's interests lay elsewhere, namely in whaling. As a result, in 1836 the land, which later became known as 'Underbank', was advertised 'at the request of the grantee' in favour of John D Lord, who was also a merchant ('Grants of Land', 24 December 1836, p.4). Lord then built the Underbank Estate. Subsequently, in 1843, Lord fell victim to the economic depression of the early 1840s. He like so many others became insolvent and proceedings were undertaken against him by the NSW Insolvency Court ('Insolvency Proceedings', 20 July 1843, p.2).

Two years after Lord became insolvent the Underbank Estate was advertised for sale by auction in 1845 ('Advertising', 30 April 1845, p.4). It didn't sell. It was then advertised again, throughout 1846 ('Advertising', 13 August 1846, p.4) and 1847 ('Abstract of Sales by Auction This Day', 2 March 1847, p.2), this time for a five-year lease with the option to purchase the estate at any point during that period. Again, this was without success. The Bank of Australia, which had foreclosed on Lord's property, then offered Underbank as the first prize in the lottery. The Underbank property consisted of 8,320 acres with a 'mansion', stockyards, sheds, implements, supplies, a vineyard, 3,700 head of cattle and forty horses ('Partition of the Bank of Australia', 6 January 1849, p.2).

Cryon Station, the other property included in Angus's (2) winning prize, was a pastoral run on the Barwon River, situated on the Liverpool Plains between Narrabri and Collarenebri ('Partition of the Bank of Australia', 6 January 1849, p.2). Cryon Station was previously held by Helenus Scott ('Transfer of Runs', 10 August 1849, p.4), but he had become insolvent and the Bank of Australia foreclosed on his assets ('Insolvency Proceedings', 7 August 1852, p.2). Cryon Station, which was 'beyond the settled districts', included 64,000 acres and had the capacity for 2,000 head of cattle ('Claims to Leases of Crown Lands Beyond the Settled District', 30 September 1848, p.2).

Most of the tickets in the lottery were purchased by stockmen, labourers, servants and other lowly paid workers like Angus (2). Some people used all of their savings or pooled their money to buy a ticket. Other people even drew on their future wages to secure a chance at winning a prize. All were hopeful, but in the end very few were happy. The terms *'Fitz Royed'* and *'Hastinged'* were coined to refer to the sentiment felt by many of those who won worthless properties for their hard earned £4 investment ('Another Lottery Scheme', 22 January 1849, p.2). The terms were in reference to the 2,156 lots of land at Fitzroy and 6,714 lots at Hastings which held no value ('Bank of Australia Lottery [?]', 23 January 1849, p.2). Many of the properties were so poorly thought of, and worth so little, that they were never claimed by those who had won them (Sykes, 1998). A writer in *The Sydney Morning Herald* ('Another Lottery Scheme', 22 January 1849, p.2) argued that, 'if the miserably few gainers were in every instance rendered perfectly happy, what set off is this against the thousands upon thousands of poor people who have made shipwreck of their little all'.

The lottery raised £44,992, a considerable amount of money but it wasn't enough to pay all the debits of the Bank. Due to the success of the first lottery, there was almost immediately talk of running another lottery. The Bank of Australia still held some properties which hadn't made it into the first draw in time, as they were 'encumbered with trusts, mortgages, marriage settlements, etc' (Butlin, 1968, p.349). These properties included 'Sydney properties, the racecourse at Maitland, properties in the town of Melbourne at Jika Jika, and mineral and alluvial land in Adelaide' - all of which had formerly belonged to the merchants, John Terry Hughes and John Hoskings. So, a 'Second and Final Drawing' was scheduled for Easter Monday, the 9 April 1849 ('Advertising', 1 February 1849, p.1).

Also, only weeks after the first lottery was drawn, Wentworth announced he planned to run his own lottery. Wentworth's lottery was backed by twenty-three members of a 'committee of friends and political supporters.' According to an advertisement posted in *The Sydney Morning Herald* ('Advertising', 2 February 1849, p.1), Wentworth intended to relieve himself 'from the large demands upon his time and attention occasioned by his very extensive private concerns'. These 'concerns', which were unsaleable in the depressed property market, included 12,000 properties which would make up the lottery prizes. The properties, according to the advertisement, were valued at £60,000, including £20,000 worth of property in the 'heart of the city' of Sydney, £10,000 of suburban Sydney property and £30,000 worth of rural property. As a significant shareholder of the Bank of Australia, Wentworth would have received a large number of properties in the first lottery draw, presumably many of which he was intending to offload in his lottery.

The tickets in Wentworth's lottery were to be sold at £5 each, which was £1 or 25% more, than the cost of the tickets in the Bank of Australia lottery ('The Lottery System', 24 February 1849, p.2). Wentworth's lottery was intended purely for his personal financial gain. The idea that public contributions from the working class could be used for rich landed gentlemen to offload their unsaleable assets was clearly too good for Wentworth to pass up. However, after considerable negative publicity,

Wentworth changed tack and declared that he owned the properties in partnership with other parties, who he didn't name. He also put up the value of the properties within a week of his first announcement to claim they were worth £135,000 ('Mr Martin's Vindication of the Patriotic Lottery', 21 February 1849, p.2).

Not surprisingly, after the first lottery which saw so many working-class people lose money, there was little appetite among the public to support any more lotteries. *The People's Advocate* ('The Lottery Scheme', 27 January 1849, p.6) suggested 'The citizens have been so tolerably well diddled by the first scheme, that we imagine they will scarcely be such fools as to suffer a second attempt'. Due to the change in public sentiment, the Attorney General John Plunkett QC, decided that Wentworth's lottery was illegal under the *Lottery Act* and that it wasn't to proceed ('Advertising', 31 March 1849, p.3). Plunkett also informed Mr Samuel Lyons, who was the agent for the Bank of Australia, that the second Bank lottery was not to take place ('Advertising', 21 April 1849, p.3). It was the end of lotteries in the colony.

Angus McDonald (2) though, was one of the winners. After feeling like they would never be able to own their own property, Angus's (2) lottery win was unbelievable and life-changing for Catherine and their young family. Undoubtedly, it was an incredibly joyous occasion with much celebration among their family and friends. A spin of the wheel had literally changed the course of their lives in unimaginable ways. Their new home, in the NSW colony had presented them with resources beyond their wildest dreams.

A few weeks after their big win, Catherine, her husband Angus (2), their four sons and various other members of their extended family headed to Underbank, via Dungog, to view their new property. As the party travelled through Dungog, which was the nearest service town to Underbank, their arrival was noted in the local newspaper. The *Maitland Mercury* referred to them as 'the fortunate highlanders' ('Dungog', 31 January 1849, p.2). It would have been a very joyful journey for all who went along for the ride to view their new estate and the place they would call home.

THE Angus MacDonald

However, Angus's good fortune didn't last long. Three months after their lottery win, Catherine, Angus (2) and their sons, were still living at Dunmore Estate, waiting for the ownership of their new estate to be finalised. They hadn't yet moved in and taken possession of their new landholding at Underbank. Angus (2) had just employed Donald McLachlan as the station manager to look after his new property. There was a lot to attend to before they could move.

As such, on the 6th of April 1849, Angus (2) rode to Maitland for the day to do some business. He was with Donald McLachlan the new station manager he had employed and Hugh McFadyen, who was Angus's (2) brother-in-law (married to his sister Christina McDonald). The three men were riding back home at the end of the day. They had spread out along the road and were about a mile or so past the Falls, when Angus's (2) horse appeared on the road without a rider in the saddle. Neither of the men saw Angus (2) come off his horse, but when they turned back to look for him, they found him lying on the road in a pool of blood. He died shortly afterwards ('Fatal Accident', 7 April 1849. p.2). The news of Angus's (2) death would have been an incredible shock to Catherine. Her world turned upside down. In an instant, her joy at winning their new property must have changed to grief and uncertainty about the future.

At the Coronial Inquest, Donald McLachlan and Hugh McFadyen (the two men who were riding with Angus (2)), suggested to the coroner that Angus (2) was not a 'skilful rider' and that he was riding with his stirrups poorly adjusted down a steep part of the road. As a result, the Coronial Inquest made a finding of 'accidental death' ('Fatal Accident', 7 April 1849, p.2). There was no will, as until now Angus (2) did not own anything of much value ('McDonald v Elliott and Another', 8 September 1852, p.1). However, with Angus's (2) premature death, before he had even taken possession of the property, the legal situation was merky at best.

The new property at Underbank was Catherine's only chance of securing her family's future. A court hearing was convened to decide the matter of who owned the property. It was argued in the court that Catherine's second eldest son, six years old Angus McDonald (4), was the holder of the winning ticket in the Bank lottery, rather than his deceased father Angus (2). It was claimed that the estate had originally been delivered to the father, Angus McDonald (2) on behalf of his young son, Angus McDonald (4) ('Re Angus McDonald, an Infant', 19 May 1849, p.4). The court was told that young Angus (4) was THE Angus McDonald, whose name was on the winning lottery ticket.

Neil Radford (2017) writing in the *Dictionary of Sydney*, suggested that Angus McDonald (2) had bought tickets in the lottery for each of his four sons, all of whom were under eight years old at the time. There is no evidence for this. It is highly unlikely that a poor tenant farmer would have had £16 spare to buy four lottery tickets, given the worth of even £4 at the time. As we know Angus (2) tried to sell half of his ticket to a neighbour, so he probably regretted the extravagance of buying even one ticket. It also seems unlikely that Angus would have bought a ticket for his *second* eldest son. If he was going to buy a ticket for just one of the children, it would most likely have been for his eldest son, eight years old Ewen McDonald.

The reporting of the inquest, which was published in the *Maitland Mercury* ('Fatal Accident', 7 April 1849, p.2) the following day, had suggested that the father, Angus McDonald (2), was the winner of the first prize in the lottery. There was no mention of his son being the winner. Also, the tone of an article in *The Maitland Mercury* ('Re Angus McDonald, an Infant', 19 May 1849, p.4) reporting on the court case to prove the ownership of Underbank, implied that there was a considered plan by the family to suggest that young Angus was the owner of the winning ticket. It could well have been, as at the time of the accident Catherine had no money, there was no will, and Catherine could not read or write, let alone fight an expensive, protracted legal battle to claim any right to the Underbank property for herself.

All in all, it seems unlikely that the ticket was purchased for the child. However, the court accepted the argument that it belonged to him, apparently seeing no harm or illegality in it. According to the report on the court case in *The Maitland Mercury* ('Re Angus McDonald, an Infant', 19 May 1849), 'His Honour directed usual and necessary references to the

Master, to be made' to young Angus (4). The judge asserted that young Angus was, in fact, the owner of the winning ticket.

A petition was then presented to the court on behalf of young Angus (4) to have a guardian appointed for him. A couple of months later, in the Supreme Court, His Honour Mr Dowling granted the request for Angus's mother Catherine McDonald to be appointed as his guardian. The Judge also stated that a 'fit and proper allowance for maintenance' was to be paid to Catherine as the guardian of the owner of Underbank ('Supreme Court', 14 July 1849, p.2). The transfer of Cryon Station from Helenus Scott to young Angus McDonald (4) was finally completed a month later in August 1849 ('Transfer of Runs', 7 August 1849, p.1165).

Catherine was now a widow with four children under eight. She was only twenty-six herself. She was a single parent, responsible for a large property, employees, tenants and stock. The move to Underbank was a big step. It was approximately seventy kilometres (forty-four miles) from her home at Dunmore Estate to her new home at Underbank. That was a significant distance by horse and cart. Dunmore had provided a ready-made community of Gaelic speaking Scots from her home on the Isle of Skye. Nevertheless, she made the move and settled in with her children and they made it their home.

The Gringai

The Gringai (Guringay or Guringai people) are the traditional custodians of the land Catherine and her family now called home. It is thought that the Gringai were most likely a clan of the Wonnarua Nation (History in the Williams River Valley, n.d.). According to Syron and Russell (15 August 2018), Gringai traditional land stretches 'From modern day Newcastle to Singleton, on the northern side of the Hunter, through the Barrington's and back down the Manning to the ocean'. This includes the land around Underbank and Dungog, the upper Williams, Paterson and Allyn River valleys and up to the Barrington Tops. Syron and Russell (15 August 2018) also describe how the Gringai lived in 'Nurras' or groups with each group having had between six and nine huts. The Nurras were spread out across the district, giving each group enough space for hunting and gathering food.

Europeans first settled in the area in the 1820s. However, little is known about the first contact between the Gringai and the colonists (Syron & Russell, 2018). From quite early though the Gringai acted as trackers, helping to capture escaped convicts, bushrangers and livestock. They also guided new settlers through bush tracks, as the road networks were limited. Aboriginal trackers were usually paid for their time with flour, tobacco or sugar (Gilpin, 29 October 1889, p.3). Reynolds (1996, p.103) suggests that First Nations people often had excellent 'linguistic skills' and they could pick up a 'working knowledge of English in a matter of weeks.'

There were also violent conflicts between the new settlers and the Gringai in the early days of contact in the area. Some of these encounters resulted in massacres. An example of a violent conflict which ended in a massacre, took place north of Dungog, near Gloucester, in the early 1830s. A group of local Aboriginal men had speared some cattle on Bakers Creek Station and run others into the bush. The European station hands mixed arsenic into damper (a type of bread) and left it where the Aboriginal men would find it. The arsenic resulted in the deaths of all of the men. The site, 'Belbora' (or Baal Bora) became known as a place of death to be shunned by First Nations people ('Conflicts with the Natives', 25 April 1922, p.2).

Yet another tragic example of violence happened in 1835, just two years before Catherine arrived in Australia. It became known as the 'Kiripit (now Rawdon Vale) massacre'. Five shepherds working for a settler were killed by a group of Gringai men. The shepherds were outnumbered by the Gringai and the last one was chased and speared in sight of the homestead at Underbank, when it was still owned by John Lord. After the attack, the Aboriginal men dispersed into two groups. A group of settlers from the Williams and Allyn Rivers areas then chased one group of Gringai on to a cliff top on the Mackenzie Tableland in the Barrington Tops. From here they surrounded them and fired as the men jumped, or were pushed, over the cliff. The other group was hunted down on the Bowman River where they were all killed ('Conflicts with the Natives', 25 April 1922, p.2).

One Gringai man who survived was hung for murder in Dungog in 1835 as a warning to other First Nations people. His name was recorded only as Charley. There are various interpretations of what happened. However, Charley claimed through an interpreter that he was authorised by the tribe to carry out Traditional Law and punish the shepherds who had destroyed a sacred talisman in front of an Aboriginal woman they were holding captive (History in the Williams River Valley, n.d.). This was just one example of Traditional Law coming into direct conflict with the laws of the white settlers.

The following year, in 1836, due to the number of conflicts between the colonial settlers and the local Aboriginal people in the area, the Dungog Magistrate Thomas Cook made a request to the Police Command in Maitland. Cook asked for two mounted troopers to 'aid the constabulary' in managing the Aborigines ('Cook to the Officer in Command Maitland Police', 29 January 1836). Lawrence Myles JP suggested in a letter to the Colonial Secretary in 1836, that 'the Blacks are becoming more troublesome' ('Myles to the Colonial Secretary', 20 May 1836).

The Gringai, like First Nations people across the colony, were suffering from the impacts of colonisation. It is believed there were around 300 Gringai people before disease and conflict with the white settlers wiped out large numbers of their people (History in the Williams River Valley, n.d.). There were smallpox epidemics in 1789, and again in 1830, that killed many First Nations people (Davidson, 1994, p.89). Children were particularly susceptible to European diseases such as measles. In 1847, measles killed thirty Gringai children in just one season. This was about thirty percent of their young people (Williams, 2014). The introduction of previously unknown infectious diseases took a heavy toll.

The white settlers often anointed chiefs among First Nations tribes and hung brass name plates around their necks. These so-called chiefs were usually men who were working with the colonists and they were given rewards and responsibilities by the settlers. King Tom of Dunmore ('Original Correspondence', 25 August 1877, p.10) was one such man; and King Darby of Dungog ('Hunter River District News', 21 November 1846, p.2) was another. However, First Nations tribes did not traditionally have chiefs. Instead, respected elders in clan groups consulted with each other over decisions. The colonists often by-passed the elders and appointed 'chiefs' of their own which further disrupted the traditional way of life for Aboriginal people.

By the time Catherine and her family arrived at Underbank in 1849, the conflicts between the new settlers and the Gringai people had mostly ceased. As the number of their people had significantly declined, the Gringai were gradually accommodating the white settlers (see Figure 10). For example, some Gringai men were known to join in playing cricket with the local settlers (Miller, 1985). No doubt, this included cricket matches held at Underbank.

Many First Nations people who learned European ways integrated these ways into their own 'cultural and spiritual practice'. According to Case (27 July 2023), the European violin is one example. The violin was originally taught to some Aboriginal people, as a way of 'civilising' them. However, many Aboriginal people used the violin 'on their own terms'. They fused it with their own traditional culture and incorporated it into community events and campfires in the bush. Karskens (2020, p.11) suggests that rather than the elimination of First Nations people and their cultures, there is a 'meaningful space for contingency and ambiguity, for relationships and resistance'. She posits that some Aboriginal people who adopted European ways, clothing and language, showed a 'cultural dynamism'. However, as time went on, many Aboriginal people lost the connection to their culture.

Dungog

Catherine's new home at Underbank was twenty-five kilometres (about sixteen miles) from Dungog, which was the nearest service town. Dungog could be reached by horseback, as long as none of the river crossings was flooded. The name Dungog was derived from the local Gringai dialect. The Gringai name for the area was Tunkok (or Tungog) which means, 'the place of thinly wooded hills' (Bennett, 1964, p.2).

Figure 10. Last of his tribe, n.d. A Gringai man who was identified only as 'Brandy'. He was born in the Tillegra /Underbank area in about 1829. He was not actually the last of his tribe (Photo by H. Pardy courtesy of Dungog Historical Society Inc, 17 April 2021, NSW, Australia).

A court of petty sessions was built at Dungog in 1833, and the town was first gazetted in 1834. Although it wasn't surveyed until 1838, an 'unofficial settlement grew up' in the meantime (Karskens, 1986, p.53). By the late 1840s when Catherine arrived, Dungog had quite a few houses, a courthouse, police barracks, two inns, two schools, a steam flour mill, a church, and even a band (Williams, 2014). A post office was established in 1835, but a regular mail service didn't begin until 1847. The mail was sent twice a week from Sydney on the steamer to Raymond Terrace, where the contractor had to pick it up. The contractor then rode on horseback to Dungog, which was an eight-hour ride, stopping at Clarence Town and Seaham on route ('Arrival and Despatch of Mails in the Hunter', 13 January 1847, p.2).

Dr Ellar McKinlay, was a well-respected Scottish doctor who lived and practised in Dungog from the 1840s until his death in 1889 (Williams, 2014). Dr McKinlay advertised in the *Sydney Herald* ('Advertising', 13 April 1840(a), p.2) on his arrival. His advertisement was addressed to the 'inhabitants of Dungog and surrounds'. It suggested that he would 'pay strict and unremitting attention to the cases entrusted in him' and that 'for the convenience of the settlers' he would 'always have on hand an assortment of Horse and Cattle medicines'.

In order to reassure people that life was good in Dungog, the 1848 Wells Gazetteer (cited in Karskens, 1986, p.79) suggested to its readers that 'the only reminder of the bad times of the 1840s was Mrs Hooke's boiling down works at the edge of the town'. The boiling down works was where cattle and sheep, when they were worth little at the saleyards, could be boiled down for tallow. The tallow was then used to make soap and candles and fetched a reasonable price. 'Boiling down' was a saviour for many pastoralists in times of drought and depression in the colony ('The New Australian Staple', 24 June 1843, p.2). The Gazetteer confidently suggested that Dungog was 'a prominent place in the list of the habitations of civilised man'. This was just as well, because Catherine and her family would have needed to make regular trips to Dungog for supplies and to take care of business matters.

Four McKinnon siblings

In 1851 Catherine's brother, John McKinnon, paid a bounty for their younger siblings, Angus William McKinnon and Margaret McKinnon, to travel out from Kendram on Skye to join them at Underbank. John paid £3 for his brother Angus (Angus McKinnon, 9 June 1851) and £2 for his sister Margaret (Margaret McKinnon, 9 June 1851). The two siblings arrived in Sydney on the 6th of June 1851, onboard the *Emperor*. Angus was twenty years old when he arrived, and he could both read and write (Angus McKinnon, 6 June 1851). He had come to live at Underbank and help manage the large estate ('McDonald v Elliott & Another', 8 September 1852, p.1). Catherine's sister, Margaret, was twenty-three years old and could read, but not write (Margaret McKinnon, 6 June 1851).

Catherine's older brother, John McKinnon was also living at Underbank (Margaret McKinnon, 28 August 1851) and had been helping with the management of the Underbank Estate ('Maitland Circuit Court', 24 August 1853, p.2). Margaret also initially resided at Underbank. The four siblings were all living close by to one another. It must have been a joyous occasion for them to reunite. They had not seen each other for fourteen years, since Catherine and John had left Skye aboard the *Midlothian*. A lot had happened in that time. Angus and Margaret would have had news of their parents, their two sisters, Ann and Dorcas, who had remained on Skye, their aunts, uncles, cousins and friends. They would have heard about the joys and sorrows which followed from the many marriages, babies and deaths that had happened since they last saw each other.

Angus and Margaret's emigration suggests there was some communication between the family back at Kendram and Catherine and her brother John at Underbank. Initially, before the mail came as far as Dungog in 1847, letters would have been transported between Skye and NSW, and vice versa, by passengers travelling on ships. It probably took five or six months for a letter to travel between Kendram and Underbank, making it about a year to send a letter and to receive a reply. Communication between the families was difficult and undoubtedly infrequent.

Only three and a half months after arriving in Australia, Catherine's sister, Margaret McKinnon, married John McMillan (1812-1896). They were married at Underbank (Margaret McKinnon, 28 August 1851). John McMillan was also originally from Kilmuir parish, on the Isle of Skye. He had arrived in NSW in 1840 on the ship, *'Henry Porcher'* ('Lower Clarence-MacLean, Friday', 7 March 1896, p.4) some eleven years earlier. He was a tenant farmer on land near the Williams River, to the east of Dunmore Estate, which was known as 'Portree'.

The year after Catherine's younger brother, Angus McKinnon, had arrived in Australia he acted in court, on behalf of his nephew nine years old Angus McDonald (4) who was the owner of Underbank. The case came about when Catherine was accused of selling cattle which did not belong to her. It was a complicated story and the accuser, Mr Davis, eventually won the case. Catherine claimed to the judge that she, herself, only owned ten or eleven head of cattle which had belonged to her deceased husband. Nevertheless, the judge ruled that Mr Davis could recover the debt from Underbank, with the sale of 268 cattle because Catherine was the guardian of the owner of the estate ('McDonald v Elliott & Another', 8 September 1852, p.1).

When he was giving evidence Mr Robert John Lees, the overseer of Underbank, claimed to have witnessed the agent for the Bank of Australia handing over the Underbank property to Angus McDonald (2), on behalf of his young son ('McDonald v Elliott and Another', 8 September 1852, p.1). Presumably this was to support Catherine's earlier claim that her son, young Angus (4), was the rightful winner of the lottery.

During the court proceedings a witness also told the court that Cryon Station, which was the other property involved in Angus's (2) original lottery win, had previously been sold ('McDonald v Elliott & Another', 8 September 1852, p.1). Joseph Pearse had purchased Cryon Station from young Angus (4) in February 1852 ('Classified Advertising', 17 April 1852, p.1). Cryon Station bordered on land Pearse already owned which was called Gorien ('Claims to Leases of Crown Lands Beyond the Settled District', 30 September 1848, p.2). Joseph Pearse was a large landholder in the colony, and he is a man who will make an appearance again later in this story. Cryon

Station was approximately 400 km (250 miles) from Underbank, making it difficult for the family to manage. No doubt, there would have also been a shortage of cash for paying wages and running Underbank. Liquidating Cryon Station would have helped solve the problem - in the short term at least.

Gold fever

After the initial group of Indian labourers was brought to NSW to work for members of the squattocracy, the practice of importing Indian labour continued. Between 1837 and 1846, 166 Indian men were brought to the colony as indentured labourers to work as shepherds on remote properties owned by the squattocracy (Ohlsson, 2013, p.153). However, the practice was stopped in 1846, by the Governor General of India, when a boatload of Indian men arrived in the colony in a state of starvation ('The Coolie Immigrants per "Orwell"', 11 April 1846, p.134).

Benjamin Boyd was from a wealthy Scots family who had been associated with the African slave trade. He was a ship owner, whaler, banker and prominent squatter in his own right. Boyd, who had arrived in the NSW colony at the end of transportation, became a voice for the squattocracy around issues of labour supply. He argued for lowering the wages of free immigrant workers and he wanted to reinstate transportation. Twice in 1847, he sent ships to the Pacific Islands of Tanna (Vanuatu) and Lifou (New Caledonia, to secure workers to act as shepherds on his various NSW stations. In total, Boyd lured 192 people (mostly men, but also a few women and underage children) to his ships. He had them 'make a mark' on a five-year contract of employment (Dunn, May 2021, p.2).

Some members of the Legislative Council suggested that the Islanders had no idea what a shepherd was, yet alone where they were being taken to and why. It was argued that Boyd's scheme constituted a 'traffic in human creatures, obviously unable to contract for themselves, and who must therefore be brought from their native land either by force or fraud' ('Legislative Council', 2 October 1847, p.2).

In reaction to Boyd's controversial measures, the Legislative Council amended the *Masters and Servants Act 1847* to specifically exclude workers from the South Sea and Pacific Islands, meaning Boyd had no legal hold over the men. As a result, he was compelled to abandon his controversial labour scheme. The workers he had already imported to NSW left *en masse,* and tried to find their way home. Boyd's scheme became associated with the term 'blackbirding'. The term was coined some thirty years later in the 1870s to refer to the practice of intimidating and kidnapping Pacific and South Sea Islanders to work as labourers in the colony of Queensland (Dunn, May 2021, p.2).

Neither the practice of blackbirding, nor the importation of Indian labourers continued in the NSW colony after 1847. Despite this, the importation of Chinese men as indentured labourers continued. The practice of importing indentured labour was openly referred to in the colony, at the time, as 'slave labour'. Rev Lang argued that while there were those in the colony who would advocate for a 'mitigated slavery', he believed British immigration was the answer. He said 'our only chance, as a people, of ever attaining a high and influential position, morally, intellectually, and politically, in the civilised world, depends upon our getting a thoroughly British population' (Lang, 1852, p.67). The squattocracy though, were set on paying very low wages.

There was a lot of debate generated in the newspapers about the situation. According to one correspondent in the *Peoples Advocate* ('Chinese Coolies', 3 March 1849, p.6), 'These lawless sons of robbery and spoliation having obtained land for nothing, require labour also for nothing; in short they wish to revive the slave-trade and the feudal system with all their attendant barbarities'.

Notwithstanding any ideas of the men being slave labour, racist sentiment towards the Chinese immigrants was evident from the beginning of Chinese immigration. The Chinese were unfairly considered by many to be 'a coloured and inferior race...distinguished for its vices rather than its virtues'

('Chinese Immigration', 29 November 1851, p.2). This notion of the perceived inferiority of the Chinese immigrants was, according to Feng (2017), embedded in the idea that only white Australians were entitled to non-indentured jobs and resources. The influx of cheap, able bodied men from China was seen to diminish the opportunities for European men in the colony at the time.

As one commentator ('Our Social Prospects', 3 March 1849, p.6) argued, the Chinese immigrants work for very low wages and they have no families to support, yet they contrive to save money. 'They *(the Chinese)* have only one idea-they have only one aim, and that is to acquire wealth and oppress the labouring man'. Another writer ('Chinese Coolies', 3 March 1849, p.6) suggested 'Give a Chinese a pound, he starts as a hawker; at the end of the year he has £50, takes a small shop, then a larger, and so on till he accumulates great wealth, and all this through his penurious, scheming, swindling, cheating habits'. Clearly, there was fear among the colonists about the new immigrants perceived ability to make a success of opportunities at their expense.

In 1849, just prior to the discovery of gold in NSW, 2600 people had left the NSW colony for California in search of gold. The Californian gold rush had begun and many mostly single men left in earnest with the hope of striking it rich ('Reminiscences of Maitland and the District', no.13 1849, 20 January 1894, p.13). Apparently, there was money to be made in California but the conditions were very poor, the cost of living was very high and there was considerable sickness and death.

Many Americans believed that all of the Australians were convicts. As a result, a statement was made by a Californian newspaper, *Alta California*, which called for legislation to prevent the landing of the Australians in California. The paper suggested that 'thousands of Jack Sheppards [sic], living, moving, murdering cutthroats' were arriving from the colonies and causing 'depradations [sic] and depraving the morals of the community'

('Reminiscences of Maitland and the District', No.14 1851, 17 February 1894, p.16).

It is interesting to look at the portrayal of the Australians who went to the gold rush in California. They were not exactly welcomed with open arms. They were generally stereotyped as convicts, and not to be trusted, or given fair opportunities. It compares in many ways to how the Chinese were viewed in the Australian media as resentment towards them grew within colonial society.

In 1851, just two years after Catherine and her children moved to their new life at Underbank, the gold rush began in NSW. The first 'payable find' in the NSW colony was made at Ophir near Bathurst and it started the rush to find gold all around NSW. In 1851, an article titled 'The Gold Fever', (17 May 1851, p.4) in the *Bathurst Free Press* stated that

> A complete mental madness appears to have seized almost every member of the community, and as a natural consequence there has been a universal rush to the diggins [sic]'....'Servants of every description are leaving their various employments and the employers are per necessitatum [sic] preparing to follow.

Many of the Chinese immigrants who had been imported as indentured labourers were leaving severe poverty, war and political instability in their own country and hoped to send money home to their families. They were generally very badly treated by the squattocracy that had brought them to Australia and invariably they hadn't improved their circumstances in any way. Therefore, as news of the gold rush spread, many of the Chinese workers caught 'gold fever' and headed to the goldfields (see Figure 11). In December 1852, Mr Wentworth informed the Legislative Council that most of the Chinese men who had been brought to NSW as indentured labour 'had absconded in masses from their masters and the laws of the country had been proved to be powerless' to stop them ('Legislative Council', 15 December 1852, p.2).

Figure 11. Chinese leaving for the diggings. Cobb's caoch [sic], Castlemaine, 1853 (Photo courtesy of the *State Library of Victoria*, Australia, Acc no: H2407 Image no: a14848).

Nearly 3000 Chinese men were brought to NSW between 1847-1853 to work as farm labourers and shepherds until the process was stopped in 1855 (Ohlsson, Nov 2013). Chinese immigration then started up again from 1858, due to the gold rush, but this was mostly the voluntary immigration of men who were working the gold fields ('Chinese Immigration', 10 July 1858, p.4).

The local newspapers were full of stories about the gold miners' successes, spurring others on with 'gold fever'. For example, the *Maitland Mercury* ('The Gold Fields', 1 December 1852, p.4) had one story that stated that new diggings at Lambing Flats, which was near Sofala in the upper part of the Turon River in NSW, had been discovered 'whence gold to a "startling" amount has been brought into town'.

Catherine, her family and those in her community were not immune to the excitement generated by these stories. The discovery of gold in NSW started a frenzy which led to some people striking it rich, while others ended up working for next to nothing. Many of the young men who lived in the area around Underbank went to try their luck at striking it rich. Catherine's step-son, from her first husband's wife, Murdoch Graham, was one of them. He left Underbank and headed to the gold rush on the Turon in 1852 ('The Late Mr M Graham', 11 April 1891, p.8). Her eldest son, Ewen McDonald also spent some time at the Abercrombie River goldfield some years later, although it was said that he 'gained little more than experience' ('Obituary', 14 July 1916, p.6). The discovery of gold in NSW changed the nature of the colony practically overnight. Gold increased the general wealth of the community and meant many people were able to better their circumstances, although not everyone struck it rich.

The first partially democratic elections which were held in the colony in 1843 only served to increase the all-pervasive power of the landed class. The *Squatters Act* then put land ownership even further out of reach for most ordinary working-class people in the colony. Catherine was forced to confront the turbulence of the times. She took the necessary measures which were needed in order to secure her future and that of her children.

As a widow with four children to feed, the threat of disadvantage and destitution would have loomed large. Without Underbank their lives would have been very difficult. Land ownership meant everything to their survival. As luck would have it, and no doubt the good will of those who helped her through the process, she was able to safeguard their home at Underbank, at least for the time being.

However, running the large estate would not have been an easy task. Catherine relied heavily on help from her siblings, particularly her two brothers, in order to negotiate the finances and the day-to-day management of the estate. Labour shortages continued to be an issue in the colony. The short supply of stockmen, labourers, shepherds and drovers was further exacerbated by the gold rush which enticed many men to leave their employment, and take a gamble on their future at the gold fields.

Chapter 6
Catherine Ballard

Caroline Chisholm - Thomas Lewis Ballard - more children - Dorcas' death - birthing options - white male suffrage - Chinese Immigrants Regulation and Restriction Act 1861 - Crown Lands Act 1861 - Felons Apprehension Act 1865 - Captain Thunderbolt

'Angels of the house'

Catherine was very much part of a general worldview, characteristic of British and colonial society at the time. This worldview was based on 'an emerging ideology of domesticity' which saw the home as a refuge from the outside public world. Inherent in this view was the idea that it was a woman's role to uphold morality and Christian family values in the home. Women were expected to be, as Lake (2020, p.139) puts it, 'angels of the house' who were 'agents of both religion and civilisation'.

As we have seen, this was also very much Rev Lang's view and one of the motivating factors for his bounty scheme which brought Catherine and the other Presbyterian Scots families to NSW. Caroline Chisholm also exemplified this view of the world. Both Rev Lang and Caroline Chisholm held strong religious convictions, which were based on narrowly defined roles for women. Even though they didn't always agree with each other, their conservative Christian views were very influential in colonial society.

Chisholm was a devoutly religious English woman who lived in the NSW colony with her husband and children. By the 1850s Chisholm and her work were well known across Britain, India and Australia (Iltis, 2006). Chisholm lobbied to increase family re-unification among former convicts and free immigrants in the colonies, believing that women as wives 'civilised' men. She procured housing and employment for women arriving in the colony, and she set up a scheme to 'disperse [female] immigrants into the interior' of

NSW to live and work with respectable families. Chisholm hoped that they would find husbands among the single men working on the land (Iltis, 2006).

Chisholm reasoned that if Her Majesty's 'paternal government' was really invested in seeing a 'well conducted community' in the colonies, then more female immigration was needed. She (cited in MacKenzie, 1852, p.115) famously said:

> For all the clergy you can dispatch, and the schoolmasters you can appoint, all the churches you can build, and all the books you can export, will never do much good, without "God's police"-wives and little children - good and virtuous women.

According to Anne Summers (2016) women who deviated from the standards of femininity inherent in this ideology were often seen as fallen, or as 'whores'. However, Summers argues that the ideal of domesticity was a middle-class ideal. Many working-class women didn't have a choice: they had to work, particularly if they were living without the 'protection' of a husband.

Even though Chisholm led a very public life herself, she didn't encourage other women to do the same. As a result of her deeply held Christian convictions and family values, Chisholm was against any behaviour that deterred women from marrying and having children. She believed in the sanctity of marriage, and that a women's place was in the home tending to the moral, as well as the physical, needs of her family. As such, it was assumed that a young Christian widow like Catherine would remarry. For without a husband in colonial NSW, she lacked respectability and social status among her peers.

Thomas Ballard

So it was, that four years after Catherine's first husband Angus (2) had fallen to his death from his horse, Catherine was a very eligible widow. No doubt she had many suitors. She was financially independent with her guardianship-stipend and she had a comfortable home. She also had four sons, aged between six and twelve, from her first marriage. It would have been expected that she would remarry and indeed she did. Catherine married Thomas Lewis Ballard, her second husband, at St Ann's Scots Church, in Paterson on the 23rd of June in 1853. They were married by the Rev James Brotherston Laughton (Catherine MacDonald, 1853). The previous reverend at St Ann's, was Rev Ross who was a respected Gaelic speaker and had preached in Gaelic. This made the church a favourite among the Scots community. Rev Laughton didn't speak or preach in Gaelic but he was a 'prolific writer on theology' and a Moderator of the Synod of Australia (Archer, & Sullivan, 2004, p.30).

According to their wedding certificate, Catherine was a thirty years old widow and Thomas was a thirty-four years old bachelor. Thomas signed his name on the marriage certificate, but Catherine remained illiterate and signed the marriage certificate with the mark of a cross (Catherine MacDonald, 1853). It is unknown to what degree Thomas was able to speak or understand Gaelic. But it could be assumed, that by now, Catherine was comfortable speaking English, albeit with a strong Scots accent.

Catherine's new husband, Thomas, was born in 1819 in Northiam, in the Rother District of East Sussex in England. He migrated to Australia on the *Woodbridge* in 1838 when he was nineteen. He had travelled with his parents, Edward Ballard, who was forty-three, and Mary Ballard (nee Lewis), who was forty-four years old, and his five younger siblings, Lydia, Luther, James, Sarah and Emma Ballard. His father, Edward Ballard, was a 'native' of Northiam Sussex and a 'Calvinist' (Edward Ballard, 1838). Edward was a 'farm servant' and was engaged by Mr Fletcher to work in Maitland (Edward Ballard, 1838). Thomas' mother Mary had died two years before his marriage to Catherine in 1851, and his father Edward died only a few years later in 1857. They both died in Newcastle ('Catherine's Ballard Family', n.d.).

Thomas's sister Emma Ballard, and his brother Luther Ballard were the witnesses to Catherine and Thomas's wedding. Thomas's sister Emma married Duncan Edward Swinden in 1878 in Maitland, after his first wife had died. Emma was forty-seven when she married and she didn't have any children (Emma Ballard, 1878). Luther Ballard and his wife, Sarah Walker also lived at Underbank for many years. The first six of their fifteen children were born there before they moved to Bowraville in the Nambucca Valley of NSW ('Catherine's Ballard Family', n.d.). Underbank was a vibrant place which offered a home to many people over the years, including from the extended McKinnon, McDonald and Ballard families. The various family members who lived at Underbank also provided a ready labour force to work the estate, as the on-going labour shortages across the colony made it difficult to find workers.

Apparently, Thomas worked cutting red cedar before his marriage to Catherine ('Catherine's Ballard Family', n.d.). Cedar trees grew on the banks of the Williams River and were hauled with bullock carts and floated down stream to Clarence Town, and then on to Newcastle and further afield. Cedar was in high demand and the trees became scarce due to the huge quantities that were being harvested. Cedar cutters had to go further and further up the rivers to find the trees. They would live in bush camps while they were logging (History in the Williams River Valley, n.d.). There was a local account of a cedar tree which had a circumference of nine metres and it was estimated it would produce nine kilometres of valuable timber ('Dungog, NSW', 2020). However, cedar cutting was a dangerous occupation which led to many accidents including the loss of limbs and death (History in the Williams River Valley, n.d.). As a result, once they were married, Thomas stopped cutting cedar and took up farming ('Catherine's Ballard Family', n.d.).

Thomas became involved in the running of Underbank. The year after he married Catherine, Thomas advertised 'clearing leases' in the *Maitland Mercury* for two farms he was letting which were part of the Underbank Estate ('Classified Advertising', 15 March 1854, p.3). But managing Underbank wasn't without its challenges. In the same year Thomas placed another advertisement in the newspaper as the 'Manager for the Guardian of the Underbank Estate' ('Classified Advertising', 14 January 1854, p.3). The advertisement stated that he was offering a £5 reward to anyone who gave information which led to the conviction of those people who were stealing or disposing of cattle carrying the Underbank brands. He also offered ten shillings per head to any person who returned the branded cattle to a secure paddock on the estate. There were ongoing issues with people stealing cattle, although this certainly wasn't isolated to Underbank.

Livestock was the currency of rural Australia. West (2005) suggests that due to cash shortages in the colony, stockmen were often paid in cattle. The skilled horsemen sometimes helped themselves to a few extra head. The stockmen knew the lay of the land, and while mustering semi wild cattle, they sometimes cut some out for themselves and went back later to collect them. Animals could be traded or swapped. In some instances, West (West, 2005) suggests that neighbours were not shy to help themselves to a cow or two; and butchering a neighbour's cow might be tolerated as long as it wasn't too many, too often. These thefts were often difficult to prove and 'served to blur the line between legal and illegal' in the rural parts of the colony. Furthermore, Karskens (2009, p.300) suggests that some cattle thieves even accrued their own herd which they then drove into the interior of the colony, away from the settlers. Some of these men amassed vast fortunes and joined the ranks of the squattocracy.

Catherine was once again a married woman. As she and Thomas went about establishing their new life together as husband and wife, Catherine's role largely centred around her family. In particular, she was focused on fulfilling her obligations as a good Christian wife and mother, caring for the well-being of Thomas and her children. She would have also expected to increase the size of her family.

Child mortality

In May of 1854, the year after they were married, Catherine and Thomas had their first child together. She was a daughter and they called her Mary Ann Ballard, after Thomas's mother. Then the following year at Kendram in

Skye, on the 18th June in 1855, Catherine's older sister, Dorcas Ross (nee McKinnon), also gave birth. Dorcas was in her early forties and it was to be her last child. Sadly, Dorcas died while giving birth that day (Dorcas Ross, 18 June 1855(b)) and she was buried in the Kilmalaug cemetery, across the way from Kendram (Dorcas Gormhail Ross, 1855(a)).

Baby Dorcas, as the infant was called, later died in a tragic accident when she was only four years old. According to her death certificate, baby Dorcas died 'by her clothes taking fire'. It took nineteen days for her to die. It would have been horrific. Baby Dorcas is also buried in the Kilmalaug cemetery (Dorcas Ross, 24 October 1859). Dorcas had already lost two children who both died in 1850 (Dorcas Ross, 18 June 1855(a)). It wasn't unusual for infants to die at this time in the nineteenth century. Still, it is difficult to reconcile the amount of death and heartbreak that happened in Dorcas's family.

As we saw earlier, Catherine lost her own child, her first Angus (3), when he was only four years old (Catherine Ballard, 16 May 1904). Child mortality rates in the NSW colony were still persistently high. In 1860, the infant mortality rate in the Australian colony was 391 deaths per 1000 births. This meant that just under forty percent of children didn't survive to be five years old (O'Neill, 2019). These figures only represent the deaths that were recorded. Many infant and child deaths in remote places would not have been officially registered.

There were various causes for the high infant death rate, such as gastroenteritis, pneumonia, whooping cough (pertussis), scarlet fever and measles. There were influenza pandemics in 1836-38, 1847 and 1850. Then, the 1860s saw a measles pandemic which was closely followed by an outbreak of scarlet fever (scarlatina). All of these diseases are highly infectious and can be particularly fatal for children (de Looper, 2015). According to de Looper (2015, p.83) 'with few effective medical therapies epidemics of infectious disease were feared'. As we will see in this story, many of Catherine's grandchildren didn't make it to adulthood.

Birthing options

Catherine went on to have five more children with Thomas. Maria Catherine Ballard was her second daughter. Maria was born in February 1856. Then in October of 1858, Catherine and Thomas had a son, Thomas Edward (he was known as 'Edward', presumably after Thomas's father). David followed in August 1860. Cyrus was born in June of 1862 and the youngest child, Allan, was born in 1864 when Catherine was forty-one ('Catherine's Ballard Family', n.d.).

Many children were born at Underbank over the years that Catherine lived there, including Catherine's own Ballard children and some of her grandchildren. This is evident by the many birth records referred to in this story, but there would have been many more families who lived in the various cottages scattered around the Underbank Estate and in the local area whose children were also born at Underbank. At this time, women didn't labour in hospital. Babies were born at home.

According to Glenda Strachan (2001(b)), women in remote areas were sometimes assisted to birth by local Aboriginal women who had experience and traditional knowledge. Some women stayed with relatives to give birth, or had mothers or sisters stay with them, while others were supported to birth by neighbours or friends in their community. Strachan says that this process of women assisting each other to give birth was known as 'neighbouring' and it was often reciprocated.

Strachan also suggests that, in some instances, older women with a lot of experience, particularly widows, became lay midwives or what was known as 'handywomen'. These handywomen were sometimes paid for their services, but not always. The amount of pay they received, whether it was in money or goods, often reflected their level of skill and the support they offered.

There has been very limited research into early birthing practices in the NSW colony. Little information was kept about the act of giving birth, who attended and what they did to help (Strachan, 2001(b)). So, in order to find out more about birthing practices in the area, Strachan (2001(b)) investigated civil birth registrations of non-Aboriginal women in the Dungog and the Upper Williams Valley between 1856 – 1896. She found that particular women were present as 'witnesses', or even listed as 'nurses' (with no qualifications or formal training) on multiple birth registrations in the area. Strachan posits that these women were either neighbouring or assisting at births as handywomen. Mrs Redman was one such woman who frequently appeared as a witness or nurse on the civil registrations of births. She clearly attended many births in the area, most probably as a 'handywoman' (Strachan & Henderson, 2005). Strachan (2001(b)) also noted that many of the women listed on birth registrations were illiterate and signed their name with 'the mark of an X'.

The findings of Strachan's (2001(b)) research suggests that in and around Dungog and the Upper Williams Valley about half the women were attended by a female neighbour or relative. These women were 'neighbouring'. The other half were attended by a midwife or 'handywoman'. Her findings also point to a clear preference by women to be attended to by other women. Strahan believed this was most probably due to tradition and a Victorian sense of decorum.

Another researcher, Madonna Grehan (2009), maintains that birth in the colony in the nineteenth century was only discussed by women in private. She found from her research that even literate women who wrote in their diaries about the experience of giving birth or suffering a miscarriage, did so in 'the most euphemistic of terms'. As was the case with many aspects of women's lives in the colony, the experience of giving birth was rendered invisible.

The exception to this invisibility was when a woman died during, or shortly after, giving birth. By the 1850s, maternal deaths had to be reported to the authorities and a coronial inquest was mandatory. Witness statements were taken to establish the cause of death (Callanan, 2019). Janine Callanan (2019) utilised Victorian Coronial Inquest reports from 1850-1880 to investigate childbirth in the colony. Even though many of these reports were brief, they offered a glimpse into what was otherwise a very private experience.

Callanan (2019) found the majority of women, particularly rural women, didn't have a doctor in attendance when they gave birth. She posits that doctors charged more than midwives for their attendance. So, if a 'medical man' was even available, they were generally only called upon to attend a birth when serious complications arose. Also, not all 'medical men', as they were referred to at the time, had medical qualifications, yet alone training in obstetrics. There were no female doctors and for rural, working-class women, a doctor generally wasn't even an option.

What Catherine's story suggests is that the women of Underbank would have, in most instances, supported each other in delivering their babies at home. There were many family members living at and around Underbank. So presumably Catherine had ample help from the 'neighbouring' women when it came to giving birth. No doubt she also assisted many other relatives and neighbours to labour and birth the next generation. In some instances, a midwife or handywoman may have also attended the women at Underbank when it was necessary.

Despite being largely invisible in the nineteenth century, childbirth was a common occurrence. Many women, like Catherine, had large families, giving birth every couple of years. It was a fundamental aspect of life which most women had to endure in private. Even though birthing was fraught with the very real possibility of death or injury, not to mention pain, in the majority of cases women and their babies survived the experience.

White male suffrage

Not surprisingly, given the growing population of people who were born in the colony and the number of immigrants who had made the colony their home, there were mounting calls for improved representation in the governing of NSW. As a result, in 1853 Mr Wentworth headed a committee to draft a constitution 'for responsible self-government'. In 1855, the *New*

South Wales Constitution Act 1855 (UK) was finally passed and on the 22nd of May 1856 the new bicameral (two house) NSW parliament had its first sitting ('Towards Responsible Government-1843 to 1855', 2023).

However, the Governor, and therefore the British parliament, retained considerable power over the NSW parliament and its ability to govern, including the ability to disallow colonial legislation. The new parliament consisted of a Legislative Council with twenty-one members nominated by the Governor, and a Legislative Assembly with fifty-four members to be elected by the 'inhabitants' of the colony. Those inhabitants were as before - men over twenty-one who had property and were a subject of her Majesty. Men who met the qualifications in more than one district could cast multiple votes ('New South Wales Constitution Act 1855 (UK)', 16 July 1855).

Just two years later, in 1858, voting by secret ballot was introduced, which lessened the ability for voters to be intimidated or coerced. The requirement for men to own land in order to vote was dropped, giving men over twenty-one, who were British subjects, full suffrage ('Australian Voting History in Action', 16 September 2020). This change would have enabled Catherine's husband Thomas to vote in the next election. The NSW colony was developing, and all white men now had suffrage. However, the development did not benefit everyone and there were still considerable inequalities in the community.

Among the many new legislations introduced by the NSW government, there are three Acts which will be explored further. As we will see, all three Acts had a considerable impact on the nature of colonial society in the nineteenth century and beyond.

Chinese Immigrants Regulation and Restriction Act 1861

The first legislation to be considered is the *Chinese Immigrants Regulation and Restriction Act 1861* ('*Chinese Immigrants Regulation and Restriction Act 1861 No28a*', 22 November 1861). Between 1851 and 1860 about 3,280,969 ounces of gold was found in NSW, transforming the economy of the colony and bringing an influx of immigrants seeking to make their fortune ('Towards Responsible Government-1843 to 1855', 2023). Initially, the Chinese men working on the gold fields were seen as somewhat of a 'curiosity'. Apparently, it was thought that they possessed 'great industry, frugality and unlimited perseverance' (Walker, 1966). However, the viability of small scaled, self-employed mining was increasingly becoming unprofitable and larger mining companies were taking over in NSW as they did in the Victorian goldfields ('Chinese on the Goldfields', 2023). This made it more and more difficult for many men to make a decent living on the goldfields.

As a result, the Chinese men working on the gold fields were being targeted by the European gold miners who were increasingly resentful of their success. On the 30th of June 1860 riots broke out at Lambing Flats gold fields on the upper Turon River where Catherine's stepson, Murdoch Graham, had gone in search of gold. Between 2,000 and 3,000 European miners gathered together and brutally beat the Chinese miners. It was reported that many of the Chinese workers also had their *'tails,'* or hair plaits, cut-off by the rioters in such a way as to also cut the skin from the back of their head ('Lambing Flat', 18 December 1860, p.7). It was a bloody and barbaric riot. However, it didn't deter the Chinese miners. By the 1861 census in NSW there were more Chinese males working on the upper Turon River goldfields than European men (Virtue, 2014).

Later that year, as a result of the growing resentment and racism towards Chinese immigrants in the NSW colony, the NSW government passed the *Chinese Immigrants Regulation and Restriction Act 1861*. The *Act* stated that the ships master of any vessel which arrived 'in any port in NSW having on board a greater number of Chinese passengers than in the proportion of one to every ten tons of the tonnage of such vessel' would have to pay a penalty. The penalty was £10 for each Chinese passenger in excess of the above amount ('Chinese Immigration Act', 28 November 1861, p.2). The *Act* placed restrictions on the number of Chinese people arriving in the NSW colony and legitimised the discrimination that Chinese immigrants experienced from the British settlers who were, of course, immigrants themselves. The *Act* also served as a precursor to the White Australia Policy, which will be discussed later in this story.

Crown Lands Act 1861

The second legislation to be discussed is the *Crown Lands Act 1861*. The *Crown Lands Act* is legislation which was to directly affect Catherine and her family. It consisted of two Acts: The *Crown Lands Alienation Act 1861* ('*Crown Lands Alienation Act 1861 No26a*', 18 October 1861) and the *Crown Lands Occupation Act 1861* ('*Crown Lands Occupation Act 1861 No27a*', 18 October 1861).

The new *Act* made crown land in the colony available, before survey, for selection and conditional purchase. The *Act* made it possible for settlers to purchase between forty and three hundred and twenty acres of crown land at £1 per acre. A deposit had to be paid which was one quarter of the land price. The purchase was also conditional on the selector residing on the land and staying there for three years. Improvements had to be undertaken such as clearing and fencing to the value of £1 per acre. If the conditions weren't met ownership of the land was withdrawn and it was auctioned off ('Conditional Purchase of Crown Land Guide', 2023).

The NSW Premier, John Robertson, who introduced the legislation, wanted to make land affordable for new settlers. At the same time, he wanted to break up the monopoly of the squatter-pastoralist class who leased large expanses of prime grazing land beyond the nineteen districts of previously established settlement ('Conditional Purchase of Crown Land Guide', 2023). The *Act* inevitably led to conflict and tensions between the already established pastoralists/squattocracy and the new selectors. Processing land selections could be slow and was only done in Sydney. The only way to know if land was selected, leased or set aside as a reserve was to read the Government Gazette notices. Subsequently, between 1861 and 1883, there were three separate *Acts* proclaimed to ease the situation for selectors who unknowingly had settled on land that was not available for settlement ('Department of Lands/164955', n.d.).

The *Crown Lands Act* was particularly designed to encourage intensive agriculture, such as the growing of wheat and sugar. As a direct result of the *Act*, a large Scots community, including many people from the Isle of Skye, settled around the Maclean district in the Clarence Valley in northern NSW. Maclean was about 500 kilometres (310 miles) north of Underbank. The Clarence River was large and the soil was rich and ideal for small land holdings.

This burgeoning community around Maclean included a number of people from Catherine's extended family. Catherine's older brother John McKinnon, his second wife Christina Cameron and their five children, also moved to Woodford Island near McLean. John made a selection of Lot 97 and Lot 98 in 1862 on Woodford Island, an inland island on the Clarence River (Potts & Lester, 2002). Catherine's younger sister Margaret, together with her husband John McMillan and their first four children Duncan, Ewen, Dorcas and John were also among the first settlers at Woodford Island ('Obituary', 9 July 1912, p.2).

Flora Graham, Angus MacDonald's (2) step daughter who travelled with him from Skye on the *Midlothian,* had married William Sherwood (1820-1902) in 1842, some twenty years previously at Dunmore Estate. She and her husband also moved to the Maclean area with their family (Flora Sherwood, n.d.). Her brother Murdoch Graham who, as mentioned earlier, had spent time at the Turon goldfields, also moved to the area at about the same time as his sister. Murdoch had never married. He was described as being a 'staunch Presbyterian' who was known for 'his honesty and straightforwardness' ('The Late Mr M Graham', 11 April 1891, p.8).

The more intensive style of farming which was encouraged by the *Crown Lands Act*, together with the gold rush, further disadvantaged First Nations people. A second wave of dispossession took place as a result of the increasing destruction of traditional food sources and ever diminishing access to traditional land. One commentator in the *Maitland Mercury* ('A Plea for the Blacks', 2 April 1863, p.2) expressed his concern that 'death in various forms soon thins the tribes of the Aborigines wherever European settlement and civilisation have gained a footing upon their soil'. He goes on to say that

> the very act of settlement is to the aboriginal possessor a trespass and a provocation; and a friendly feeling towards the trespasser is not to be created or promoted by treating the party aggrieved as if he were a mere dingo, to be shot on his approach.

The lack of food and increasing dispossession meant many First Nations people who had survived the first invasion of white settlers were now reliant on government handouts. The author of the *Mercury* article concludes by stating that 'New South Wales has her duties to discharge towards the remnant of her aboriginal population, and those duties are not to be hid from sight by a few bales of blankets' ('A Plea for the Blacks', 2 April 1863, p.2).

The author is referring to the annual distribution of blankets by magistrates to so-called 'worthy' Aboriginal people, a practice which was first instigated by Governor Macquarie in 1814. Blankets were also being distributed annually by the magistrate in Dungog. The distribution of blankets was an attempt to encourage cooperation between First Nations people and government officials. However, it also increased the control that the authorities had over Aboriginal people. The people who took the blankets had to register with the authorities and their movements could then be tracked (Bennett, 1964).

The new settlers were being given more opportunities to take up land under affordable conditions. However, that meant even more land was being taken from First Nations people without any thought for their history, their family connections, their connection to country or their very survival.

Felons Apprehension Act 1865

The third Act which will be considered here is the *Felons Apprehension Act 1865* ('*Felons Apprehension Act 1865 No11*', 8 April 1865). Bushrangers were a continuing concern for those living in the NSW colony in the nineteenth century, particularly those like Catherine and her family who lived in remote situations. They were vulnerable to attack from bushrangers when they were at home, working on their land and on the roads and bush tracks when they travelled. In fact, during the 1860s, a 'bushranger epidemic' was said to be taking place (Watson, 2016).

A second wave of bushrangers had begun with the discovery of gold in NSW in 1851. The gold fields became an obvious place for bushrangers to operate, and many gold miners were held up and robbed of their new found wealth. There was also an increase in the amount of traffic on the roads which was too hard for many bushrangers to resist ('The Gold Fields', 1 December 1852, p.4).

Whereas the early bushrangers were mostly escaped convicts of British origin, the later ones tended to be young men who were born in the colony (there were very few female bushrangers). The second wave of Australian-born bushrangers had grown up in the bush and they were mostly uneducated and unemployed. Many were sons of ex-convicts and immigrants with small landholders and uncertain incomes. More often than not, these parents didn't pay their sons any wages but expected them to work hard. The young men were generally excellent horsemen, they had well-developed bush skills and they were at ease in the colonial landscape. They saw their 'bushcraft' as a power which could be brandished against those in positions of authority (West, 2005). West (2005) argues that,

> bushrangers utilised their environment just as it was, in opposition to the urban middle class who, harking back to the English view of the countryside saw the land as something to be tamed and to be made profitable through agriculture.

During the 1860s more than 400 men were convicted of armed robbery in NSW (West, 2005). Between 1863 and 1864 alone, at least sixty highway robberies were committed (A written return for NSW, 18 October 1863 - 18 October 1864). The bushrangers were so successful in part due to the poor state of the existing small, localised police force in the colony. Therefore, in March 1862 a centralised NSW police force was established. However, the new force depended on a militaristic style of policing. The centralisation of decisions and instructions made the force slow to react to evolving situations, and the men were mostly unskilled and untrained. Some city police officers even feared the bush. They usually had weaponry which was inferior to that of the bushrangers and there was little infrastructure to support them. They were also very reliant on First Nations trackers (West, 2005).

The new wave of bushrangers was often swayed by stories of injustice and the brutal treatment of prisoners at the hands of the wealthy pastoralists, the police and the judicial system. According to Ward (1958, p.151,) many of these young men became bushrangers 'partly out of a misguided romantic sense of adventure'. Furthermore, Seal (1996, p.197) argues they were frequently attributed qualities which meant they inhabited 'the grey area between criminality and political or pre political protest'. Some people from the 'rural working class' had also found themselves clashing with the police, due to their heavy-handed approach. Police shortcomings meant many people chose to side with the bushrangers in order to assert their opposition to the authorities. As a result, some bushrangers were seen as 'sympathetic characters' (Ward, 1958, p.151).

The most famous of the bushrangers in the area where Catherine lived was Frederick Ward, who was known as 'Captain Thunderbolt'. Thunderbolt had a reputation for being polite and never robbing anyone poorer than himself, and as such was one of those bushrangers who elicited empathy from many of the new settlers. In 1860, Thunderbolt - who was on release after a stint in prison - settled with his Aboriginal wife, Mary Ann Bugg and their children in the Dungog area ('Bushrangers of NSW', 2021).

Before long though, Thunderbolt was charged with breaking the conditions of his parole and was taken back to jail on Cockatoo Island to serve a second term. He was sentenced to nine years without parole ('Mudgee Quarter Sessions', 9 October 1861, p.3). He later escaped Cockatoo Island and from November 1863 to January 1864, together with his wife and children, carried out a spree of robberies in the Dungog, Stroud and Singleton areas ('The Empire', 8 May 1865, p.4).

During one of these robberies, Thunderbolt and his family were chased in the rugged mountain country and across flooded rivers near Underbank by troopers and volunteers ('Ward, The Bushranger – Close Pursuit, and Escape', 23 February 1864, p.2). Apparently, Ewen McDonald Catherine's eldest surviving son, also affectionately known as 'Big Hughie' - was one of the men who were engaged to chase Thunderbolt ('Obituary', 14 July 1916, p.6).

The troopers rode into Ewen's camp in the bush where he was cutting cedar with a group of men and ordered them 'in the Kings name' to assist in the chase of Thunderbolt. Thunderbolt's wife Mary Ann, and their two children, had escaped early in the pursuit. With the help of an Aboriginal tracker, the men set off after the bushranger. Apparently, after a dramatic chase through the mountains, Thunderbolt leapt to freedom over a steep bank on his horse (see Figure 12). The story goes that Thunderbolt was later heard to say that 'McDonald was so close to him at one time that he thought he would have to shoot him, but he passed on without seeing him' ('Obituary', 14 July 1916, p.6). Thunderbolt escaped this time but he was eventually captured. More about that later.

In 1865, due to the increasing pressure on the legislature to take action and after heated debate, another piece of legislation was enacted called the *Felons Apprehension Act*. The *Act* stipulated that a person who was armed and had been declared an 'outlaw' could be shot dead without notice 'by any of her Majesty's subjects whether constable or not'. Also, anyone found to be aiding an outlaw could have their land taken and face imprisonment with hard labour. A process for declaring an individual an outlaw was included in the Act ('The Felons' Apprehension Act', 20 April 1865, p.4). The *Act* lasted for a period of two years, and only six people were deemed outlaws in NSW under the *Act*. One of those so-called outlaws was Ben Hall. Hall was born in Maitland, the son of ex-convicts and he was shot dead by police only days after the *Act* came into force (West, 2005).

Figure 12. Thunderbolts leap, 1910 (Monckton, W. & Pratt, A., 1910, *Three Years with Thunderbolt*, The States Publishing Co., Sydney, *National Library Australia*, p.94, http://nla.gov.au/nla.obj-52861897).

Colonial Australia was a place where life for settlers was fraught with challenges, including violence and hardship, as well as adventure and opportunity. The new police force did eventually serve its purpose and by about 1867 the so called 'bushranger epidemic' was considered over (West, 2005). It seems that Ewen was known as a good storyteller, who could spin a great yarn. So, no doubt Ewen entertained his family and friends on more than one occasion with the tale of how he chased Thunderbolt through the bush.

While the occurrence of bushrangers in the area made for a good yarn, it also meant that many people lived in fear of being held up or raided. Women travelling on the roads or alone on remote properties must have felt particularly vulnerable. Even though ordinary people may have empathised with the plight of some bushrangers, not all of them were gentlemen and an encounter with a bushranger could be terrifying and dangerous. Karskens (2009, p.304) makes the point that most bushrangers were desperate men and, as she puts it, 'decidedly unromantic robbers', who would not think twice before using violence or intimidation to get what they were after.

The three *Acts* which have been discussed above are just a sample of those passed by the NSW Government. Once the requirement for men to own property in order to vote was dropped, the balance of power slowly began to change. Previously, the squattocracy and wealthy men with property held enormous sway over conditions in the colony. Even though Britain still had control over the colony, once ordinary men could vote they had a voice, and the colony took a step closer to genuine democracy.

Women and First Nations people were still not considered worthy of a vote. The colonial government held scant regard for women's needs, yet alone their rights. Women were very much viewed as fulfilling a role in the home, or private sphere of the family, and they were generally considered to be subservient to men. First Nations people were still far from achieving any entitlements or justice from the colonial government.

Chapter 7
Underbank Lost

Angus McKinnon - Ewen McDonald's marriage - a grandchild - loosening the ties that bound them - the New England Tablelands - a happy home - an expanding family - Underbank lost

Angus McKinnon

Catherine's youngest brother, Angus McKinnon, left Underbank a couple of years after Catherine's marriage to Thomas. Angus purchased a block of land at Tinonee, near Taree NSW, in 1855 (Colonial Secretary Town Purchases, 16 April 1855). Apparently, Angus had taught at a school in his home parish of Kilmuir on Skye for a couple of years before he emigrated. He intended to go back to teaching and in pursuit of this, in 1861, he undertook a one-month teaching course in Sydney at the Model National School (Catherine McKinnon's Family, n.d). When he finished the course, he was appointed as the teacher at the newly opened National School at Taree, which was to later become the Taree Public School ('The Big Flood', 1 September 1931, p.5).

Angus met Anne Geddes Shearer in Taree and they were soon engaged. The Shearer family were originally from Caithness in Scotland. They had travelled to Australia in 1853, when Anne was about ten years old, on the ship the *Prince of the Seas* ('The Shearer Family', 2 January 1940, p.2). It seems that Anne's brother Donald was against the marriage, as he considered Angus to be a lowly paid teacher and therefore not a suitable husband (Catherine McKinnon's Family, n.d.). Despite Donald's objections, Angus and Anne were married at her sister Christina and brother-in-law John's home, called 'Purfleet' near Taree, on the 17th of April in 1863 (Angus McKinnon, 17 April 1863). Angus was twenty-nine and Anne was twenty.

Angus was a very active member of the Taree community. He helped to form the first Teachers Association on the Manning ('Meeting of the Teachers', 4 July 1868, p.2), and he was the secretary for the committee to build the new Taree Presbyterian Church ('Tenders for the erection of a Presbyterian Church at Taree', 19 September 1868, p.3). Angus was also interested in astronomy and gave a lecture on the subject at the Taree Literary Society ('Taree Literary Society', 2 March 1867, p.3). He was a keen photographer at a time when photography was still quite new. For an example of one of his photographs see Figure 13, which is a photo he took of his three eldest surviving children Ewen, Flora and Annie. Ewen and Flora were named after their paternal grandparents from Kendram, on the Isle of Skye.

Figure 13. Ewen, Flora, Annie, c1870 (Angus McKinnon photographer, Taree, NSW, Australia, photo courtesy of Margaret Rouhan, Rosemary McFayden and John Nolan).

A new generation

In June of 1868, when he was twenty-seven, Catherine's eldest son, Ewen McDonald also married. Ewen married Emily Weller. Ewen was well respected by all who knew him. He was known as a 'sincere and earnest Christian' and he was described as a kind and generous man who could not tolerate injustice. Apparently, he was also a talented cricketer and he played for the Underbank team along with his stepfather Thomas Ballard ('Obituary', 14 July 1916, p.6).

Ewen's new wife Emily was from Lostock, which was not far from Underbank, so no doubt they had known each other for some time. Emily's parents were William Weller and Sarah Ann Wallace, who were from Sussex in England. Ewen was the first of Catherine's children to marry and he and Emily lived at Underbank ('Generation No.3', n.d.).

The following year, on the 14th of May in 1869, Ewen and his wife Emily had their first child. Catherine and Thomas were in their late forties and they were now grandparents for the first time. The baby's birth was registered in Dungog and he was most likely born at Underbank. He was named Alfred McDonald (Alfred McDonald, 14 May 1869). This would have been a very joyous occasion for all of the family. Alfred was to be the first of many, many grandchildren for Catherine and Thomas. He was the start of the second generation of Australian family members who were born in the NSW colony.

Even though Catherine's children were first generation Australians, they had been exposed to considerable Scottish influences, not the least would have been Catherine herself. Her first four sons had grown up only speaking Gaelic, and they had lived in a small enclave of Gaelic speaking Scots at Dunmore Estate. Apparently, Catherine's eldest son Ewen, didn't learn to speak English until he was a teenager (Angus MacDonald, 7 January 2023). More than likely, it was the same for Catherine's other three boys Angus (4), Malcolm and John.

Even when Catherine and her four sons moved to Underbank, they were still largely immersed in their extended Scottish family with Catherine's siblings and their cousins living close-by. As we know, language and culture have a closely intertwined relationship. Culture is largely transmitted through language, and language is transmitted as part of culture. In the process of learning a language, we also learn about culture because language is embedded with the values and beliefs of a culture ('Language and Culture', 2023). Once Thomas came into their lives, English was his first language and it would have been more common for them to hear English spoken at home. Catherine's six children with Thomas may well have been bi-lingual and spoken both English and Gaelic.

Catherine and her siblings were the threads that bound their children to Kendram, on the Isle of Skye, and their Highland heritage. However, with each new generation, the threads which connected the family to their Scottish origins were loosening. Alfred and his generation would be more removed from their Scottish heritage and their ancestors. They would come to see themselves as 'Australians', as they forged their own sense of cultural identity.

Distant memories

With the many years which had passed since Catherine left the Isle of Skye, her memories of her parents and her childhood at Kendram must have faded. Catherine's father, Ewen McKinnon had passed away at Kendram in 1861 when he was eighty-seven. He died from 'mortification in the right foot'. His daughter Ann, Catherine's sister, was with him (Ewen MacKinnon, 1861, p.1). According to the 1851 Scottish census, Ewen and his wife Flora had employed a 'servant', a young eighteen years old woman, called Catherine Matheson (Catherine Matheson, 1851). So, they must have needed help to manage at home for some time. Then in 1870, Catherine's mother Flora McKinnon (nee Cameron), who by then was a great grandmother, also passed away at Kendram. She died of 'gradual decay' from 'old age'. She was the grand age of ninety-two (Flora MacKinnon, 1870, p.1).

Catherine's sister Ann, her husband William McLeod and the youngest of their eight children, had been living with Flora (Flora MacKinnon 1861). When Ewen died, nine years previously, Ann and her family had moved from where they were living at the neighbouring crofting settlement of Conista (Ann McLeod, 1851), to live with Flora at Lot 1 Kendram ('Kilmuir Estate Rental Book', 1875-1879, p.140). Ewen and Flora were most likely buried at the local Kilmalaug cemetery where the other members of the family at Kendram were also interred.

Catherine's parents both lived long lives at Kendram- which was surprising given their poor diet, the lack of medical care and the hard conditions in which they lived. When Ewen and Flora died, they hadn't seen their four children, John, Catherine, Margaret and Angus, since they left Scotland and emigrated half way around the world. They didn't get to see four of their six children grow into adults, which would have been a difficult loss for any parent. They also never got to know their many Australian grandchildren, or their great grandchildren that followed. As we saw earlier, they had also lost their daughter Dorcas only six years before Ewen's passing. The only child who remained was their daughter, Ann, who stayed close by and was seemingly a dutiful daughter.

Sadly, on the 9th of January 1872, only two years after their mother had passed, Catherine's older brother, John MacKinnon who was living at Woodford Island, McLean, in NSW also died. He was sixty-four (John MacKinnon, 9 January 1872). Then his wife, Christina died in July, the following year (Christina McKinnon, 24 July 1873). According to their death registrations, they are both buried in the Maclean Cemetery. Catherine's sister Margaret, who also lived in the Maclean district, had remained close to John and her husband was the executor of John's will after he passed (Potts & Lester, 2002). Catherine would have keenly felt the loss of her older brother, who had travelled out from Scotland with her all those years ago. John was a link back to her parents and her distant childhood on Skye.

A great adventure

The future was unknown, and Catherine's life was still unfolding in ways she could not have imagined. She would come to forge new bonds in a new place which was, as yet, unfamiliar to her. This 'new place' can be glimpsed in a story which was written by an author identified only as 'an occasional contributor', and published in April 1872 in the local *Maitland Mercury* newspaper ('Notes of a Trip from Bandon Grove to Bindera', 20 April 1872, p.5).

The story is about an expedition which was undertaken by a small group of men from the area. The men travelled with two Aboriginal men and a pack horse to carry supplies, including some food and their billies. The author does not explain the purpose of the journey, nor does he give the names or the number of the men in the group. Even though it is not a certainty, as you will see, it is probable that Thomas Ballard and at least one or more of Catherine's McDonald sons were among the group.

The group went overland from Bandon Grove, near Underbank, north west up to the tablelands, then on to Bingera (which later became known as Bingara). Bingara is 136 kilometres (about 85 miles) west of Glen Innes in NSW. Some of the journey was along well-worn routes (lines) where squatters sent their sheep. Other parts of the journey involved following routes marked out by the Aboriginal trackers with white rags on trees or poles. The two Aboriginal men who, would have been Gringai, went ahead and, according to the author, 'opened a marked tree line from the Williams River to the Tumally line, which leaves the road on the Williams about eleven miles from Underbank'. This was not unusual, as according to Reynolds (1996) from the beginning of English settlement in the colony European travellers had taken Aboriginal guides with them when they trekked into the bush. They were often totally reliant on the guides to find the way, and to find enough fresh water and food to sustain them on their journey.

When the group of men reached the top of the tablelands the view over the precipice was, according to the author, 'grand in the extreme'. The author went on to say 'the chasms and glens are almost underneath you, and the distant view is wonderful'. The author suggested that one member of their group named the spot Ballards Landing. So, it is fairly safe to assume that Thomas Ballard was one of the men.

Then at a later point, when they were on to the tablelands and past the head of the Little Manning River 'a few miles from Eckfords old station – Baan Baan', the travellers came across a large plain. Apparently, another man in the group named this spot the McDonald Plains. So possibly, at least one of Catherine's McDonald sons, Ewen and/or his brother Angus, were also part of the group.

The group then rode on to Tumally Station, where the author described how a 'Scotch mist' was falling when they arrived in the evening. The trip took them through Mr Campbell's Glenrock station, and Mr Hungerford's Glencoe station and on to Hanging Rock. The author described Hanging Rock as having 'a somewhat wild and romantic appearance'. Leaving in the morning, they then rode a few miles further to Nundle and on to Tamworth. That section of the journey was level road and they made it in a day.

The men travelled the final leg of the journey from Tamworth to Bingera in Mr Chaffey's express coach. The author described the road as being 'eight or ten inches deep in dust' which made travelling 'anything but pleasant'. Bingera was a gold mining town. Gold was first found there in 1851 and was still being mined at the time the men arrived. The author did not think much of the town itself but suggested that some of the gentlemen in the group 'took up twenty acres, and intend to open a reef and begin quartz crushing'. He does not say who these men were, so we are left to wonder.

The story is a fascinating, first-hand account of travelling in a remote part of the NSW colony. Along the journey from Bandon Grove to Bingera and back, the travellers encountered wild cattle, they camped by magnificent rivers and they saw beautiful country. The men were caught in torrential rain and 'a violent thunderstorm occurred, accompanied by sharp and fierce lightening'. They were shown hospitality by strangers, and met prospectors, station owners, and a candidate from the Son of Temperance movement, who was running in the local election. The journey to the New England Tablelands was most probably Thomas Ballard's first sighting of this part of NSW. His experience may well have influenced his later decision to settle there. All-in-all, a great adventure was had by the group of men.

A happy home for a growing family

In the meantime, the extended family were happily settled at Underbank. Apart from the main house at Underbank, there were seven cottages where other people lived and farmed on the estate. Various family members lived in these cottages over the years, as well as numerous friends and tenants. As was mentioned earlier, the journey from Underbank to the service town at Dungog included river crossings which could be impassable for periods of time due to flooding. Also, the roads were very poor. Therefore, as the community around Underbank had grown, the number of local amenities which were available to the residents had also increased.

Underbank, like other settlements in the area, had developed as a small village serving the local community. For example, there was a post office near the main house at Underbank ('Advertising', 25 December 1875, p.4), there was a small school which had opened in 1867, a Church and, by the early 1870s, there was also a general store (Williams, 2014, p.70). Even so, regular trips to Dungog would have still been necessary in order to attend to banking, business matters and to buy supplies which were not available at the Underbank store.

Catherine's family home at Underbank was apparently a warm and welcoming place to visit. According to one account, 'for the stranger and traveller the hospitable doors of Underbank were ever open'. Furthermore, Angus McDonald (4), who was by now an adult and running Underbank, was known for his appreciation of and 'liberality toward any worthy object that appealed to him' ('Angus McDonald', 17 June 1927, p.2). As a result, Underbank had all of the modern conveniences available at the time. Angus (4) was also known for his talent as an excellent chess player ('Angus

McDonald', 17 June 1927, p.2). Many of the local residents and visitors alike would have been enticed into a game of strategy with Angus (4) on the chessboard when they were visiting.

Karskens (1986, p.43) suggests that in the second half of the nineteenth century, houses were no longer merely a place of shelter. She argues that they had become 'a symbol of its owner's success and prosperity, a material statement of his conquest of the land and its difficulties, and a proclamation of European supremacy and the arrival of 'civilisation'. Furthermore, Russell (1993, p.30) posits that houses were a place where 'civilised' women were involved in colonising the land. Many Gringai women had taken on working for the new settlers in their homes, doing domestic work, such as laundry. Russell (1993, p.30) argues that training in domestic living and domestic service was one of the ways that the new settlers attempted to 'reform' Aboriginal women. No doubt, Gringai women were employed at Underbank by Catherine and the other women to do laundry and other domestic chores.

Catherine's older children had all grown up to be fine men and women and they were starting to make their own way in the world. Four of her children married over the next three years. Firstly, in 1872, her youngest son from her first marriage, John McDonald, married Elizabeth Hutchinson when he was twenty-five. Elizabeth's parents, John Hutchinson and Ellen McDonald, had emigrated from Ireland and they lived near Dungog. John McDonald was a farmer at Underbank and he later became a magistrate (Justice of the Peace). He was a tall man and was described as being 'one of nature's gentlemen' who was 'big in stature and big in heart' ('Deaths', 16 January 1920, p.2).

Then two years later, in 1874, the next of Catherine's children to marry was her second daughter Maria. Maria married James Cornish. She was the first of the Ballard children to marry. James, who was known as 'Jim', was the son of James Stewart Cornish and Eliza Jane Smith from Bendolba, near Underbank. Maria was eighteen years old and James was twenty-four (Maria Ballard, 1874). They also lived at Underbank ('The Late Mrs M. C.

Cornish', 4 May 1935, p. 2) and their first child, a daughter, Catherine (Kate) McKinnon Cornish was born later that year.

Also in 1874, there was yet another wedding. Catherine and Thomas's eldest daughter Mary was married. In 1868, when she was fourteen, Mary had gone to live in the Manning River district near Taree with her uncle Angus McKinnon, his wife Anne and their three young children. The school where Angus was teaching had a teacher's residence attached to it, where they lived. Mary spent three years living there with the family. It is not clear if Mary went there to help Anne with the children at home, to help Angus in the classroom, or to go to school herself ('The Late Mrs Mary Bignell', 9 June 1934, p.2).

Mary had been back living at Underbank for several years, when she married Robert (Koft) Bignell. They were married in May of 1874, when she was twenty years old ('Catherine McKinnon's Family', n.d.). Her husband Robert was the son of James Bignell and Amelia Kingston from Bandon Grove, which was near Underbank. Robert was also a well-known cricketer in the area ('Obituary', 20 February 1925, p.2). No doubt he played cricket with Mary's father, Thomas and her brothers, who were also keen cricketers. Mary and Robert had their first child, Robert Edwin Bignell later that year, but sadly he died soon after birth ('The Late Mrs Mary Bignell', 9 June 1934, p.2).

Finally, the fourth wedding to take place was that of Catherine's son, Angus McDonald (4). Angus (4) was thirty-one by now and the owner of Underbank. Less than a year after his sister Mary's wedding on the 17th of February 1875, Angus (4) married twenty years old Helena George O'Keefe (see Figure 14). Angus (4) had been appointed a Magistrate (Justice of the Peace (JP)) for the district of Dungog a couple of years previously, so he was considered an upstanding gentleman of sound judgement ('New Magistrates', 9 September 1873, p.2). As a JP or magistrate, Angus was authorised to keep the peace in the colony. This entailed being able to hear minor crimes, such as trespass and extortion. He was also able to arrest and take bail from a criminal and mandate a criminal to good behaviour ('Classified Advertising', 9 January 1830, p.1).

Angus (4) and Helena's wedding was held at 'Wiregully' (Wirragulla), near Dungog. Wiregully was the home of the prominent pastoralist Benjamin Hooke Esq, and the marriage was presided over by the Rev John Gibson. Helena was born in Adelaide, in South Australia, but was living at Wiregully. She was a governess ('Marriages', 25 February 1875, p.1), so she was obviously well educated herself and most probably teaching Benjamin Hooke's children.

Figure 14. Left: Helena McDonald (nee George O'Keefe), n.d. Right: Angus McDonald (4), n.d. (Photos courtesy of Angus MacDonald).

The family was expanding rapidly as Catherine's older children were marrying and starting families of their own. The many weddings would have provided an excuse for the family to celebrate and welcome new members into the fold. It also meant that Catherine and Thomas could look forward to the joy of more grandchildren running about their feet.

Underbank lost

Underbank was a comfortable home to Catherine, Thomas and their growing family, including Angus (4) his wife Helena and numerous other family members who resided in the many cottages on the estate. However, managing such a large estate in the NSW colony presented many problems. There was a prolonged drought in the colony and no one knew how long it would continue. As a result of the prevailing dry period there wasn't enough feed for the stock ('The Present Drought', 4 April 1876, p.4). Much of Underbank remained covered in forest and unfenced ('Underbank Estate', 29 January 1876, p.1), making it difficult to contain the cattle in one area to graze on what little there was, while allowing the grass in another paddock to recover. Livestock were dying of starvation and the price of buying feed was exorbitant as most of NSW was in drought ('Armidale', 4 April 1876, p.6). The poor condition of the cattle also meant that they were worth very little, even if they could be mustered and taken to the saleyards. According to one stock report, 'The consequence of this unfortunate state of affairs is a general stagnation of pastoral business' ('Pastoral News', 28 December 1875, p.3). Maize crops throughout the district were also very poor with very low yields ('Paterson', 2 February 1875, p.3). All in all, it was a difficult time.

By 1875, the problems running the large estate had increased to the point where something had to be done. Angus (4) had married Helena that same year and undoubtedly felt the added responsibly of a family of his own to support. As a result, Angus (4) mortgaged Underbank Estate to Joseph Pearse. Joseph Pearse, as mentioned earlier in this story, had purchased Cryon Station from Angus McDonald back in 1852, when Angus was just a young child, months after the initial lottery win.

According to Foster (21 November 1979, p.2), Angus (4) then used the money from Pearse to invest in gold mining. He clearly wasn't immune to the gold fever that had gripped the colony. For many Christians in the NSW colony gold was seen as a gift from God. Indeed, Rev Lang (1852, p.5) wrote,

> Are we not told in the word of God that the earth is the Lords and the fulness thereof? The silver and the gold it contains are His, for He made it, that is, the

earth, and deposited these precious metals in it, as in a bank deposit, thousands and perhaps tens of thousands of years ago, that it might be searched for and found, and drawn forth, and turned to account by intelligent, enterprising and energetic men.

So, no doubt believing God was on his side, Angus (4) decided to take his chances, thinking it was a sure thing and the answer to their problems.

However, the major gold rushes were mostly finished in NSW by the mid-1860s. Despite this, gold was still being found in some areas up until the 1880s, although mining in the areas near Underbank had only limited success. Little River, near Underbank, was a reef which was worked and abandoned several times by various prospectors ('Dungog', 7 December 1878, p.16). The main reef with any payable gold wasn't discovered on the Little River until 1879, at the Wangat reefs (Karskens, 1986, p. 178) and this was too late for Angus (4).

Also, by 1876 *The Maitland Mercury* suggested that people should not be deluded into thinking there was much, if any, money to be made at the nearby Barrington Tops diggings ('Latest News from the Barrington Diggings', 18 July 1876, p.3). It was estimated there were about two hundred men there digging for gold, including some of the most experienced miners in the colony. It was very cold working the long winter in the mountain gullies of the Barrington Mountains and a lack of sunshine made the digging difficult. In the best cases, a small number of men were said to be earning £2-£3 a week. However, according to the *Mercury* most were 'not earning salt' ('Latest News from the Barrington Diggings', 18 July 1876, p.3).

It is unknown exactly where Angus (4) invested his money, but clearly he didn't make anything on the investment. As a consequence, he couldn't afford to pay back the mortgage to Pearse and the Underbank Estate was advertised for an unreserved sale. A number of other 'valuable grazing and agricultural estates' were also being advertised for sale at this time, so Angus (4) was not alone in needing to sell ('Maitland Stock Reports', 11 December 1875, p. 7). The fact that other properties were up for sale also made it a buyers' market.

The auction for Underbank was to take place on the 17th of January 1876 ('Advertising', 25 December 1875, p.4). According to the advertisement for the auction, Underbank had 'substantial and extensive improvements.' The house was described as being a brick cottage with,

> 8 rooms, kitchen, with 4 rooms attached, large underground cemented tank, stable, coach houses, sheds, stock, milking yards etc. The whole combined form a comfortable homestead, furnished with every convenience.

There were also seven other houses in good repair attached to different portions of the land, and a post office close to the main homestead. The Underbank Estate was described as 8,460 acres of 'highly productive', 'substantially fenced' and 'luxuriantly grassed' land. It included an abundant and continuous supply of water, with five miles of river frontage as well as various creeks and tributaries. It was said to 'abound with valuable timber, including cedar'. Apparently, the family were still residing on the estate at this time (Advertising, 25 December 1875, p.4). However, Underbank didn't sell and Joseph Pearse, the mortgager, took possession of Underbank in early 1876. Pearse had also purchased Dunmore Estate from the Lang family four years previously (Dunmore House, 2018).

According to a report in the *Maitland Mercury*, several families of farmers had left Underbank by the middle of the year, and several more had made arrangements to leave shortly. The report suggested it was 'a state of things much to be regretted' ('Dungog', 24 June 1876, p.7). The families who had already left Underbank included Catherine, Thomas and their children.

At the same time as taking possession of the Underbank Estate, Joseph Pearse advertised for men to ringbark 5,000 acres of timber and to erect eighteen miles of post and rail fencing at Underbank ('Underbank Estate', 29 January 1876, p.1). It was a huge and costly undertaking. Pearse also had his share of problems managing the large estate. An advertisement in *The Maitland Mercury* the following year ('Advertising', 30 June 1877, p.2) offered a £100 reward (an enormous amount at the time) for any information leading to the conviction of people stealing cattle and horses branded with any of the Underbank brands or that of JBP.

In December 1877, Joseph Pearse instructed that the Underbank Estate be sold by public auction ('Sales by Auction', 27 December 1877, p.8) and it was advertised again in February 1878 ('The Famous Underbank Estate', 22 February 1878, p.7). This time Underbank was sold to Mr Langton Parker Esq who purchased the Estate for £12,500 ('Latest Telegrams', 28 February 1878, p.5). Underbank Estate was bought, sold and sub-divided many times over the coming years (see appendix).

Catherine had lived in the upper Hunter area for nearly forty years since arriving as a young girl. Catherine and Thomas were not young when they had to leave Underbank. Catherine was fifty-three and Thomas was fifty-seven. The idea of starting over would not have been an easy prospect at their age.

Catherine's children were all growing up. Her eldest son, Ewen McDonald, already had four children of his own who I believe were all born at Underbank. Angus (4) was married with his first child on the way. Her son Malcolm McDonald, was not yet married but he was an adult of thirty-two. Her youngest McDonald son, John, was married with two children, Angus and Clementine, whose births were both registered in Dungog. It is probable they were also born at Underbank. Her two Ballard daughters were also married and had a daughter each.

However, Catherine's four Ballard sons were not yet adults. Edward was eighteen, David was sixteen, Cyrus was fourteen and the youngest child Allan, was twelve. Catherine and her extended family had lived a very comfortable life at Underbank. Even though it had presented them with some enormous challenges, it was also their home and it had offered a sanctuary to many people over the years. It must have been difficult to go, but Catherine and her family didn't have a choice. With their home at Underbank lost, they had to pack up what they could carry and leave.

Chapter 8
A New Start at Red Range

A new selection at Red Range - new acquaintances - eating the wildlife - a skeleton is found - the Ngarrabul Nation - Glen Innes - the newspapers - Cobb & Co coach connections

Red Range

In early 1876, after Underbank was repossessed, Catherine and Thomas Ballard, together with their sons Edward, David, Cyrus and Allan, travelled north to their new home. Their daughter Maria, her husband James Cornish and their daughter Kate, also went with them. Mary was the only Ballard child not to move with the family. Catherine and her family were starting over again from scratch, at a place called Red Range.

Red Range is nearly 400 kilometres (250 miles) north of Underbank, in the New England Tablelands district near Glen Innes. It was a long journey and they travelled by horseback and carried all of their worldly belongings in horse drawn carts. Apparently, Catherine's daughter Maria rode side saddle with her daughter Kate, who was a toddler at the time, sitting in front of her ('The Gulf Country', 7 July 1969, p.3).

They were a very close and resilient family and they had a lot of work ahead of them. Shortly after their arrival, Catherine and Thomas's daughter Maria and her husband, James Cornish, made a selection at Red Range near what was then called Rusden's Lagoon (Historical Lands Record Viewer, 1958(b)). Maria and James called their property 'Roseville'.

Thomas also made a conditional purchase of 200 acres of land under the *Crown Lands Act* ('Local Intelligence', 5 April 1876, p.2). They called their original selection 'Albion Forest' ('Government Gazette Notices', 24 January 1882, p.467). 'Albion' was an old, poetic name for Britain ('One Hundred

Victorian Boys Names and Meanings', 2023). Then a few months later Thomas took up a pre-emptive lease on 600 acres ('Local Intelligence', 19 July 1876, p.2). The Ballard selection was part of the rugged, mountainous country known locally as the 'Gulf Country'. Apparently, it was 'a part of the old Yarrow Creek squatterage', it was said to be 'in its virgin state' and 'mostly untouched by European settlement' ('The Gulf Country', 7 July 1969, p.3).

Thomas and his sons must have been capable horsemen, as the country was not easy going. By many accounts it was, and it still is, a beautiful place. One author suggested that the first sighting of the Gulf Country generated 'feelings of reverence, of astonishment, of undefined pleasure to flow through the heart', and caused the viewer to marvel at 'the wonders of creative power' ('The Gulf Country', 7 July 1969, p.3).

There is no evidence to indicate the type of house Catherine and Thomas built on their selection. However, they would have had to start with an outside camp fire and a tent or lean-to when they first arrived until they could build something more permanent. Fortunately, with their four sons living with them, they had many hands to help with the task of building a comfortable home.

Most houses of that era in the New England area were made of timber slabs. There was ample timber available and the slabs were usually laid vertically. Some houses were also made of wattle and daub (mud), or built from local stone. The roof was most probably made of flattened stringy bark, or initially at least. It would have been similar to the style of home in this photo of Stonehenge homestead (see Figure 15). Then later, the stringy bark roof may have been replaced with corrugated iron, or wooden shingles ('Early European Settlement in New England', 2018).

They needed to build something weatherproof fairly quickly. Red Range gets hot in summer and very cold in winter with heavy frosts and the occasional snowfall. New England has an altitude of over 900 metres above sea level and strong winds can blow from the eastern escarpment (New England (NSW), 2022). Catherine's family of six also had to be fed, which would have been no mean task in a bush camp in all weather conditions. Therefore, a good fireplace was essential. As well as cooking, a fire was needed for staying warm, heating water for bathing and laundry, and generally creating the warmth of a 'hearth', the centre of the home.

Figure 15. Stonehenge homestead, 1869. Mr and Mrs Colin Fletcher in foreground and J J R Gibson in background (Photo courtesy of Glen Innes Historical Society Archives, NSW, Australia, No.01279, 30 August, 2023).

Thomas paid five shillings for a timber license to log hardwood on their property the year after they arrived in Red Range ('Timber and Other Licenses', 17 April 1877, p.1546). As well as timber to build their house, they needed timber to build sheds to house their horses and equipment and for fences, which were post and rail in those times. Thomas may have also made some money selling the timber.

Other people at Red Range

George and Harriet Kempton from Cambridgeshire, in England, were most probably the first Europeans to have settled at what was to become the township of Red Range. They made their first selection in Rocky Valley in 1854, on what is now the Red Range Road. Then a few years later, they selected another block called 'Splitters Home' ('Red Range, NSW', 2023).

According to William Sargeant ('The East', 12 October 1939, p.2), John Heaney was also one of the early small land holders to make a selection at Red Range in the 1870s. Sargeant says that Heaney was closely followed by Thomas Ballard and his sons, James Cornish, Phillip Hottes, John Ryall, James Taylor and W Potter. He suggested that Mr William Woollings of Square Range, and Messrs William and Henry Pettit of Pinkett, were also early settlers in the Yarrow Creek area.

As we will see later in this story, many of the settlers mentioned became friends of the Ballard family and attended meetings at their home. No doubt these early settlers also exchanged goods and services with each other. They would have shared their produce, their tools and their various skills, as well as helping each other out when it was needed - not the least of which would have been the birthing of babies. Many of the women, like Catherine, had experience in child birth and presumably they were able to support the younger women to birth the next generation of babies. According to William Sargeant, 'stout hearts were needed in those days to carve a farm out of the virgin forests' ('The East', 12 October 1939, p.2).

Catherine, Thomas and the boys might have also been friends with a local Aboriginal man called Black Tommy. Tommy spent time around the Yarrow Creek area ('Black Tommy', 10 April 1878, p.2), which was part of the Ballard selection. Tommy had been getting into trouble with local law enforcement for some time. He was said to hold up the occasional traveller from a lookout on the Mann River, known locally as 'Tommy's Rock'. Apparently, Tommy was well liked by many of the new settlers and had managed to evade capture, sometimes with their help (AMBS, 2010).

In 1878, a £50 reward was offered by the NSW Government for the capture of Tommy ('Black Tommy', 10 April 1878, p.2). A year later, he was fatally wounded by police at Bald Knob, not far from the Ballard's selection. The £50 reward was divided between two local policemen, Constable Wainwright who received £28 and Constable Goodhew who was given £22 ('Local and Other Notes', 10 June 1879, p.2).

Kangaroo steamer

As well as working, building, fencing and clearing their land, the Ballards also had to source food. The meat from native wildlife was consumed by new settlers when there wasn't any beef or mutton to be had. This would have been the case most of the time, because of course there was no refrigeration. A dish called 'Kangaroo Steamer', was widely eaten in the NSW colony by European settlers throughout the nineteenth century. It consisted of kangaroo meat that was cooked slowly in either a glass or an earthen ware vessel with bacon, onion and various seasonings. The vessel was sealed so that it could be stored for longer before spoiling. The meal resembled the British dish known as 'Jugged Hare' (Singley, 2017). The consumption of such dishes, particularly for those living in remote and rural settings, would have been a necessity.

According to Singley (2017), most of the new settlers went to lengths to maintain their traditional British identity. Those who did the cooking, which was mostly the women, tried to transform native fauna such as kangaroos, bush turkeys, possums, koalas and echidnas into meals that resembled traditional British fare (Singley, 2017). Singley (2017) argues that this consumption of native wildlife was 'mediated by deeply held cultural prejudices', such as the belief that the native wildlife was inferior to European meat. Edward Pierson Ramsay (1875, cited in Stubbs, 2001) who was the curator of the Australian Museum in Sydney, suggested that the increasing consumption of native fauna in the NSW colony was

> ...in distinction to the formerly widespread belief that there was little or no game in Australia; a belief as senseless as the commonly heard statements that Australian flowers had no scent and, Australian birds had no song.

No doubt, Catherine and her family enjoyed their share of kangaroo steamer, roast echidna, bush turkey, kangaroo tail soup, parrot pie, smoked echidna and roast wallaby (see Figure 16).

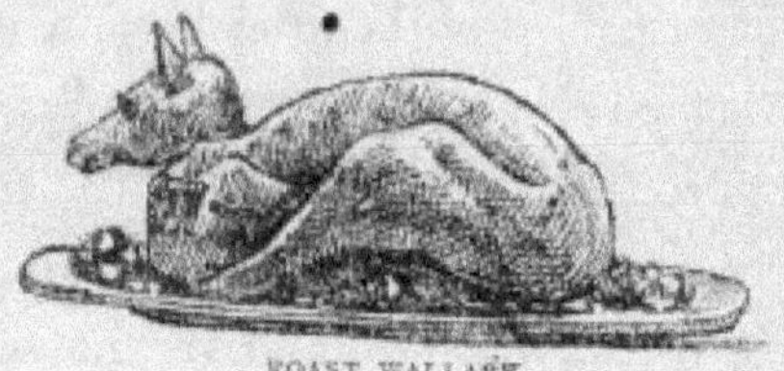

2858.—ROAST WALLABY.

Ingredients.—Wallaby, forcemeat, milk, butter.

Mode.—In winter the animal may hang for some days, as a hare, which it resembles, but in summer it must, like all other flesh, be cooked very soon after it is killed. Cut off the hind-legs at the first joints, and, after skinning and paunching, let it lie in water for a little while to draw out the blood. Make a good veal forcemeat, and after well washing the inside of the wallaby, stuff it and sew it up. Truss as a hare and roast before a bright clear fire from 1¼ to 1¾ hour, according to size. It must be kept some distance from the fire when first put down, or the outside will be too dry before the inside is done. Baste well, first with milk and then with butter, and when nearly done dredge with flour and baste again with butter till nicely frothed.

Time.—1¼ to 1¾ hour.

Sufficient for 6 persons.

Seasonable.—Best in cold weather.

ROAST WALLABY.

Figure 16. **Roast wallaby, c1880** (Beeton, I., c1880, *Mrs Beeton's Book of Household Management,* Ward, Loch & Co, London, *Sydney Living Museums*, R89/80, NSW, Australia).

Skeleton Creek

Clearing some of the trees would have enabled the Ballard family to grow food such as potatoes, wheat and corn to accompany their roast wallaby. It also meant they could plant pasture to feed their livestock. However, once the new settlers had started to clear the land of trees and the pasture grew, the kangaroos came to eat the sweet, new grass, particularly when the rainfall was low and feed was scarce elsewhere. As a result of the land clearing being undertaken in the area, the local newspaper, the *Glen Innes Examiner* ('The Marsupial Plague: Meeting of Stock Owners', 4 September 1878, p.2) made reference to the 'marsupial plague' and a spokesperson for local landholders around Glen Innes, Mr Somerville, suggested 'the evil was assuming alarming proportions.'

One day, either due to the so-called marsupial plague or in order to get some kangaroo meat for dinner, or perhaps on both accounts, one of Catherine's sons and her son-in-law James Cornish went out shooting kangaroos. They were walking through the bush at Shannon Vale, about a kilometre or two (one mile) from their selection looking for game when they came across human skeletal remains, lying on the ground. The remains were later identified in a post mortem as those of an Aboriginal man. There was no sign of violence to his body, and it was never known who he was, or how he died. It was thought he had died about six years previously, most probably of natural causes ('Local and Other Notes', 6 February 1878, p.2).

Interestingly, Skeleton Creek appears on an old Lands Registry Map (Historical Lands Record Viewer, 1958 (a)) of the area. There is also a modern-day road, called Skeleton Creek Road, near the area in Shannon Vale. It is not surprising that there was the skeleton of an Aboriginal man in the bush at Red Range. It was Aboriginal land and First Nations people had lived and died on the land for many thousands of years before the Ballard family arrived.

The people of the Ngarrabul Nation

The traditional custodians of the land are the people of the Ngarrabul (also spelt Ngoorabul, Nugumbul, Narbal, Narbul) Nation. According to Ngarrabul elder, Keith Byrne (cited in Australian Museum Business Services (AMBS), 2010, p.17), the land of the Ngarrabul people includes 'Glen Innes, Deepwater, and Torrington State Recreation Area, to Bolivia Station and the escarpment country of Washpool National Park in the north east, and the Mole River in the north'. This area includes the Ballard selection at Red Range. Apparently, the Ngarrabul people called Red Range Gundamba ('Crumbs', 8 January 1897, p.3).

In 1842, the population of First Nations people in the New England region was thought to be about five to six hundred people (AMBS, 2010, pp.17-19). However, as noted by Barry McDonald (2000), statistics are difficult to rely on as First Nations people moved around between the tablelands and the coastal plains according to the season. It has also been suggested that they moved from the Glen Innes area to the west in summer to avoid the March flies (Gardner, 1854). Furthermore, McDonald (2000) posits that they may have deliberately avoided contact with the white authorities and the process of being counted. Regardless of the size of the population, the local Aboriginal people suffered the effects of colonisation as they did elsewhere.

According to numerous reports, between about 1838 and 1844, there had been some very violent encounters in the area between the local Aboriginal people and the early European settlers, with 'fatalities on both sides' (AMBS, 2010, p.29). There were a number of occasions when Aboriginal people stole sheep from pastoralists, and there were instances where shepherds were speared. The pastoralists for their part tended to use excessive force and often retaliated against Aboriginal people indiscriminately, resulting in the deaths of many innocent people. The massacres of First Nations people that are known about in the area, occurred on the Beardy Plains, Deepwater Station, Bluff Rock, Bolivia, and the Beardy and Mole rivers (AMBS, 2010, p.29). There may well be others.

An example of the indiscriminate use of excessive violence by pastoralists in the New England district became known as the 'Myall Creek Massacre'. The massacre happened long before the Ballard's arrived in the district but the repercussions of the killings are evident to this day. On the 10th of June 1838, at least twenty-eight innocent men, women and children from the Wirrayaraay people at Myall Creek, near Inverell, were massacred. Seven British men were hung in Sydney jail on the 18th of December 1838 for their murders. The three men who were in charge of the group, and had supposedly encouraged the massacre, escaped without punishment. Nevertheless, this was the first-time white men had been hung for killing First Nations people in the colony (Plevey, 6 July 2022).

The hanging of the white killers had reverberations around the colony. There was some public sympathy with the condemned men. This was evident in editorials which were published in the *Sydney Herald* at the time, which argued vehemently to have the white killers released, referring to the Aboriginal people as 'savages' and 'aggressors' ('Editorial', 14 September 1838, p.2). Even so, not all of the British settlers sympathised with the killers. Many of the settlers actively campaigned to have the white killers punished ('The Lords of the Soil', 12 December 1838, p.2). According to History Professor Bain Attwood (13 July 2017, pp.24-43), after the Myall Creek prosecutions the 'colonial front lines and allegiances became a little murkier'.

Six years later in 1844, another massacre happened in the area. This time it was at Bolivia Station sixty kilometres (thirty-seven miles) north of Glen Innes, on the way to Tenterfield. There are conflicting accounts of what took place at Bolivia Station. However, it appears that a group of Aboriginal people, either Ngarabal or Jukembal people, stole a flock of sheep at Bolivia and speared the shepherd, a man named Robinson. Then in another example of excessive force and indiscriminate retaliation, Edward Irby from Bolivia Station, together with Major Windeyer from Deepwater Station and two other men who were all on horseback, tracked the group of men, women and children through the landscape. When they reached Bluff Rock, they drove the group off the cliff. Ten people were killed that day and many more were injured (Richards, 2013). According to Richards (2013, p.26), the stolen sheep and the murder of the shepherd were reported to the Colonial Secretary, but the retaliatory killings were not included.

Edward Irby (Irby & Irby, 1908, p.80) himself, wrote in his memoir about the incident. He said,

> The blacks saw us coming and hid themselves among the rocks. One in his haste, dropped poor Robinsons coat so we knew we were on to the right tribe. If they had taken to their heels they might have got away, instead of doing so, they got their fighting men to attack us. So we punished them severely and proved our superiority to them.

Furthermore, Irby (1908, p.80) suggested that they 'had no alternative' but to act as they had. If Irby and Windeyer truly thought they had no alternative and they had acted within the law, they would have reported the deaths of the Aboriginal people when they reported the stolen sheep and the murder of Robinson. Most likely, the killing of the Aboriginal people at Bluff Rock was not reported because of what had happened after Myall Creek. Clearly the white settlers knew they would be punished for the killings if the authorities found out about it. However, in this case it still wasn't enough to stop them from doing it.

By the time Catherine and her family settled at Red Range, there was little direct conflict between the traditional owners and the new settlers. Most of the violence had taken place well before the Ballard family arrived in the area.

The service town of Glen Innes

When Catherine and Thomas first arrived at their new home in Red Range, there weren't any shops or services and it wasn't yet a town, as such. They were truly early colonial pioneers. Their nearest service town was Glen Innes, which was about thirty kilometres (nineteen miles) from Red Range.

European settlement had begun in the Glen Innes area in the early 1840s. In 1844 the Scotsman, Major Archibald Clunes Innes, had acquired 25,000 acres in the area around Glen Innes, which he called 'Furracabad Station'. Sometime between 1844-1852, Innes sold the station to Archibald Mosman (Stephen, 2006). Coincidentally, Archibald Mosman, who you may recall from earlier discussions in this story, originally owned the land which became Underbank Estate before Catherine and her family lived there.

The township of Glen Innes was first gazetted by the colonial government in 1852, twenty-five years before the arrival of the Ballard family. In order to survey the newly gazetted town, John James Galloway took his bearings from the Furracabad Station store. The store, which was owned by Archibald Mosman, was managed by Mather and Gilchrist, and it became the first store in the new town of Glen Innes (Stephen, 2006). In 1854, once the land was surveyed, the first land sales took place (Donald, 1987) and the population in the town started to gradually increase.

According to the NSW census, the total population of Glen Innes township in 1871 was 343 people. This included 204 males and 139 females (Byron, 1883-4). Tin was then discovered nearby at Vegetable Creek (later named Emmaville) in 1872 which added greatly to the prosperity of the town ('No Title', 4 August 1875). A decade later, in 1881, the population of Glen Innes had more than tripled with 1,327 residents, including 761 males and 566 females (Byron, 1883-4).

In 1876 when the Ballards arrived in the area, Glen Innes had a post office, a telegraph station, a courthouse, police barracks, five hotels, three churches, a school and seven shops, including Grover's Hay, Corn, Chaff and General Produce Store (see Figure 17). The town also had a variety of other useful services such as a Lands Office ('No Title', 4 August 1875, p.2) and a branch of the Bank of NSW (Chappell, 14 September 2021).

Figure 17. Looking from Wentworth Street North along Grey Street – Glen Innes c1875 (Photo courtesy of *Mitchell Library, State Library of NSW*, Australia, At Work and Play 02509, Ref.390549).

There was even a Temperance Hall in Glen Innes, which included a lodge of the Sons of Temperance ('Prince of Wales's Birthday', 11 November 1874, p.2). Glen Innes was where the Ballard family would have gone to buy supplies, to do banking and to take care of business matters.

There were two local newspapers which serviced the Glen Innes area. *The Glen Innes Guardian* had been publishing for a few years when a second paper was started by the Vincent brothers in 1874. The brothers called their paper the *Glen Innes Examiner and General Advertiser*. The *Examiner* eventually acquired the *Guardian* in 1924 ('Land of the Beardies', 2016-2021). Also, the *NSW Government Gazette* ('NSW Government Gazette, 1832-2001') was an official government publication which was available all over the colony. It was first published in 1832, and provided important information about government proclamations, government employment appointments, as well as notifications about land selections and other aspects of government business.

The traditional Aboriginal name of the area around Glen Innes is Gindaaydjin which refers to the large smooth, round rocks that lay on the open plains in the area ('Land of the Beardies', 2016-2021). The European name of Glen Innes is generally thought to have been conferred on the town by Archibald Mosman in tribute to Major Innes. Cities, towns and geographical features in the colony, were often named after Scottish individuals and places. The use of 'Glen' to precede a name was also sometimes added to give the name a Scottish flavour. Wilkie (19 May 2018) argues that giving places Scottish names 'gave the landscape social and cultural significance for Scottish immigrants, and made reference points for identity and community in an alien environment'. In fact, according to Wilkie, about seventeen percent of non-Aboriginal place names in Australia are of Scottish origin.

This certainly was the case both for Glen Innes and for the surrounding district where Scottish names such as Glencoe, Dundee, Armidale, Ben Lomond etc abound. No doubt for the Ballard family, and Catherine in particular, this touch of Scottishness added a sense of familiarity or significance to her new home. Watson (1984, p.xx) argues that by imposing their own Scottish (or British) ancestors on the landscape, they were in fact able to substitute 'their own ancestors for Aboriginal ones, and establish[ing] permanent and familiar symbols to ease the passage of new settlers from the old world to the new, from the frontier to civilisation'.

Cobb & Co

The Newton Boyd Road had joined Glen Innes to south Grafton on the NSW coast in 1867. It was about 177 km (110 miles) of road over rivers, springs and steep, rough mountainous terrain, although three bridges were added to the Newton Boyd Road over the next decade, which improved its reliability. The road passed through a number of thriving gold towns and large stations along the way and included a carved rock tunnel known as the 'Dalmorton Tunnel'. The Dalmorton Tunnel is 'about 100 feet in length, through a mass of rock projecting on the river in advance of the general mountain side. Two tiers of bales are said to pass through this tunnel upon a wool dray' (it is only 3.3 metres high). The road was narrow with a vertical drop to the river. It was apparently a formidable journey to travel along the road in a coach or on a buggy ('Gwydir Highway: History and Development', n.d.).

By 1876, Glen Innes was also well connected to both Sydney and Grafton by Cobb & Co coaches. Cobb & Co was the most successful horse-drawn coach service in Australia at the time. They had started in Melbourne in 1854 and moved into NSW in 1862 (Riley, 18 October 2011). In 1867, a Cobb & Co coach began to travel between Newcastle and Glen Innes (Land of the Beardies, 2016-2021) and they had a booking office in Grey Street ('Under the Colonnade', 4 August 1875, p.2).

Cobb & Co also added routes to Inverell and the Queensland border at Wallangarra. At its peak in the 1870s, Cobb & Co coaches travelled 45,000 km (27,962 miles) a week over 11,200 km (6,960 miles) of routes, harnessing up to 6,000 horses. They travelled from the north of Queensland through NSW to southern Victoria, and provided passenger mail and gold-escort services. They had changing stations positioned every sixteen to thirty-two km (ten to twenty miles) along the route where the horses were changed. Fresh horses could go faster, making the Cobb & Co coach service the most efficient way to travel (Riley, 18 October 2011).

According to one account, the coaches travelled at about twelve kilometres an hour (seven to eight miles) ('Notes on a Trip from Bandon Grove to Bindera', 20 April 1872, p.5). Another source (Riley, 18 October 2011) suggested that a 200 kilometres (124 miles) coach trip could take about three days, with meals and overnight accommodation provided at 'bush inns', often run by families, along the way.

For example, on one trip in 1878, travelling from Glen Innes south to 'the metropolis', a passenger described how the trip began with a 'brief sojourn' at the Stonehenge Hotel. He said the next stop was at Mr Campbells of Glencoe just twenty-eight km (eighteen miles) from Glen Innes, where fresh horses were harnessed. Then at 9 am a breakfast of eggs, bacon and roast beef, was served at Mr Walsh's at the Ben Lomond Hotel, and so the journey continued ('Southward Ho!', 12 November 1878, p. 2).

Cobb & Co used strong, but lightweight Concord coaches, which had been designed for use in the American West. They suited the Australian conditions better than the English coaches which were previously used. However, the roads were often very rough. The coaches had to cross flooded creeks, they became bogged in mud, their drivers had to try to outrun bushrangers and they were faced with all sorts of inclement weather. One passenger described a coach journey as like riding 'a baby camel in a hell of a hurry' (Riley, 18 October 2011). As you can imagine, the journey was very uncomfortable and serious accidents were not infrequent. 'Mr Loveday's American coach wagon' left Glen Innes for Grafton every alternate Tuesday and cost £2 10s or £4 4s return ('Jottings by the Way-New England', 26 August 1871, p.18).

Grafton, on the Clarence River, became the port which serviced Glen Innes. A paddle-steamer transported passengers and goods such as wool and tin, from Grafton down to Sydney and other goods were then sent back up the coast. The steamer journey took about thirty hours ('Advertising', 12 January 1876, p.1). Therefore, if any of the Ballard family wanted to travel to Sydney (or anywhere along the way), they could get the coach from Glen Innes to Sydney, or the coach from Glen Innes to Grafton, and get on the steamer down to Sydney. It also meant that other family members could travel on the coach to Glen Innes and then out to Red Range to visit them.

It would have taken a lot of hard work and tenacity by everyone in the family to start from scratch on their selection at Red Range. Catherine, Thomas and their children had to depend on each other for everything, particularly in the beginning. The family developed many skills between them over the years they lived at Underbank and Dunmore Estate. These skills were needed to carve out a comfortable and sustainable life in the Australian bushland.

Once they settled into life on the Range, the Ballard family soon developed relationships with the other new settlers. In a small, isolated community such as Red Range, friendships were important for the stability of the community and the progress of the town. We can only assume that the Ballards also developed relationships with the local Aboriginal people on whose land they were living.

Although it was still early days when the Ballard family arrived, the town of Glen Innes was starting to grow as a service town with an increasing population. Regular trips to Glen Innes were necessary as it offered them many of the services they needed, as well as providing regular coach access to other regions of the colony.

It is clear that from the time they first arrived at Red Range, the Ballard family relied on newspapers to keep them informed of what was happening. The newspapers afforded a much needed and valuable source of information to people in the colony. Many of the events described in the next part of Catherine's story were reported in *The Glen Innes Examiner* and the *NSW Government Gazette*, which the Ballard's themselves would have read. As a family, they shared a fervent interest in politics and current affairs, something which will be explored in later chapters.

Chapter 9

Life on the Range

Death of Rev Lang - Lang's legacy - Public Instruction Act 1880 - secular education - supplementing their income - 'using' the land - Aboriginal workers - cricket and other social events

Rev Dr John Dunmore Lang

On the 8th of August 1878, the Rev Dr John Dunmore Lang (see Figure 18), who had initiated the bounty scheme which brought Catherine and her kin to Australia, died of a stroke. Rev Lang was an important figure in the NSW colony in the nineteenth century and his death was discussed widely in the newspapers across the colony. His passing would not have gone unnoticed in the Ballard household at Red Range.

Rev Lang's funeral was held at the Scots Church in Sydney, where he had ministered for fifty years. His funeral was one of the largest ever seen in the colony. It was estimated that over 70,000 people lined the streets to witness the funeral procession. More than 3,000 people walked in the procession, including five hundred Chinese men who walked at the front ('Public Funeral of the Rev. John Dunmore Lang, 12 August 1878, p.3).

Rev Lang had worked to abolish the poll tax on Chinese migrants. He opposed convict transportation and was the first public figure to advocate for Federation, democracy and a republic ('Public Funeral of the Rev. John Dunmore Lang, 12 August 1878, p.3). He also lobbied for the better treatment of First Nations people and openly questioned the violence being perpetrated against Aboriginal people in the name of progress.

Figure 18. Rev Dr John Dunmore Lang, n.d. Chromolithographic portrait. Artist unknown (Digby, E. (ed), 1888, *Australian Men of Mark 1788-1888*, Maxwell, Sydney).

In 1834, Lang didn't hold back when he wrote in his published volume, *'An Historical and Statistical Account of New South Wales, Both as a Penal Settlement and as a British Colony'* about the poor treatment of the Aboriginal people (Lang, John Dunmore, 1837). Lang argued that,

> There is black blood, at this moment, on the hands of individuals of good repute
> in the colony of New South Wales, of which all the waters of New Holland would
> be insufficient to wash out the deep and indelible stains!

Rev Lang was a Presbyterian Minister, a politician, an historian, he owned three newspapers, he wrote and published books, pamphlets and poems and he was the founder of the first Australian college of higher learning in 1831 (Dunmore Lang College, 2023.). Even so, Rev Lang was a controversial character and not without his detractors. There were those, such as Dr Mclean and Dr Martin, who publicly accused Rev Lang of deceiving the Scottish immigrants who had arrived in 1837 on the *Midlothian* with unrealistic expectations. These allegations were later proved wrong ('The Dunmore Highlanders', 7 September 1841, p.2).

He also established the Presbyterian church in Australia, but his financial record keeping was 'unconventional' which landed him in jail a couple of times. He was convicted of libel on another occasion. He had ongoing power struggles with the Presbyterian church hierarchy and was criticised for his many absences from the pulpit (Baker, 2006).

Rev Lang continued to recruit Protestant migrants and German Protestant missionaries and preachers to the colony. He wanted to quell what he saw as the rise of Catholicism. As the *Glen Innes Examiner* aptly put it, 'for over half a century the deceased clergyman formed a conspicuous figure in colonial history' ('Death of Dr Lang', 14 August 1878, p.2).

Among his greatest achievements was the promotion of education in the colony. Rev Lang was a tireless advocate of education for both women and men. He had long argued for a national and secular education system to be available to everyone in the colony (Dunmore Lang College, 2023).

Secular education across the colony

Due in no small part to Rev Lang's efforts, the NSW colonial government was in the process of building new schools across the colony at the time of his death. The aim was to have schools within easy reach of all townships and small settlements in order to comply with the new *Public Instruction Act 1880* which was to come into force the following year ('Bathurst Free Press-*Magna est veritas et prvalebt*', 20 February 1891, p.2).

Under the *Public Instruction Act 1880,* primary school education was to be made compulsory. Parents or guardians would be required to ensure their children, aged between six and fourteen years, attended school for at least seventy days out of every six months ('Public Instruction Act 1880', 5 November 2019). There were approximately 147,000 children in the NSW colony in the six to fourteen age group who would be required to attend school, or receive educational instruction at home ('Education', 16 September 1881, p.8).

The decision to make schooling compulsory under a government system of education came about at a time when ideas about the role of children in society were changing, and notions of national cohesion were emerging. The building of hundreds of primary schools was intended to ensure that children were prepared to take their place in 'civilised' society (Clark, 2022).

One newspaper commentator remarked that 'it is painful' to find a boy of twelve, as is common throughout the colony, who 'cannot make his autograph' or read basic English in 'so highly favoured and enlightened an age as the present' ('Compulsory Education', 11 December 1869, p.2). Another commentator wrote that 'education was designed to promote human happiness, morality and virtue'. Furthermore, he suggested that the education of girls 'should be to render them fit for their duty as wives and mothers to society at large' ('Editorial', 16 October 1869, p.2). The education system was generally seen as an effective way of indoctrinating children with the required virtues needed to forge a so-called civilised society and to shed the stereotype of the convict colony.

As a result of the government objective to make school compulsory for all children, a school was built at Red Range in 1879. Mr Ruming of Red Range was the contractor who undertook the construction of the new school building. He was said to have 'made a good job of the work'. When the school first opened, there was an average attendance of twenty-five children ('Provisional School at Red Range', 3 June 1879, p.2). Catherine's sons were all too old to go to the Red Range school, but her Cornish grandchildren all attended over the coming years.

Due to the new *Act* which made education compulsory, there was a twenty-five percent increase in enrolments in government schools in NSW in 1880. The increased number of students also led to an increase in the number of teachers employed throughout the colony opening up many work and career opportunities ('Public Instruction Act 1880', 5 November 2019). Since the 1850s, most teachers had started their training as pupil teachers, similar to apprentices. Pupil teachers had to successfully complete a written exam, and an assessment of their practical teaching skills was conducted by a school inspector from the Department who was responsible for maintaining educational standards (Strachan, 2001(a)). Even though Catherine herself had no formal education, education was highly valued in her family. As we will see, three of Catherine's children and a number of her grandchildren later became school teachers.

The new *Act* also required that the instruction given in all public schools should be secular and include 'only general religious teaching' rather than 'dogmatic or polemical theology' ('Public Instruction Act 1880', 5 November 2019). This was a significant change, as previously many schools had been run by churches and included comprehensive religious study. Furthermore, the *Act* stated that students should be instructed in the history of England and Australia ('Public Instruction Act 1880', 5 November 2019).

The Australian history referred to in the *Act* only related to history since colonisation. The belief at the time was that Australian history only began with colonisation and there was no recognition of First Nations people history, or the invasion that saw the beginning of white settlement (Clark, 2022, p.144). In 1888, the colonial historian, teacher, poet, novelist, scientist, philosopher and journalist Alexander Sutherland (1888 cited in Clark, 2022, p.305), argued that 'A truly savage race can have nothing that we may narrate as history'. He went on to explain that,

> ...the Australian colonist dates the commencement of history of his country from the arrival of the first white men' because 'his sable predecessors...have left material for the antiquarian, their bygone ages may offer scope to the geologist, but of history they have none (1888, cited in Clark, 2022, p.145).

Clark (2022, p.305) suggests that 'this dismissiveness confirms prevailing views at the time that the colonisation of Australia was providential and reflected the superiority of the British race and its Empire'.

The mail run

Late in 1879, as Catherine and the family settled into life on the Range, Thomas went about supplementing the family income. Thomas successfully applied for the contract to operate the mail run between the Glen Innes Post Office and Red Range. He was paid £20 a year to undertake the journey once a week ('Government Gazette Notices', 31 October 1879, p.4877).

Thomas' younger brother, James E Ballard, had purchased eighteen acres of agricultural land in Glen Innes ('Advertising', 2 March 1880, p.4). James had been living in Tamworth, but he had relocated to Glen Innes. At about the same time as Thomas began his mail run, his brother James was appointed as the new 'Post and Telegraph Master' at the Glen Innes Post Office ('Local and Other Notes', 20 January 1880, p.2). However, James left Glen Innes eighteen months later for Coonabarabran ('Local and Other Notes', 23 August 1881, p.2).

In 1882, Thomas was awarded a further three-year contract with an increase in payment to £40 per year to do the mail run twice a week. He picked up the mail from the post office in Glen Innes and rode back to Red Range on horseback ('Government Gazette Notices', 24 January 1882, p.467). The newspapers were also delivered to Red Range, along with the mail ('Local & Other Notes', 1 March 1881, p.2).

The first conveyance of mail to Glen Innes began in the 1850s, when mail was transported between Newcastle and Glen Innes. However, it was haphazard and couldn't be counted on with any certainty. Then in 1867, when the Cobb & Co coach began to travel regularly between Newcastle and Glen Innes, the mail was sent along with the coach. From 1875, the mail also went with the coach between Glen Innes and Grafton. There were mail deliveries between Glen Innes and other destinations where the coach travelled, such as Inverell and Armidale ('Land of the Beardies', 2016-2021).

Mail deliveries were prone to being held up by bushrangers. Robbers were an ongoing danger that went with the job. The mail often included cash and other valuables which were sent to new settlers from their families ('No Sydney Mail', 2 March 1880, p.2). This made the mail a very tempting source of revenue for bushrangers.

The well-known bushranger Captain Thunderbolt, who had been in the Dungog area when the Ballard family lived there, had moved his bushranging to the New England district in the late 1860s. Once there, he had taken on an orphan boy, Will Monckton, as his companion and accomplice. Monckton was captured by police in 1869, and served a fourteen-month jail sentence. He was released early due to his good behaviour in jail and his young age. Monckton later settled in Howell, in the New England district, and raised a large family (Pratt, 1905). He became a respectable member of the community and many of his descendants still live around the district today. However, by the time Thomas was delivering the post, Thunderbolt was no longer a threat. He had been killed nine years earlier on the 25th of May in 1870. He was shot at Kentucky Creek near Uralla NSW, by an off-duty policeman, Constable Walker ('New South Wales Police', 16 July 1870, p.4).

Notwithstanding the death of Thunderbolt, there were many other bushrangers and desperate men who were disposed to holding up the mail. For example, on one occasion a man, who said his name was Riley held up the coach between Inverell and Glen Innes. He helped himself to seven bags of mail. There were three passengers on board but none was 'interfered with' ('Mail Robbery', 29 May 1883, p.2). No doubt, Thomas stayed alert and kept an eye out for anyone suspicious when he picked up the mail in Glen Innes, and on the ride back out to Red Range.

It is impossible to say if letters were sent between Kendram, on the Isle of Skye, and Catherine at Red Range, in the NSW colony. As we have discussed, the mail was becoming more reliable as time went on, but it is unknown if the families corresponded, or if they just lost contact. They were living worlds apart. Even though, like Catherine's own children, her nieces and nephews and cousins from Skye were most probably literate, they had never met their aunts, uncles or cousins who lived in Australia.

So, when Catherine's sister, Ann McLeod (nee McKinnon), died of pneumonia in 1881 at the age of seventy-two (Ann MacLeod, 4 May 1881), it is impossible to know if anyone wrote to tell her. Ann and her husband, William McLeod, were living at the family croft at Lot 1 Kendram with their son, Donald and his wife Marion Cameron (daughter of Catherine's cousin, Malcolm Cameron from Balnacnoc on Skye) and their four grandchildren (Ann MacLeod, 1881).

Only a few years before Ann died, an 1876-78 Ordnance Survey Name Book described Kendram as 'a small district on which there are a number of croft houses, all one storey in height, thatched and in the very poorest of order inside and out on Captain Frasers property' (Ordnance Survey Name Book, 1876-78). They were very poor and their croft was clearly very run down by this time.

Ann was the last member of Catherine's immediate family to die at Kendram. As with the deaths of her younger sister Dorcas and those of her mother and her father, it is unknown if Catherine would have even heard about Ann's death. If in fact, her nieces or nephews in Skye did write to let Catherine know about her sister's death, the letter would have taken at least four months to arrive in Sydney by sailing ship. Compound steam ships, which were more efficient than sail, began transporting the international mail after the granting of a mail subsidy from the government in the 1880s. However, it was probably too early for a steamship to have carried this particular letter ('Journeys to Australia', 2024).

If there was a letter, once it arrived in Sydney it would have been transported to Glen Innes either via steamer to Grafton and then coach to Glen Innes, or inland by coach from Sydney. Finally, Thomas as the Red Range postman, would have picked the letter up in Glen Innes and delivered it to Catherine.

Of course, Thomas would have also needed to read the letter to her and break the sad news of her sister's passing.

The colonisation of nature

As a condition of their land selection at Red Range, the Ballard family like other settlers who obtained land under the *Crown Lands Act,* were required to clear their land of trees and fence it. The need to 'improve' the land was inherent in the *Act* ('*Crown Lands Alienation Act 1861 No26a*', 18 October 1861, pt18). The Ballard family worked hard to achieve this. There was a general understanding in the nineteenth and twentieth centuries in Britain and Australia that the natural environment was to be tamed, improved and exploited. The historian Andrew Fitzmaurice (2007, p.14) suggests that 'attitudes to the exploitation of nature and the belief that property is created by use, permeated the entire experience of European expansion'. As we discussed earlier, in order to justify taking land, the English colonisers had argued that First Nations people did not 'improve' the land.

By all accounts, the land on the New England Tablelands, including Glen Innes and Red Range, was abundant with native wildlife and covered with forest and native flora before the white settlers set about colonising it. However, due to their attitudes about the land, the new settlers often had a complex relationship with the natural environment in which they lived. As they cleared more and more native forest on their selections, the kangaroos and wallabies continued to come in even larger numbers. The native marsupials ate the sweet new pasture that came up after the land was cleared, or indeed any crops that the settlers had planted.

There were various *Acts* passed by the colonial government over the years which attempted, on the one hand, to eradicate native wildlife and, on the other, protect it. For example, in an attempt to manage the so called 'marsupial problem', the NSW government passed the *Pasture and Stock Protection Act 1880*. Under the *Act,* kangaroos and wallabies were declared 'vermin'. Bounties were paid for each marsupial killed and farmers were responsible for seeing that their land was cleared of the 'pests'. In 1884 alone, over 250,000 bounties were paid in NSW for kangaroo scalps and 86,000 for scrub wallabies with many of these killed in the New England district. The main justification for the killing was the protection of the pastoral industry. The skins were also sold for footwear, rugs, clothing and souvenirs, so they also had an economic value beyond the bounties (Boom, Ben-Ami, Croft, Cushing, Ramp & Boronyak, 2012).

At about the same time, in 1879, the *Animals Protection Act* was first implemented in NSW. The *Act* was passed in order to protect animals during the breeding season, to prevent their extinction. The Committee for the Protection of Native Birds and Mammals was formed, which was the beginning of the conservation movement in the colony (Stubbs, 2001).

The local Ngarrabul people hunted kangaroos, wallabies, goanna, echidna, wild duck, fish, honey ants, witchetty grubs, bird eggs and other native animals. However, according to an Aboriginal Heritage Study which was undertaken for the Severn LGA, Ngarrabul people didn't eat or kill the koala. The koala was very significant to the Ngarrabul people, as it was their tribal totem (Australian Museum Business Services, 2010, p.21).

As a result, the koala population in the New England district was said to be very large before colonisation and up until the late nineteenth century. European settlers in the district suggested that over the span of a twenty-four km (fifteen-mile) journey in a horse and sulky, you would expect to see over a hundred koalas up in the trees ('About Glen Innes', 2016-2022).

Regrettably, koalas - like kangaroos - were also killed in huge numbers by the new inhabitants of the NSW colony, mostly for their beautiful pelts. The koala's pelt is soft and very dense which makes it waterproof and gives it great insulation qualities. The pelt made excellent hats, gloves and coat lining. The marsupials were mostly hunted in the winter months when their fur was thick, and the pelts were then sent to the Sydney markets where they were mostly exported overseas. The fur was highly sought after in cold climates such as Britain, Canada and the United States. It is estimated that about eight million koalas were killed across eastern Australia, including a huge number in the New England district. As a result, the koala population was decimated and the fur trade was eventually banned in NSW in 1906 ('AKF: Shocking Figures Reveal the Devastating Impacts of the Koala Fur Trade', 25 August 2015).

Unfortunately for the wildlife and the environment as a whole, in the second half of the nineteenth century there was a global, volunteer movement of European colonists known as 'Acclimatisation Societies'. Their aim was to introduce wildlife from one country to another. The NSW branch of the society began in 1861. The members of the society quickly began introducing exotic species into the Australian environment ('Acclimatisation Society of New South Wales Annual Report, 1861).

They introduced wildlife mostly from the northern hemisphere into the Australian landscape, including carp into the Murray River system, deer to the mountains as well as starlings, thrushes, Indian myna birds, blackbirds and sparrows. They did this in order to 'improve' the Australian environment by introducing animals they viewed as 'useful' (Gallacher, Jokiranta & Marie, 4 November 2022). 'Useful' animals were those they knew and liked, as well as those animals they were familiar with on their dinner plates. Native Australian animals were seen to be peculiar!

Rather than 'improve' the environment, many of these introduced species became invasive and had unforeseen consequences. One of the major scourges on the Australian landscape, which was introduced in 1859, was the rabbit. Thomas Austin released thirteen European, wild rabbits on his land in Victoria on Christmas Day in 1859. Supposedly, they were to be hunted for sport and eaten. DNA testing has recently confirmed that these were the first rabbits to become feral across Australia. By 1880, the rabbits had reached the NSW colony, and by 1886 they were in Queensland (Dettre, 23 August 2022). The Ballard's would have probably first seen rabbits at Red Range in the early to mid-1880s.

Native birds were also plentiful in the New England district during the nineteenth century, including the eastern rosella, wonga wonga pigeon, curlew, lyrebird, kookaburra and whistling eagle, just to name a few. Frank Cornish would later recall visits to his grandparents, Catherine and Thomas, at their selection. Frank said his most vivid memories were of 'the songs of the birds in the early morning' ('The Gulf Country', 7 July 1969, p.3). Sadly, by the turn of the century, there was huge habitat loss due to land clearing, which heavily impacted the bird population. In addition, the use of poisons for baiting invasive species, such as rabbits, foxes and feral pigs, dramatically decreased the bird populations ('About Glen Innes', 2016-2022).

Hughes-de' Aeth (2018) argues that the environment was not, as most of the new settlers thought, something passive that needed to be exploited or improved. Rather he suggests it was a 'dynamic system of interrelated parts, where every action had cascading consequences and complex repercussions.' Unbeknown to the new settlers at the time, the colonisation of the Australian environment had far-reaching consequences for the ecological health of the environment long into the future.

Aboriginal workers on the Range

Once the number of new settlers increased in the area, traditional seasonal movement became more difficult for Ngarrabul people. This resulted in many people having to remain in the district through the cold winter period. It also meant they often required clothing and food rations, which were distributed by The Aborigines Protection Board, in order to survive the winter (Australian Museum Business Services, 2010, p.32). With limited access to traditional land to make warm possum skins cloaks, First Nations people also became more and more reliant on the annual distribution of blankets from the court house in Glen Innes to survive ('Local & General News', 29 May 1888, p.2) (see Figure 19).

In 1882, the Aborigines Protection Board was established in NSW to manage a number of missions and reserves on land set aside by the government to 'protect' the estimated 9000 First Nations people who lived in the colony at the time ('Missions, Stations and Reserves', 2022). The missions and reserves gave their managers, who were mostly Christian groups or religious individuals, authority over the movements of First Nations people and stripped them of their autonomy.

Figure 19. Glen Innes Court House, 1865. Annual Blanket Distribution of Blankets to Aborigines (Photo courtesy of Glen Innes Historical Society Archives, NSW, Australia, No.2728, 30 August 2023).

The Honourable George Thornton wrote 'the hitherto uncared for blacks of this colony will at least be protected and preserved from cold and hunger by the kind and wise action of the Government' ('Aborigines', 11 September 1882, p.4). However, Doukakis (2006) argues that a protectionist policy was instituted to try and control First Nations people under the guise of providing welfare. Despite the best attempts of the government, only about seventeen percent of the known First Nations people in NSW lived on land controlled by the Aborigines Protection Board in the nineteenth century (Doukakis, 2006).

Most of the First Nations people living in the area near the Ballard farm at Red Range lived in camps, on land of their own choosing. These camps were either situated on small remnants of their traditional land, or on the fringes of towns (Doukakis, 2006). There were Aboriginal camps close to Red Range at Oban, Kookabookra and at several other nearby stations such as Aberfoyle, Lyndhurst and Camperdown. Barry McDonald (2000) estimates there was a population of about sixty Aboriginal people living in the area in the 1880s.

The restricted access to Country and their traditional way of life also meant many Ngarrabul people looked for employment with the new settlers in the area (Australian Museum Business Services, 2010, p.32). It is more than likely that the Ballards employed Aboriginal people to work on their farm. By 1884, according to a stock return that Thomas Ballard had submitted for that year, they had 1000 acres, twelve horses, eighty cattle and ten pigs on their farm (Descendants of Edward Ballard, n.d.). Subsequently, they would have needed to employ extra workers including stockmen, drovers, farm hands and domestic help. It is most likely they employed Aboriginal workers to do these jobs.

Like most other new settlers at the time, they would have paid the First Nations people who worked for them in rations rather than cash. These rations usually included flour, sugar, tea, clothing, tobacco and alcohol. Given their strong Presbyterian faith, and most likely their aversion to alcohol, it seems unlikely they would have used alcohol as payment, although many others did. The introduction of alcohol and tobacco, as well as sweet and starchy foods to the diet of the Aboriginal people by new settlers, may have been well - meaning at the time. There were always cash shortages in the colony and these goods were valued by the settlers themselves. However, this change from natural bush tucker to processed foods and stimulants adversely affected the health of many First Nations people (Australian Museum Business Services, 2010, p.32).

According to an *Aboriginal Heritage Study* (Australian Museum Business Services, 2010, p.32) which was undertaken for Severn Council, most First Nations people who worked for new settlers tried to maintain their participation in traditional life by attending ceremonies and fulfilling their tribal obligations. As a result, they could at times suddenly disappear, or leave their job, to attend to their cultural duties, behaviour which was not generally understood by their employers. However, as the population of new settlers increased, it became harder for Aboriginal workers to fulfill their traditional way of life and many became dislocated, leaving them caught 'in limbo between two worlds' (Australian Museum Business Services, 2010, p.31-32).

Despite the obvious tensions, it is interesting to note that there were many instances of new settlers and First Nations people who formed good working relationships, as well as friendships. Apart from the benefits of companionship and good will, there were many other benefits for new settlers who maintained good relationships with the first Australians. Goodall (2008) suggests these included a source of cheap, readily accessible, skilled labour. Increasingly, First Nations workers had become skilled in European farming methods and the handling of livestock. Aboriginal workers also had many traditional bush-skills and traditional knowledge, which they could teach new settlers. What's more, they were largely self-sufficient, as many Aboriginal workers continued to gather their own food and build their own houses. They were comfortable living and working in the bush, which many non-Aboriginal labourers found too remote. Clearly, First Nations people played an important role in the establishment and on-going success of farms in colonial NSW. Without the available workforce, the new settlers would have struggled to survive, particularly in more remote locations such as Red Range.

Life wasn't all hard work

Life wasn't all hard work for the Ballard family at Red Range. Catherine and Thomas's four sons and their son-in-law, James Cornish, were all keen cricketers. The men all played in the Red Range team which was founded by David Ballard ('Red Range', 5 April 1923, p.4). On occasion, they made up nearly half the team. Thomas had been a keen cricketer in his younger days and had played on the Underbank team (Obituary, 14 July 1916, p.6). However, he must have left playing to the younger lads at Red Range, and just cheered them on from the sidelines, as his name didn't appear in any of the regular matches which were reported in the newspaper.

Apart from the match itself, there were other rewards to be had from a game of cricket. On one occasion, when the Red Range team had played the Warwicks on home soil, an article in the *Glen Innes Examiner* gave a glowing description of the event ('Warwicks v Red Range', 15 November 1881, p.4). The article stated that the Red Range team had 'made ample provision by way of a capital lunch for the visitors' and 'the proceedings were very enjoyable and the most was made of the outing'. I think it is fair to think that Catherine and the other mothers, wives, grandmothers and daughters most probably provided the 'capital lunch'. In fact, in another instance, when Red Range played against Glencoe, the newspaper commentator suggested 'the day was fine, and a fair sprinkling of the fair sex put in an appearance to witness the contest'. He went on to thank Mrs Cornish, Catherine's daughter Maria, and Mrs McDonald who had presided over the provision of a splendid lunch ('Glencoe v Red Range', 13 December 1881, p.2).

There weren't any women playing in the Red Range cricket team. However, there was mention of a cricket match in Glen Innes between 'married and single ladies' ('Local and Other Notes', 14 January 1879, p.2). And another at Vegetable Creek, played 'between a number of young ladies' in 1879 ('Held Over', 10 June 1879, p.2). Women started to play cricket more regularly in the 1890s in Australia, in all-women's teams.

However, their long dresses and undergarments inhibited their ability to run (see Figure 20). By the early twentieth century, as the style of their dresses became less cumbersome, women often played in mixed gender, community teams, particularly, in country areas when there weren't enough men available. It wasn't until the 1920s that women started to play cricket in long white trousers, like the men, enabling them to move with ease (Howell, Howell & Brown, 1989). Despite the improvement in their playing attire, cricket was still not considered to be a sport which was suitable for all women, due to 'medical reasons' ('Women in Print', 19 December 1922, p.7).

Mostly though, women attended cricket matches in the nineteenth century to socialise with other women and to provide support, in the form of refreshments and encouragement, to the menfolk. No doubt community cricket also provided important opportunities for young, single people such as Catherine's sons to meet other young people from further afield. In a small community such as Red Range, the pool of potential partners was limited.

Figure 20. Ladies' cricket match-Glen Innes NSW, c1900 (Photo courtesy of *Mitchell Library, State Library of NSW*, Australia, At Work and Play 02655, Ref.390695).

Aside from the regular cricket matches over the years, there were other events on the Red Range social calendar. Apparently, the annual Red Range school picnic was a big event not to be missed. There were one hundred and seventy people, including seventy-three children in attendance, at the 1883 picnic which was quite a large gathering for a small school community. A concert had been arranged by 'Messers Ballard' and others to entertain the crowd, and it was said that the 'very earth quaked with the good things provided by the ladies' ('Red Range', 21 August 1883, p.2). The Red Range School picnic, which raised much needed funds for the school, continued throughout the years and brought much pleasure to both the students and the local community.

In early 1885, Thomas Ballard entered a selection of produce from their garden in the Farm Produce section of the Glen Innes Show. His entry consisted of six watermelons and some early cobs of corn. His son-in-law, James Cornish, also entered potatoes, cucumbers, onions and local game. Both Thomas and James won small monetary awards for their entries. It was estimated the crowd attending the show reached 2000 spectators on the Friday alone. Clearly, it was a popular event which drew a large crowd from all around the district ('The Glen Innes Show', 24 February 1885, p.2).

On another occasion, there was a sports carnival fundraiser and luncheon (for 1s) held at Mr Petitt's Garden Palace Wine Vaults at Red Range. The races included a walking race, a sack race and a three-legged race, and there were high jump and long jump events ('Advertising', 3 November 1885, p.5). Horse races were also held at Red Range ('Advertising', 8 May 1888, p.5) and Catherine's son, Edward Ballard, was known to breed a good sprinter ('A Wonderful Old Horse', 1913, p.2). Yet another community event was organised by David Ballard in his capacity as the secretary of the Red Range cricket team. David had arranged a 'Ball and Supper' to raise money for the team. The tickets were advertised as 7s 6p ('Advertising', 8 December 1885, p.5). No doubt, the women of Red Range also provided the food and drink for the ball.

Once Catherine, Thomas and their sons left the family sociality of Underbank, their lives changed. They went from living among a community of extended family and friends to relative isolation. The school building program which was instigated by the NSW government provided many small communities, such as Red Range with their first public building. Apart from providing an education for the local children, this public infrastructure also provided a focus for the families at Red Range to start building a strong community.

Regular events such as those held at the school, cricket matches, balls, shows, picnics and community race days were a very important part of life on the Range over the years. These events afforded opportunities for people in the area to catch up with each other and enjoy themselves. Certainly, many of the social events held in Red Range would have been looked forward to by members of the Ballard family, and the community at large. By engaging with the local community, having shared experiences and building relationships, Catherine and the other people living in the Red Range area were able to develop strong bonds, which would help to see them through difficult times.

In order to stay in touch with family members and friends who lived further away, regular mail deliveries provided an important source of communication. Even though Catherine couldn't read the letters herself, the mail would have helped to ameliorate some of her sense of isolation from her family. Her family were now quite scattered around rural NSW. The mail could deliver bad news, such as deaths, but it was also a means of arranging celebrations like weddings, as well as visits from family members.

Chapter 10

Family

*Welcome visitors - a new baby - health care - a fatal coach accident -
Malcolm McDonald's wedding - the death of Angus McKinnon*

Family visits

Visits from family members would have been welcomed by Catherine and
Thomas at Red Range, no doubt bringing much joy. Family visits enabled
Catherine and Thomas a chance to catch up on the news of their family
and get better acquainted with their grandchildren. The photo below is of
Catherine with two of her grandsons, William and George McDonald (see
Figure 21). The photo was taken in about 1878. William and George are the
children of Catherine's eldest son Ewen McDonald and his wife Emily. Ewen
and his family (which included three more sons, Alfred, John and Herbert)
were still living somewhere near Dungog at the time of the photo (David
James McDonald, 1882). The photo suggests that either Ewen, and at least
some of his family, were visiting Catherine at Red Range, or *vice versa*.

Initially, after Underbank was repossessed, Catherine's youngest son from
her first marriage - John McDonald, his wife Elizabeth, and their first two
children Angus and Clementine - had moved to Inverell west of Glen Innes.
John and Elizabeth had two more children while they were living in Inverell
who they named Catherine and Ewen. Inverell was close enough for the
families to have regular visits, which must have been valued by both sides.
However, in 1881 John and his family moved back to Munni, a small
agricultural village on the Williams River near Underbank. They bought a
property there which they called 'Heatherbrae' ('Deaths', 16 January 1920,
p.2). Elizabeth's family lived near Dungog and perhaps that drew them back
to the area.

Figure 21. Catherine with two of her grandsons, c1878. George Frederick McDonald (1878-1947) and William Angus McDonald (1872-1960) (Photo courtesy of Angus MacDonald).

In 1882, Catherine and Thomas had a visit at Red Range from their son Angus (4), his wife Helena and their three sons, Eldred, George and Victor. After Underbank was repossessed, Angus (4) and Helena had moved to Gunnedah on the Liverpool Plains of NSW. In Gunnedah, Angus (4) had become a respected school teacher with the Education Department ('Mr. Angus McDonald', 13 June 1927, p.5). While they were visiting Catherine and Thomas at Red Range, Helena gave birth to another son. He was their fourth child (Cyrus EDA McDonald, 1882).

Doctors still didn't usually deliver babies or attend births so the baby must have been born at either Catherine or Maria's home at Red Range with help from the women of the family. Both Catherine and Maria would have attended many births by now and would presumably have been quite experienced at supporting women in labour and through the delivery. Even though maternal mortality rates in the colony were still high (Lewis, 2014), the mother and child were both fine. The baby was named Cyrus Edward David Allan McDonald. It is testament as to how close the brothers must have been that the child was named after all four of Angus's (4) Ballard brothers. The safe arrival of another baby into the family would have been a happy occasion and a joy to be shared by all.

Health care

The Ballard family, like other settlers living in remote parts of the NSW colony, would have had to rely on their own resources, as well as each other, to treat and attend to their health and medical needs. No doubt, as well as delivering babies, they stitched cuts, dressed wounds, removed decayed teeth, nursed snake bites and perhaps even set broken bones for each other.

There were a number of doctors practising in the town of Glen Innes in the early 1880s. The doctors in Glen Innes did what they could for medical cases and they even undertook some surgery. Dr Charles Creasy Clayworth was a surgeon from Edinburgh who had settled in Glen Innes. Apparently in 1880, Dr Clayworth rather skilfully performed a right breast amputation for a 'malignant cystic tumour' on a local resident, Mrs Williams ('Local and Other Notes', 9 November 1880, p.2). The first, rather basic section of the Glen Innes hospital, known as the South Wing, had opened in 1877 although, initially at least, there was only one ward available for up to six male patients ('Land of the Beardies', 2016-2022). So, Dr Clayworth would most likely have performed the surgery in his rooms. It was not reported how well Mrs Williams faired over the long term.

In 1880-81, there was a smallpox (variola virus) outbreak in Sydney. The outbreak led to the passing of the *Infectious Diseases Supervision Act 1881*, and the establishment of a central Board of Health. People were required to notify the authorities of any smallpox cases (de Looper, 2015, p.271). Also, as a result of the outbreak, Dr Clayworth offered government supplied smallpox vaccinations to patients ('Advertising', 21 December 1880, p.1). Since the early 1800s 'vaccine viability was maintained by inoculating unvaccinated people and transferring the 'lymph' between individuals through arm-to-arm transfer'. The process posed risks to those involved, such as the spread of syphilis. This arm-to-arm transfer was then replaced by the use of animals for the production of lymph. However, when, and to what extent, the production of vaccine was taken from animal lymph in colonial NSW is not known exactly (Weston, Gallagher, & Branley, 17 March 2014). However, Dr Wrigley, another Glen Innes doctor, advertised in 1883 that he was administering free government vaccinations having just received a fresh supply of calf lymph ('Advertising', 2 October 1883, p.4).

Chemists competed with doctors for patients in somewhat of a medico-political power struggle throughout the later part of the nineteenth century in the colony. Doctors were pushing for only those registered professionals with medical qualifications to be allowed to treat patients (Lewis, 2014). However, chemists and others continued to treat people with all sorts of medicines, balms and elixirs.

One chemist and druggist, John Hunt, who had a shop in Grey Street in Glen Innes advertised that he sold cattle medicines, trusses, syringes, enemas and 'first class perfumeries' ('Advertising', 1 March 1881, p.5). Thomas Ballard even wrote a testimonial in the *Glen Innes Examiner* for one of Hunt's veterinary medicines. Thomas said that 'Hunts Horse and Cattle Embrocation' quickly cured his horses sore back and was equally as good for 'girth and collar galls' ('Advertising', 6 September 1881, p.5).

Mr Hunt also sold homeopathic remedies and a range of his own Hunt branded pills, balms, tonics, syrups and expectorants in his shop ('Advertising', 1 March 1881, p.5). Chlorodyne was a common ingredient used in the elixirs of the day. Chlorodyne was a mixture of laudanum (an alcoholic solution of opium), cannabis tincture and chloroform. According to Doyle (2006), chlorodyne was consumed by a wide range of people, including people who were teetotallers.

Chlorodyne was used to treat a wide assortment of illnesses including insomnia, diarrhea, cancer, epilepsy, migraines and even cholera, all with mixed results. In moderation, these elixirs would have offered some sufferers temporary relief from their symptoms. When abused, however, they led to addiction (Dayton, 5 September 2022). Within the next decade, Australia became a world leader in the consumption of tonics and patented medicines (Doyle, 2006). As a result, many people who frequently imbibed the tonics found themselves addicted and even more unwell than when they started.

Another Glen Innes chemist, A J Dodd, who was also in Grey Street, advertised that he sold Dodd's anti-bilious pills and Dodd's balsams for coughs. Additionally, Dodd could extract teeth and fill cavities with gold or silver ('Advertising', 10 February 1880, p.1), although there were also dentists who visited Glen Innes. For example, Mr Adolphe Gabriel from Sydney was visiting Glen Innes for just a few days in 1881. He was seeing people in private rooms located in Brownes Commercial Hotel. He was offering artificial teeth and dental surgery ('Advertising', 30 August 1881, p.2). Dentistry was a risky business though. Mr Robert Arden Lewis died at the age of thirty-two, when he was under the influence of chloroform during an operation at Spencer's Dentist ('Family Notices', 1 March 1881, p.2).

Angus McKinnon

As was previously discussed, Catherine's younger brother Angus McKinnon, who had originally come out from Skye to help her manage Underbank, was working as a teacher at the Taree Public School on the mid north coast of NSW. He taught in Taree for about 14 years ('Port Macquarie', 20 August 1887, p.417).

Angus, Anne and their six children then moved to Port Macquarie in 1876, where he taught at the Port Macquarie Public School ('Port Macquarie', 20 August 1887, p.417). For many years, Angus also wrote articles for the local *'Times'* newspaper which circulated in Port Macquarie and the Manning district ('The "Manning Times"', 13 April 1889, p.2). Angus and Anne had five more children over the years they lived in Port Macquarie, although only four survived. Angus was intelligent, he was a good family man, he was a well-regarded member of the community, and he had a passion for teaching.

However, in just one moment his life was turned upside down. On the 8th of January in 1884, Angus, his wife Anne and one of their daughters were travelling in the mail coach from Port Macquarie south on their way to Taree. When they were about ten miles out of Port Macquarie along the Manning Road, the brakes gave way on the coach and the driver lost control of the horses. The coach was 'smashed to pieces.' Angus's wife Anne was killed in the accident. Angus and their young daughter, were also both badly injured ('Dreadful Coach Accident', 9 January 1884, p.5).

Anne died instantly as she was thrown out of the coach and her back was broken. The other passenger, a man named Mr Kenneth McKenzie, was also killed and the driver of the coach broke his collarbone. Angus and Anne had ten surviving children. The youngest child, Athol, was only nine months old ('Dreadful Coach Mishap', 12 January 1884, p.11). After their mother died, the children were sent to live with relatives and friends of Anne's family.

Catherine and Thomas's eldest daughter, Mary, had lived with her uncle Angus McKinnon and his family at Taree when she was a teenager. Some sixteen years later, in the second half of 1884, Mary, her husband and her family moved to Landsdowne on the Manning River, north of Taree ('The Late Mrs Mary Bignell', 9 June 1934, p.2). Mary had her hands full with seven children under nine, but she was close to her uncle Angus and his children. Mary was later described as 'a fine woman who devoted her life to her family'. She was 'deeply religious' and known for her unselfish service to others in their time of need ('The Late Mrs Mary Bignell', 9 June 1934, p.2). No doubt, she did what she could to help at this incredibly difficult time.

Just over a year after his wife had been killed in the coach accident, Angus took a teaching position at the Lawrence Public School on the Clarence River near Maclean ('Appointments and Employment', 16 September 1884, p.6205). However, his situation at work deteriorated when a woman called Mrs Cockburn, sent a telegram to the 'Minister for Public Instruction' making allegations that Angus was drowning his sorrows in alcohol ('Mrs Cockburn', 30 May 1884). The allegations were later backed up by Angus's daughter Anne, who happened to be dating Mrs Cockburn's son, Wemyss Cockburn ('Lawrence Head Master', 10 August 1885). Two other gentlemen, who had apparently known Angus for twenty years, also backed the allegation of his decline into alcohol (School Inspector's Report to the Under Secretary, 21 April 1885). As a result of the 'neglect and intemperate habits' suggested in the allegations, Angus was fired from his teaching position on the 30th of March in 1885 ('Angus McKinnon', 2 April 1885, p.1).

Intemperance would have been frowned upon by Catherine and the other members of Angus's family, as well as his peers. As a good Presbyterian, he would have been expected to uphold temperance, even in such trying times. The public shame associated with his drinking, and the loss of his job, would have been difficult for him to bear.

In order to try and salvage his tarnished reputation and his job, Angus wrote a letter to 'The Under Secretary' for the Department of Public Instruction ('Angus McKinnon', 2 April 1885, p.1).

In the letter he made a pledge of temperance. He stated:

> I deny emphatically the allegation of intemperance and defy the world to prove it, and to avoid even a suspicion I pledged myself to abstain from all intoxicating liquors, which pledge I mean to keep so long as I live, finding by long experience that it is the only way to be safe from the tongue of envy and malice.

The letter went on to assert his unblemished character and pointed to his impeccable teaching record. He also asked the Under Secretary for compensation for his dismissal.

Despite his letter, a couple of weeks later on the 21st of April 1885, the School Inspector recommended that Angus be removed from the Public Service. The Inspector suggested that apart from the charge of intemperance, he found sufficient evidence to the 'neglect of the school and to the gross inaccuracies both in the school records and in the Return for Decr [sic] quarter 1884' (School Inspector's Report to the Under Secretary, 21 April 1885).

After twenty-five years of flawless service, Angus was let go and denied any compensation ('Lawrence Head Master', 10 August 1885). This must surely have added to his woes. Catherine and Angus's younger sister, Margaret McMillan (nee McKinnon) and her family, were living at Woodford Island on the Clarence River near Lawrence at the time. I assume they tried to help Angus.

A wedding at Maclean on the Clarence River

On a happier note, also on the Clarence in 1885, Malcolm McDonald - Catherine's son from her first marriage - married Lydia Isabella Stanley Smith (she was known as 'Isabella'). Malcolm had bought land next to his old home at Underbank, bordering on Quart Pot Creek ('Historical Lands Record Viewer' 1893), at about the same time that Catherine and the family had left the area ('Advertising', 29 March 1877, p.1). Isabella's parents, Alexander Smith and Lydia Stanley Kingston, had both originally emigrated from Ireland (Lydia Kingston Smith, 21 May 2016). They lived at Bandon Grove, which was next to Underbank. Isabella was also the cousin of Robert Bignell (also originally from Bandon Grove) who was married to Catherine's daughter, Mary Ballard. Malcolm was forty-one at the time of his marriage and Isabella was twenty-nine. However, they must have known each other for many years.

Even though they were both living near Underbank, Malcolm and Isabella were married in the Presbyterian church in Maclean on the Clarence River (Malcolm MacDonald, 2010). The Presbyterian minister in Maclean, Rev Duncan McInnes, delivered services both in English and Gaelic due to the large Scots community who were living in the area. Gaelic was spoken freely in the Maclean area as many of the new settlers who lived there didn't speak

English ('History of Clarence', 13 January 1925, p.2). There were a number of members from Catherine's extended family living in the district at this time, some of who presumably attended Malcolm and Isabella's wedding. These included Catherine's sister, Margaret McMillan, and her family and her younger brother, Angus McKinnon. However, as mentioned earlier, Angus was not in a good way at this time. Catherine's brother John McKinnon had long since passed away but some of his children, Malcolm's cousins, still lived in the Maclean area.

It would not have been far for Malcolm's older brother, Ewen McDonald and his family to make the journey from their new home. Ewen and his family were living at 'Glencoe' on Skinners Creek in Booyung near Clunes, in north eastern NSW. It was an area of sub-tropical rainforest known as 'The Big Scrub'. There was a sizable Scots, Presbyterian community in Clunes with ties to both the Isle of Skye and the Maclean district where Malcolm's wedding was held.

Malcolm's half-sister, Mary Bignell (nee Ballard), could have made the journey from her home near Taree. Maria Cornish (nee Ballard), Malcolm's other half-sister who lived at Red Range, was pregnant with twins in 1885, so, it is unlikely she made the journey. Catherine's step children from her first marriage, Flora Sherwood and Murdoch Graham, also lived in the Maclean area. They would have known Malcolm since childhood, so perhaps they also attended the wedding.

Apart from the large Scots community, there were also many Irish settlers in the area (McSwan & Switzer, March 2006, p. 33) who may well have been related to the bride. No doubt, there were many other family and friends from both sides of the marriage who lived in the Maclean district. Hopefully, Catherine and Thomas made the journey to attend Malcolm's wedding. They could have travelled by coach, from Glen Innes down to Grafton, then travelled north by steamer along the Clarence River to family at Woodford Island and Lawrence, and then on to Maclean for the wedding. As well as celebrating Malcolm and Isabella's marriage, it would have been a good opportunity to catch up with their family and friends.

A descent into darkness

Tragically, just a couple of years later, Catherine's brother, Angus McKinnon, died of self-inflicted gunshot wounds. His death was three years after the coach accident that killed his wife, Anne. He was found dead on Anne's grave at the old cemetery in Port Macquarie. A gun and a forked stick were found beside his body. He had used the stick to pull the trigger of the gun ('Shocking Suicide at Port Macquarie' 2 August 1887, p.3). It can only be seen as an act of deep sadness and desperation on his part.

According to an article in *The Mercury* ('Shocking Suicide at Port Macquarie' 2 August 1887, p.3), Angus had been very despondent. Apparently, he had been working as a travelling salesman for a Sydney based Life Insurance Society. He was staying at the Star Hotel in Port Macquarie but he had been 'sick for several months' and was unable to pay the rent. *The Mercury* said he was a broken man with ongoing physical and mental disabilities after the accident which killed his wife.

As there were no relatives living in the Port Macquarie area, the Masonic Lodge, of which Angus was a member, made the arrangements for the funeral. They also organised the coffin and a wreath to be laid on top. A burial service was held at what was then the new cemetery in Port Macquarie, and a few friends and mourners attended the graveside. Angus's eldest son, Ewen McKinnon, who worked in a solicitor's office in Kempsey, arrived just as the grave was being closed ('Melancholy Fatality', 4 August 1887, p.2). A couple of months later, a railing was erected around the grave which was paid for by Angus's former students ('News of the World', 15 October 1887, p.3). It is unknown if Angus's grave had a monument with an inscription, but presumably his family was able to arrange for one to be installed at a later date.

A respectable burial was very important to those living in the NSW colony. It was a show of social status, but it also offered some protection to the corpse. A pauper's burial might include several bodies in one grave, which was known as the 'packing system'. Even though it was contrary to regulations, pauper's graves were sometimes very shallow. Shallow graves were easily uncovered by heavy rain or breached by a foot or a walking stick. Pauper's graves didn't have a monument to mark the identity of the deceased and as such they discouraged 'the veneration of the dead'. A pauper's grave was a burial which all respectable people and their families did their best to avoid (Murray, 2013).

By the time of Angus's suicide, it was no longer believed that suicide was a sin, a result of moral failing, or the work of the devil. Discussion of suicide had been removed from the domain of priests and theologians. The secular discipline of psychiatry was starting to emerge for the treatment of mental disturbances. During the nineteenth century people who attempted, or were successful at committing suicide, were generally believed to be unfortunate or weak and overwhelmed by the emotional strain of life (Taylor, 2022). In a large study undertaken by Dr Wynn Westcott, Deputy Coroner for Middlesex, in around 1885, misery, despair and remorse were found to be the main causes of suicide. Dr Westcott's study was reported by the *Glen Innes Examiner,* so the Ballard family would have been aware of its findings ('Some Facts About Suicide', 13 October 1885, p.5).

It was widely believed that suicide rates were rising in the western world, including Australia, in the later part of the nineteenth century. According to De Looper (2015) eight percent of male deaths in NSW between 1880 and 1884 were from suicide and 5.5 percent of female deaths. Dr Westcott (1885 cited in 'Some Facts About Suicide', 13 October 1885, p.5) attempts to explain the gender differences in suicide rates. This difference was apparent in his study, and across a number of other European studies. He posits that,

> the struggle for existence falls at the present time, and always has fallen, chiefly to
> the men of a State. The female mind is more capable, too, of accommodating itself
> to change of circumstances, and it is more marked by powers of self-sacrifice than
> the male intellect.

According to Dr Westcott's research, suicide was highest among widowed men without children, and lowest among married men in general. Married women on the other hand, were a third more likely to suicide than widowed women. Marriage appears to have offered men considerable protection from the risk of taking their own life, but not so for women. However, despite their 'powers' of self-sacrifice' and accommodation, Dr Westcott may have underestimated how much of the load in 'the struggle for existence' women carried in a marriage.

In the eighteenth century, those who attempted suicide forfeited their property rights and their right to a Christian burial. However, there was little interest in punishing these 'unfortunate people' in the nineteenth century, and the idea of temporary insanity was often used to evade criminal responsibility. People who attempted or succeeded in committing suicide generally no longer lost their property, or their right to be buried in the Christian section of the cemetery, although the legislation which enabled these punishments was not removed in NSW until 1862 (Jowett, Carpenter & Tait, 2018).

Angus was fifty-seven at the time of his death. He was described in his obituary as a 'cultured, genial and generous hearted gentleman' who was 'highly respected by all who knew him' ('The Late Mr McKinnon', 30 July 1887, p.2). Those who were acquainted with him clearly held him in high regard. The tragic death of his wife and his own ongoing problems were too much for Angus to bear. He never recovered and his life descended into darkness.

Births, weddings and deaths are all important life events which mark the passing of time and generational change. As we have seen previously, family ties were very important to Catherine and her kin. For families, such as the Ballard's living in rural NSW in the nineteenth century, family visits offered a chance to get together with those they loved and to share the highs and lows of life.

Due to the time and the distance involved, Catherine wasn't able to attend Angus's funeral. She wouldn't even have heard about his passing until after he was buried. Her brother's suicide, although illegal at the time, would not have resulted in any punishment for his family. His suicide would have brought incredible sadness and distress to all who knew him but perhaps most significantly to his ten surviving children and his extended family, including Catherine. After Angus's death, only one of Catherine's siblings remained alive: her younger sister Margaret. Catherine's family of origin had shrunk to just two.

Because of the geographic size of the colony, people often had to travel long distances to attend events and to visit family, making these occasions even more significant. The arrival of the train line to Glen Innes, which will be discussed in the next chapter, linked Glen Innes to Sydney and other locations in the colony. The train made long distance travel faster and more comfortable, and it opened up new opportunities for the people of the district.

Chapter 11
A Place of 'Civilised' Society

Cheap, reliable transport - a Union Church - a new school room - increasing civic responsibility - the temperance movement - a downturn in the economy

The new steam service

In 1884, the railway line came to Glen Innes. It was a pivotal moment for the district. The Glen Innes station was an extension of the Great Northern Rail Line from Newcastle, which previously only went as far as Armidale. In order to build the railway line, the Government purchased land from private citizens who owned property along the route. However, First Nations people who were the traditional owners of the land were not compensated for the use of their land.

The steam service meant that the Ballards, and other farmers in the area, could transport their produce such as potatoes, wheat, corn and oats to Sydney and other regional markets. They could also purchase goods from Sydney and have them sent back to Glen Innes on the train. Furthermore, the rail journey was a faster, safer and more comfortable way to travel than by stage coach. It meant that they themselves could travel south, and their family members who lived in the south could catch the train north to Glen Innes to visit them at Red Range. The railway also brought an influx of people to the area which opened up new business opportunities. The steam service inevitably had a big impact on the town of Glen Innes and the surrounding district, including Red Range.

There was a grand opening of the 'new steam service' on 19 August 1884, amid great fanfare. The opening was a big event not to be missed (see Figure 22). It may well have been attended by members of the Ballard family. According to an eye witness account ('Opening of the Great Northern

Railway', 21 August 1884, p.4) a large, confused and chaotic crowd gathered at the new Glen Innes station to see the acting Minister of Works, the honourable George R Dibbs, declare the line open to the public. This was followed by a procession consisting of a four-horse bus carrying various dignitaries, marching troopers, the town band, buggies and townspeople which headed through town to the Tattersalls Hotel. The Minister and the Mayor then ascended the balcony at the hotel and gave a toast followed by speeches to the crowd below. After the day's proceedings were finished, a celebratory ball was held in the large engine shed.

Figure 22. Opening of the Great Northern Railway to Glen Innes, 1884 (*Illustrated Sydney News NSW: (1881-1894)*, 23 September 1884, p.16, https://trove.nla.gov.au/newspaper/page/5787274).

Initially, Glen Innes was the terminus of the line and there was much discussion and division as to where the line should go from there. Businessmen, miners and farmers alike were keen to see the railway extend to the northern regions of the NSW colony to provide cheap, reliable transport. The towns that were bypassed by the steam services often lost their populations and their businesses to those with a station. Therefore, there was intense lobbying on behalf of towns to have the train reach them and to include a station stop (Lamb, 2015).

The Minister assured the crowd at the Glen Innes opening that the line would eventually extend further - which it did. The line reached north to Tenterfield in 1886. Then, in 1888, the line was opened to the border with Queensland, at Wallangarra, where it met the narrower gauge Queensland line. However, many people in the north of the colony were in favour of an extension of the Great Northern Rail Line from the New England tablelands down to the coast, in part because it would deal 'a blow to the centralising force of Sydney' (Lamb, 2015, p.27). The link would have facilitated the exchange of goods and produce between the coast and the inland such as sugar and wheat, essentially bypassing Sydney.

The idea was controversial. A rail line between the northern tablelands and the coast involved high construction costs as the line needed tunnels and bridges to cross the steep terrain. Also, there was intense rivalry between towns wanting to be the connection point. In 1884, after many surveys and deputations, it was decided to spend £2 million on the line from Glen Innes to Grafton. A loan bill passed the lower house of the NSW parliament, but it was deferred by the upper house ('The Government Railway Proposals', 28 October 1884).

The line between the New England Tablelands and the coast never eventuated. The financial crisis of the late 1880s and 1890s started putting fiscal pressure on the government. At the same time, the campaign in favour of the line terminating at Grafton became splintered as other towns such as Ballina, Byron Bay and Tweed Heads began to agitate to be the town at the coastal terminus. Despite this, the arrival of the railway line cemented the success of the township of Glen Innes and the surrounding area, in the nineteenth century.

According to Lamb (2015, p.24), the train line was 'a popular symbol of progress' across the NSW colony but it was also a 'prime target for criticism'. In summary, Lamb (2015, p.24) suggests that the railway was 'the offspring of human hopes and rivalries, a potentially disturbing agent of social change' as well as 'an economic institution with important social and political ramifications.'

A Union Church

The train line brought progress and new opportunities for the Ballard family. But as their lives became more established at Red Range, a church was needed so that they had a place where they could worship. Catherine and Thomas remained devout Christians and practicing Presbyterians. Their religion was very important to them. As there wasn't a church at Red Range when they first arrived, services were often held at the Ballard home. On Sundays, the Presbyterian Minister would preach at St Andrews in Glen Innes, and then come out to the Ballard home at Red Range to conduct an afternoon service at 3.30pm ('Local and Other Notes', 4 December 1883, p.2).

In outlying communities like Red Range, where there wasn't a resident Minister, parishioners would often have to wait until the Minister was available to officiate at events, such as weddings, deaths and baptisms. In the absence of a Minister, these events would take place with family and friends in people's homes or outside on their farms. The details would usually be entered into the family bible. Later, when the Minister arrived, there might be a number of weddings, baptisms or deaths to officiate on the same visit ('Land of the Beardies', 2016-2021).

These arrangements were all well and good in the early days of arriving at Red Range, but a church was needed if they were to consider themselves a 'civilised' Christian community. Therefore, in April 1886, Thomas Ballard, as the Secretary of the Union Church at Red Range, posted an advertisement in the *Glen Innes Examiner and General Advertiser* ('To Builders', 6 April 1886, p.2). He was seeking tenders to build the first Union Church at Red Range to serve the Presbyterian, Anglican and Wesleyan Methodist congregations.

The notice read:

> TENDERS are invited for the erection of a weatherboard Church, 3Oft. x 11ft.,
> at Red Range. For plan and specification apply to T. L. Ballard, Red Range, or at
> the Manse, Glen Innes. Tenders received up to April 12.

> T. L. Ballard

> Secretary Red Range Union Church.

The church was erected and had opened its doors by the following year ('Local & General News', 9 August 1887, p.2). Apparently, the new church contained 'some beautifully crafted cedar pews' which were made by Mr Walmsley, who was a local resident of Red Range at the time ('Red Range, NSW', n.d.).

It was not unusual in the colony in the nineteenth century, for communities without a church to join together to form a trust to build a Union Church. Once the Union Church was built, it was operated by the trust and available to parishioners from different denominations ('Union Church', 2022). The number of churches in NSW doubled between 1870 and 1890. At this time, the Sunday School movement also 'entered its golden age' with most children regularly attending (Lake, 2020, p.134).

Lake (2020, p.134) argues that church attendance was a form of socialisation whereby a particular view of the world, and how to live in it, was acquired. Attending church on the Sabbath was also a disciplinary process. The ritual instilled a sense of order and control in the lives of individuals, families and communities. Churches were seen as a symbol of a 'civilised society' in colonial NSW (Karskens, 2020, p.456). The addition of the church to the town at Red Range would have been a valuable community asset and was most probably a source of pride for the Christian families who lived in the area, such as the Ballard family.

A new school room

As was mentioned earlier, the school had opened in Red Range in 1880, but there was already a need for a new classroom and a teacher's residence. As a result, tenders were called for in 1882. However, no one applied. It was then determined the following year by the Minister of Public Instruction that only a teacher's residence be erected at the school. The intention of the Minister was to erect a new school building in the not-too-distant future ('No Title', 29 September 1885, p.2).

In the first quarter of 1885, there were forty-nine students enrolled at the Red Range school. However, the average daily attendance was rather poor with only twenty-two students attending on a regular basis ('No Title', 29 September 1885, p.2). There were fines for those who did not comply but, in reality, the obligation was poorly enforced particularly in regard to children who were never enrolled. Many children throughout the colony continued to miss school with some families dependent on their children working on farms or in factories just to survive ('Bathurst Free Press- *Magna est veritas et prvalebt*', 20 February 1891, p.2).

In early 1886, advertisements were placed in the newspaper again looking for tenders to build a new weatherboard classroom at the Red Range School ('Red Range Public School', 9 February 1886, p.2). This time the tender was successful, and the classroom was built. The annual school picnic, which was attended by over 300 people, was held at the school in September that year, with a fund-raising concert in the evening in the new class room. The amateur talent entertaining the attendees at the concert again included David and Allan Ballard ('Local and General News', 21 September 1886, p.2).

After the concert, the Red Range teacher, Mr W D Bourke, thanked the community for the success of the concert and said that the £13 which was raised (quite a sum), would be used to procure prizes for the students at the school ('Advertising', 12 October 1886, p.6). By 1887, according to the *Examiner*, there was a good turn around in attendance, with the average daily attendance being over fifty students ('Local and General News', 10 May 1887, p.2). The success of the school, like the church, must have brought a sense of pride to the community. Red Range was no longer an 'untamed, primitive wilderness'. It was now a place of 'civilised' society.

Politics on the Range

The NSW colonial elections were held in early 1887. All of the now 124 seats in the NSW Legislative Assembly were being contested on a 'first past the post' basis. This was the first time that candidates stood as members of official political parties. As mentioned earlier, white men over twenty-one who were British subjects had full suffrage; but women were still away off achieving this right and for First Nations people the right to vote was even further away.

The Free Trade Party won the election, and their candidate, George MacLeod Matheson, was elected in Glen Innes 603 votes to 567 ('The General Election 1887-Results of the Polling', 28 February 1887, p.12). The newly formed Free Trade Party was against protective tariffs and quotas, and - indeed any restrictions on trade. They argued that this would create more prosperity in the colony (Simms, 2001). At the time of the election, Thomas was in favour of free trade but, as we will see, he most likely changed his mind as times became harder for farmers to make a living.

The opposition party in the 1887 NSW colonial election was known as the 'Protectionist Party'. The Protectionist Party was also formed in 1887, just before the election. It was a political party created around the idea of advocating for protectionist tariffs and quotas against cheap foreign imports and, therefore, protecting local farmers at a time of increasing hardship in the NSW colony (Simms, 2001).

Several months after the election in May of 1887, a meeting was held at the Ballard home at Red Range to discuss the Northern Separation League. With the increasing degree of 'civilisation' at Red Range also came a sense of civic responsibility and a number of political meetings were held at the

Ballard home. The meetings, which were attended by local men, enabled them to discuss some of the current issues which they were facing. This particular meeting at the Ballard's was attended by thirty local men including Thomas, his four sons and his son-in-law. The men at the meeting decided that 'separation (from NSW) was the proper remedy for the grievances under which the district labors *[sic]*'. A unanimous resolution was passed stating that a branch of the Northern Separation League be formed at Red Range, and a 'strong committee was elected' ('Separation Meetings, Red Range', 10 May 1887, p.4).

The Northern Separation League was active in many rural areas in the north of the NSW colony at the time. Its aim was to separate from NSW and form an independent colony with its own representative government. It was a movement which asserted that 'the system of centralisation which concentrates so large an expenditure on works in and around Sydney deprives them of many legitimate advantages, and that those are of no benefit to the country districts' ('Separation', 23 August 1887, p. 2). In essence, it was thought that 'a fair return was not given for the revenue yielded' by communities in the north of the state such as Glen Innes, Red Range, Grafton, Inverell, Tenterfield and Lismore ('Separation', 23 August 1887, p.2). Separation from NSW would mean the revenue raised in the north of the colony would be spent improving the lives of local communities, rather than the lives of those in Sydney. However, the separation of the north from the south of NSW never came to fruition.

The temperance movement

Red Range was becoming a thriving village with a church, a school and a growing community. As a result, Henry Stephen opened a general store in in late 1887 at 'The Green House', which was located at Perrys Swamp in Red Range. He advertised in the *Examiner* that he 'intended to sell at Glen Innes prices.' He also stated in the advertisement that the general store would include a circulating library and, significantly, that it would be a wine depot ('Advertising', 6 September 1887, p.1).

The Licensing Court had granted Henry Stephen a 'colonial wine license' so that he could sell wine from his store at Red Range ('Local and Numeral News', 12 July 1887, p.2). Under the *Licensing Act of 1882,* the Court could grant a license to a storekeeper to sell wine or cider as long as the alcohol was sold in quantities of at least two gallons, none of the alcohol was consumed on the premises, and the wine was produced locally (*Licensing Act of 1882* No 26a, 2023). The Sunday observance law meant that no alcohol was be sold in the colony on Sundays. However, this law was not strictly adhered to and some outlets sold alcohol to patrons illegally, behind closed doors, or from under the counter (Doyle, 2006).

The temperance movement in NSW was growing. Alcohol was seen as a problem by many in the colony who believed that its consumption needed to be constrained. Between 1825 and 1883 there were no less than twenty-seven liquor Acts passed in the NSW parliament (Doyle, 2006). Then, in 1887, an alliance was formed by various groups which was called the NSW Temperance Alliance. It was a collection of independent organisations who had been advocating temperance and trying to win over individual drinkers to the cause. The alliance included the Women's Christian Temperance Union (WCTU), which will be discussed in more detail later. Also, the Band of Hope, the Rechabites, The Blue Ribbon Army, the Good Templars and the Sons of Temperance joined the alliance. Most of the advocates of the Temperance Alliance were in favour of the full prohibition of alcohol. However, they realised that this was unlikely to be achieved in Australia, and so temperance in the form of moderation or restraint was sought by the movement through government legislation (Doyle, 2006).

Historically in the NSW colony, wine, beer and stout were seen as dietary supplements. Wine had also been imbibed as a sacrament and was used as a toast by the upper - and supposedly more sophisticated - class of colonial society. Therefore, wine, beer and stout were not considered by many people to be as problematic as hard liquor such as rum and gin. There were also large brewing and distilling interests in the colony which exerted pressure on the government of the day. Moreover, wines and spirits produced in Australia were winning awards and being exported to Great Britain and Europe, which provided a good economic argument against their prohibition (Noyce, 2021).

I can only assume that Catherine and Thomas were themselves teetotallers, who supported the temperance movement, as they held a strong observance of Presbyterianism. According to Doyle (2006, p.36) 'the philosophical base of temperance was in Protestant moralism which saw drunkenness as a manifestation of moral turpitude and the drinker as a miscreant'.

Interestingly, Doyle suggests that the Catholic Church took a more lenient stance on the consumption of alcohol, perhaps because wine was used in the sacrament, but also due to the large working class, Irish Catholic population who liked to drink. Presumably, the Red Range general store, by just selling wine, avoided the direct wrath of those in the temperance movement.

A Protection Union meeting

In 1888, the year after the NSW election, Thomas held another meeting at their home. This time it was a Protection Union meeting. There was an economic downturn in the NSW colony around this time. A series of economic crashes and then a severe drought hit farmers particularly hard ('Local and General News', 11 December 1888, p.2), and the downturn made it difficult for farmers to compete against foreign imports. The *Glen Innes Examiner* ('Glen Innes Protection Union', 28 August 1888, p.2) suggests the meeting was held so that the local men could meet the Union delegates Messrs Grover, Legh, and Flanders. In attendance at the meeting were Thomas and Catherine's sons, Allan and Cyrus Ballard, their son-in-law James Cornish, J Ryall, B Goodwin, J Walmsley, R Cheney, R Ruming, J Larkins, J P Bourke, J Taylor, J Marshall, and WA Potter and J Potter. The chair was occupied by Mr Ryall, and James Cornish was appointed as the secretary.

The meeting was well attended. However, the *Examiner* ('Glen Innes Protection Union', 28 August 1888, p.2) explained that not everyone in the community who was interested could attend, as there was a bushfire on the

'Range'. Some people were worried that their fences, buildings and livestock were in danger of being burned in the fire, so they had to stay home to protect their properties and their livelihoods. For those men who made it to the meeting, the visiting delegates explained the issues. Then Thomas, as a free-trader, apparently put some 'searching questions to the delegates' which were 'satisfactorily replied to'. After some discussion among the group, a motion was carried to establish a branch of the Protection Union at Red Range.

Clearly, this was an issue of particular concern to the Ballard family. Thomas must have been convinced of the need for tariffs to protect Australian farmers from cheap foreign imports. A couple of months later, Mr Ryall reported they had fifteen paid-up members on the roll, and he said that they were expecting to soon have thirty to forty members from Red Range alone ('Glen Innes Protection Union', 2 October 1888, p.2).

Catherine and her family were prominent members of Red Range and they were actively working to develop a strong community. The addition of a church, and the extension of the school, were integral to establishing a community on the Range, encouraging both Christian and family values.

The Ballard men and their son-in-law, were also passionately involved in politics. They had a keen interest in the issues that affected them, and they kept up to date with the current news and developments, both locally and nationally. It appears that lively debate was encouraged within the Ballard family, and this is reflected in the meetings which were held in their home.

Interestingly, years later, one observer commented that Catherine's daughter, Maria Cornish, also read widely 'with taste and discrimination and her opinion on almost any question of the day was worth hearing' ('The Late Mrs M. C. Cornish', 4 May 1935, p.2). This is a noteworthy reflection. Despite the fact that an interest in current affairs was clearly not limited to the men in the family, the women were not recorded as attending any of the meetings or committees in the community. Women still had not attained suffrage and their absence from public political and social discourse is significant.

Chapter 12
The Emerging Stereotype of the 'Typical Australian'

David and Kitty Ballard - currency lads and lasses - the need for a National Government - The Bulletin magazine - the notion of a 'national identity' - the exclusion of women - Chinese workers - Kwong Sing War store - First Nations people

Native born

At the age of twenty-six Catherine's son, David Ballard, had started teaching primary school at Paradise Creek Public School just south of the Inverell-Glen Innes Road (David Ballard, 1886, p.624). Presumably, this is where David met his soon to be wife, Catherine (Kitty) Munro. Paradise Creek was not far from where she lived with her mother. At the beginning of 1888, David moved to Clearbank Public School at Matheson on the Inverell-Glen Innes Road (David Ballard, 1886, p.624). Teaching, like the Christian Ministry, was a respectable occupation but it was not well paid. In 1888, his yearly salary was just £96 (David Ballard, 1886, p.624).

Also in 1888, David Ballard married Kitty in Inverell (David Ballard, 1888) (see Figure 23). David was twenty-eight and Kitty was twenty-seven. Kitty's parents, Donald Munro and Catherine Ann McGillivray, had also been crofters on land owned by Lord MacDonald at Lower Breakish in the Parish of Strath, on the Isle of Skye (Munro, Donald, 1853). Kitty's paternal grandparents were Margaret MacInnes from Leitir Fura, in the parish of Sleat, and Donald Munro from Lower Breakish (Donald Munro, 1865). Her maternal grandparents were Mary McKinnon from Heaste and Donald McGillivray also from Breakish (Catherine Munro, 27 August 1917). Heaste and Breakish are both in the parish of Strath, which was McKinon clan land before it was lost following the Jacobite uprising of 1745.

Figure 23. David Ballard and Catherine (Kitty) Ballard, c1895 (AB Butler Photographer, Tenterfield, NSW, Australia, photo courtesy of John Gillies).

Kitty's parents, Catherine and Donald Munro, along with their first five children had immigrated to the colony of Victoria in Australia in 1853 on the *Hercules* (Munro, Donald, 1853). Kitty was born six years later in Mortlake, Victoria where her parents had bought a property. However, her father Donald Munro died of pneumonia in 1865 (Donald Munro, 1865), just before the birth of his twelfth child. It must have been a terrible shock for Kitty's mother, Catherine Munro.

Kitty's mother and her family continued to farm in Mortlake for a few years after Donald's death. Then they moved to Laen in the Wimmera before her mother, together with seven of her children including Kitty, moved to NSW (Sims, 2014). At the time of David and Kitty's wedding, Kitty's mother Catherine was a widow living near Inverell.

In 1889, the year after he was married, David was promoted to teaching class 3B ('Appointments and Employment', 12 March 1889, p.1923). Then in September 1889, he was appointed as a teacher at Fernhill Public School near Inverell (David Ballard, 1886, p.624). David and Kitty also had their first child in 1889. She was a daughter and they named her Flora Ballard.

The following year, in 1890, their second daughter Catherine Mary Ballard (Catherine (Mary) Ballard, 1890) was born. Both of the baby's grandmothers were also called Catherine, as was her mother Kitty, so it is difficult to say exactly who she was named after. However, the child was known within the family as 'Myee' (Mr & Mrs Ballard, 1921). She later baptised her own daughter, Myee Catherine. The name Myee has since been passed on to her grand-daughter and two of her great grand-daughters.

The year before David Ballard's second daughter was born Lord Carrington, the Governor of the NSW colony at the time, and his wife Lady Carrington, also had a daughter. She was the Carrington's fourth daughter. She was born in Sydney in 1889 and she was baptised with the name Judith Sydney Myee Carrington. According to a newspaper report ('Gossip', 23 November 1889, p.42), her first name Judith was after Lady Carrington's sister. Her second name, Sydney, was after the place she was born; and her third name, Myee was an Aboriginal word meaning 'native born' or born of this country. Presumably, the name Myee was in the language of one of the local Aboriginal nations from the Sydney region.

Judith Sydney Myee Carrington was described in the newspaper as a 'fine specimen of an Australian baby'. Another 'Lady Correspondent' suggested that the name Myee would before long 'find its way into the "buzzom" [sic] of society' ('From a Lady Correspondent in Sydney', 7 December 1889, p.3). Well, it appears that the name Myee, found its way into the "buzzom" of the Ballard family.

There is a noteworthy history in relation to the distinction between those British people who were born in the colony (so-called native-born), and those who immigrated from Britain. Peter Cunningham (1827, p.53), writing in 1827, suggested that the British-born colonists at that time were widely referred to as 'sterling'. This was in reference to the English currency from Britain - 'the mother-land' - where they were born. He suggested those British people who were born in the early years of the colony, were known as 'currency lads and lasses.' This reference was mostly in relation to those people whose parents had been convicts. However, the children of free settlers were generally tarnished with the same brush. This may well have been the case with Catherine's first four sons, Angus, Ewen, Malcolm and John. They may have been referred to by others as 'currency lads.'

According to Cunningham (1827, p.53), the term was first used to describe a person by 'a facetious paymaster of the 73rd Regiment quartered here, – the pound currency being at that time *inferior* to the pound sterling'. The *Currency Act* was passed by the governing Council on the 28 September 1824, which made British sterling the only legal tender in the colony. This was despite the fact that shortages of sterling persisted in the colony throughout the nineteenth century. National banknotes were not issued in Australia until Federation in 1901 ('Currency Crises', 2023).

Due to a shortage of sterling, various different 'currencies' circulated in the colony including Dutch guilders, ducats, rupees and the Spanish dollar. Promissory notes - or IOUs, as they are commonly known - were also frequently exchanged, although they were not always accepted as they were easy to forge and had no legal backing. These various alternatives were generally referred to as 'currency' and were never on par with the value of sterling (Moloney, 2000, p.25).

The term 'currency' was originally a derogatory label. So, there was an inference of illegality and inferiority attached to the term when it was applied to white colonists who were born in NSW. As a result of this perceived inferiority, the so-called currency lads and lasses were often treated as second class citizens by those born in Britain. However, after the currency lads beat the English born players in a cricket match in Sydney in 1832, Horatio Wills, who owned a newspaper which he called the *Currency Lad* (12 January 1833 cited in Molony 2000, p.131), declared in his paper that the name 'currency' was now a source of pride among the colony.

It took some time, but eventually the name was reclaimed by the native-born colonists as a positive reference. As well as the *Currency Lad* newspaper, there were plays and songs (Molony, 2020), boats and even hotels, which were named after the currency lads and lasses (Morris, 1898). The name was mostly used between the 1820s up until the beginning of the gold rush in the 1850s. Then, the term gradually fell out of use. By 1898 it was obsolete (Morris, 1898).

As early as 1830, one observer (cited in Molony, 2000, p.23) had argued that 'As there are now so many white natives in Australia, the term *native* as applied to the aborigines should be discontinued'. It became generally understood, in the colony at least (for it did create confusion back in Britain) that Aboriginal people were 'the blacks', and references to the 'natives' were meaning the white people who were born in the colony. Jones (1 March 2017) argues that this early embodiment of Australian nationalism is important, because 'it reveals how quickly indigenous roots were claimed at the expense of Aboriginal Australians'.

By 1881, at least ninety percent of people aged under twenty-four who were living in Australia were born in Australia. This was the first large-scale generation of 'native born' Australians (McDonald & Moyle, 2018). In 1883, Richard Twopenny (cited in Molony, 2000, p.23) in his book *Town Life in Australia,* felt he needed to explain to the reader that 'An aboriginal is always a "black fellow". A 'native of Australia', would mean a white man born in the colony'.

By the late nineteenth century, even though the term 'currency lads and lasses', had lost favour, the idea of being a 'native-born' Australian had taken hold. Over the second half of the nineteenth century, as the number of British people living in the colony who were born in NSW increased, more and more people were identifying themselves as 'native-born'. Many of the NSW colonists, like Catherine's children and her grandchildren, saw themselves as 'Australian'. According to Clark (2022, p.87), for most people this national identification did not diminish their sense of 'Britishness' or their loyalty to the mother country and the British Empire. The co-existence of these two allegiances was not seen as contradictory.

The push towards nationhood

Growing out of this increasing sense of Australianness, was a push towards nationhood. The Premier of the NSW colony, Henry Parkes, had given an iconic speech at a banquet which was held in his honour at the Tenterfield School of Arts on the 24th of October 1889. In his speech, he said that Australia now had a population of three and a half million people and had two thousand miles of railway. He argued that in order to preserve 'the security and the integrity' of the country, a federal army was needed and the only way to do this was by federating the colonies. The time had come for the Australian colonies to federate under one national government. He suggested that a delegation of 'leading men' from each colony should meet to decide on the constitution which was necessary to facilitate a Federal Government with a Federal Parliament ('Sir Henry Parkes at Tenterfield', 25 Oct 1889, p.8).

It wasn't the first mention of Federation, but it was the most compelling appeal to be made by a politician to the public to date. It set the process of Federation into action (Fletcher, 25 May 2001). Parkes died in 1896, before he could witness the fulfilment of his ambition. Nevertheless, he became known as 'the Father of Federation' (Fletcher, 25 May 2001). Parkes's speech at Tenterfield was discussed in all of the newspapers. By this time, there were about 600 newspaper titles being disseminated regularly to readers across the country (Lake, 2020, p.210). The Ballard family would have read about Parkes speech, including his convincing arguments about the need for a unified Australia.

In 1891, in order to learn as much as they could about the implications of the pressing issues of the day, another community meeting was held at the Ballard home at Red Range. This time it was to hear a lecture on 'The Labor Question, the Fiscal Question, and Federation' which was delivered by Mr C Legh ('Local and General Items', 26 May 1891, p.2). Public lectures were an increasingly popular mode of social interaction in the NSW colony at the time. They were particularly useful for garnishing support for political reform movements and as a way of spreading new knowledge or information across the local community (Freyne, 2010).

It appears Mr Legh was quite passionate on the subjects and his lecture made for a rather long evening. A report in the *Examiner* ('Local and General Items', 26 May 1891, p.2) suggests that Mr Legh 'proceeded to dwell at great length' on the topics 'explaining in a concise and lucid style his views on the cause and remedy of the Labor and Fiscal questions, and also the advantages to be derived from, and the evils to be averted, in the adoption of the proposed Federation scheme'. According to the report, no one had any questions at the end of the lecture as it seemed every possible angle had been covered by Mr Legh.

It is not surprising that the Ballard family were keen to understand as much as they could about these topics. The 1890s saw a worldwide recession with a downturn in the economy, the consequences of which were felt by everyone. It was a time of union led strikes by workers. The employers of labour were pitted against the workers, who were seeking better pay and conditions. The strikes were impacting both the workers and commerce across the colony ('The Finish of the Great Strike', 16 September 1890, p.2). Also, the prospect of the Federation of the states into the Commonwealth of Australia was a huge issue with broad reaching implications. Despite the lecture being rather long, the ideas which were discussed were clearly of concern in the Ballard household and were hot topics across the colony.

Many people in the colonies believed that a national government was needed to deal with issues that crossed colonial borders such as trade, defence and immigration. In 1891 the first National Australasian Convention was held in Sydney to discuss and write a draft constitution. When the constitution was finalised, the six colonies would unite as states under a national government. Power would be shared between the State and Federal governments, forming the Commonwealth of Australia ('About Parliament', 2022).

Many in the NSW colony were looking to the future to fulfil ideals of progress, development and the exploitation of resources. In a speech to the Royal Colonial Institute in 1894, the English journalist Flora Shaw (cited in Clark, 2022, p.270) wrote 'It has been suggested that Australia is uninteresting because she has no past; but the interest of Australia lies forward, not behind'. Unsurprisingly at this point in time, still no consideration was given to the rich history of the First Australians.

The Bulletin magazine

The Bulletin was a very popular illustrated, weekly publication which was established in 1880. Its content included political commentary, cartoons, sensationalised news stories, poetry and stories. However, the magazines content was openly racist and sexist. In 1886 the magazine's banner was 'Australia for the White Man'. This remained *The Bulletin's* banner for nearly sixty years ('The Bulletin', 2017).

The Bulletin was very influential in propagating the notion of a national Australian identity which was based on the exclusion of certain people. According to Jacob Hirsch (2019, p.8), the typical Australian portrayed in *The Bulletin* was a white (British), rugged, male, bushman who was anti-authoritarian, liked to drink alcohol and valued mateship above all else. He argues that *The Bulletin* advocated 'Australia for Australians'. Its nationalistic ethos endorsed national pride, the values of rural life, humour in the face of adversity and support for the struggling farmer.

Popular Australian writers and poets such as Andrew Barton (Banjo) Paterson and Henry Lawson, both of whom published in *The Bulletin*, helped to cultivate this so-called 'national identity' by romanticising tales of roguish bushmen ('Australian Literature', n.d.). Banjo Paterson also wrote the popular Australian song *Waltzing Matilda* in 1895 which exemplified the image of the 'typical Australian'. The song glorifies a lone bushman 'waltzing' (walking) through the countryside, carrying all of his possessions rolled up in a 'matilda' (a swag). The swagman steals a 'jumbuck' (a sheep) from a 'squatter' (a large pastoralist) and then escapes three 'troopers' (police) by jumping in to a 'billabong' (a small lagoon).

This construction of the quintessential Australian bushman was made despite the fact, that by now, most of the population lived in urban settings. As the rural landscape became more populated and therefore tamed, the archetype of the Australian bushman became a myth of times past. Yet at a time when federalisation was on the horizon, this myth offered a national identity for both those living in the bush and urban dwellers looking to romanticise the past (Hirsch, 2019, p.8).

The Ballard's, like most Australians at the time, were most likely in favour of Federation and a unified Australia. The Ballard family, as we have seen, were all well-read, apart from Catherine. No doubt they would have read stories and poetry, perhaps even in *The Bulletin*, about living in the Australian bush which struck a familiar chord with them. As skilled horsemen, capable bushmen and early pioneers, the males in the family more than likely identified with some aspects of the image being portrayed by Paterson and Lawson.

Even so, as firm law-abiding Presbyterians, they were undoubtedly teetotallers and would not have subscribed to all of the ideals of Australian manhood being promoted at the time, such as the consumption of alcohol. According to Lake (2020, p.229), the terms 'wowser' and Bible-basher' were coined at this time in Australia. Terms like these were used to disparage the 'straight-laced Protestant types' who disagreed with Henry Lawson's ideal of the hard drinking, anti-authoritarian Australian male. Lake (2020, p.229) argues that the invention of these disparaging terms in the Australian vernacular at the time 'points to an intense contest over the nature and future of Australian society'. The notion of a national identity being promoted in *The Bulletin* was a contested space and in no way represented all Australians.

Bushman masculinity and the exclusion of women

The 'typical' Australian being portrayed in *The Bulletin* was unashamedly male. The hyper-masculine bushman was also portrayed as heterosexual. Yet, as the sociologist Robert Bell (1973, p.3) suggests, 'the adversity of the landscape, the homosocial nature of early colonial society, along with an increasing scepticism of the puritanical doctrines of Christianity combined to create an environment where mateship and the associated sense of loyalty and brotherhood emerged as the basis for a new morality'. 'Mateship' was privileged between certain white men and for those men it afforded a basis for putting 'mates' above all others.

Catherine, her daughters and grand-daughters, like most of the women in the NSW colony, would not have seen their own experience reflected in *The Bulletin's* portrayal of the typical Australian. However, their experiences as early settler women in the colony were clearly a valid expression of a national identity. They were hard working, early pioneers. They birthed and raised children who would become the future generation of Australians. They endured hardships, losses, as well as good fortune, in their lives. Yet their lives were mostly invisible in the public arena. Kingston (1994, p.84) argues that women had mostly been written out of Australian history, the emphasis being almost solely on the male experience.

This powerful, masculine image appeared at a time when many women in the NSW colony were seeking a change to the deeply entrenched inequality that they faced both in their private lives and in society at large. Some commentators such as history professor Marilyn Lake (cited in Murrie, 1998), have suggested that the construction of the hegemonic Australian male was, in part, in opposition to the rise of the first wave of feminism happening at the time. Murrie (1998, p.70) also argues that,

> in the defence of men's interests the bushman masculinity was a powerful image. A man existing among men and without broader social ties, the bushman's freedom – his drinking, his gambling, his 'independence', and his sexual indulgence – could be celebrated in the spirit of nationalism as an 'Australian' freedom, thereby legitimising men's social practices, and masking the gender politics of the conflict.

Chinese workers were excluded

The stereotypical Australian bushman was also constructed in sharp contrast to people from cultures of non-Anglo backgrounds, such as people of Chinese heritage and First Nations people. According to Hansen (10 May 2019), *The Bulletin* was particularly anti-Chinese in its rhetoric. It contained article after article lamenting Chinese immigration, saying that Chinese workers stifled the wages of Australian working men, and spread disease, gambling, corruption, opium and prostitution throughout the colony. As discussed earlier, the competition for opportunities during the gold rush had generated a lot of racial discrimination that was particularly directed at Chinese men.

Despite this rampant xenophobia that the mostly male Chinese immigrants had experienced, many of them stayed on in the NSW colony after the gold rush. Many Chinese men went to the Glen Innes area to work on the tin mines, such as the mines at Vegetable Creek (Emmaville) north of Glen Innes itself. At one stage, there were 1500 Chinese men on the field. The town of Vegetable Creek was named after the market gardens which were run by Chinese men to feed the mining settlement ('Land of the Beardies', 2016-2021).

Feng (2017) argues that contrary to the fear generated by those writing for *The Bulletin* – the assertion that Chinese men were stifling the wages of Australian men - the opposite was true. Countless Chinese immigrants started businesses and took jobs that European men were not interested in doing. Chinese men often worked in market gardens, restaurants, laundries and shops. Many of these Chinese men were very successful.

One man of Chinese heritage called Wong Chee opened a general store in Glen Innes in 1886. It was called the Kwong Sing War store. Wong Chee employed a number of Chinese workers, some of who went on to open their own businesses ('Family History', 2000-2012). The store still operates in Glen Innes today, as the Kwong Sing store, but it is no longer owned by the same family. No doubt Catherine and her family would have shopped at the Kwong Sing War store on trips to Glen Innes for supplies. The Kwong Sing

War store sold items such as men's flannelette shirts and lady's black hose (stockings). They may have even used some of Dr Brown's Bronchial Balsam which was advertised in the *Glen Innes Examiner* (see Figure 24).

Kwong Sing War.

— OF THE —

FAMOUS : CHEAP : STORE,

DO not find it necessary to hold periodical Clearing-out Sales, for the simple reason that their PRICES ARE SO LOW, and the QUALITY of THEIR GOODS so superior, that a discerning public know where to get full value for their money, and by their liberal purchases reduce the Stock as fast as it is replenished.

Kwong Sing War, however, have overpurchased in certain lines, and these must be quitted, even at a loss, to make room for direct shipments of merchandise, to arrive August 24.

Some Bargains We are Offering:

Flannelette at 2d per yard
Ladies' and Children's Ulsters, at half our usual price
Men's Flannelette Shirts at 9d each—splendid value
Ladies' Hose, fast black, from 4d; cashmere, from 9d pair.

KWONG SING WAR,
Chinese Storekeeper, Grey-st., Glen Innes.

ADVICE ! IF YOU ARE IN WANT OF A REMEDY FOR A COUGH TRY

DR. BROWN'S BRONCHIAL BALSAM.

This is a REMEDY that has been proved by thousands all over the World.

— IT CURES —

Coughs, Colds, Asthma, Bronchitis, and all Chest and Lung Complaints.

PRICE, 4s and 2s.

Prepared only by JAMES BROWN, F.R.C.S., Jackson Ville, U.S.A.
Agent for Australia—W. G. CAINS, Chemist, Sydney, and

SOLD BY KWONG SING WAR,
GENERAL STOREKEEPERS, GREY-ST., GLEN INNES

Figure 24. Kwong Sing War advertisements, 1895 ('Advertising', *Glen Innes Examiner and General Advertiser (NSW: 1874-1908)*, 2 August 1895, p.5, https://trove.nla.gov.au/newspaper/rendition/nla.news-article217811570).

The 1891 census for the district of Glen Innes (which later in 1904 became the electorate of Gough), recorded a total of 9,353 people living in the area. Of these, 638 people were of Chinese descent ('The Census', 28 April 1891, p.2). So, there was a sizeable population of mostly Chinese men, who had settled in the area. The total number of Chinese women in the NSW colony had risen from only twelve in 1871 (Bagnall, 9 August 2016), to 109 twenty years later, in 1891 (Bagnall, 2011). As a result of this, many Chinese men married, or co-habited, with women who were not of Chinese heritage, including Aboriginal women.

Unlike many other countries at the time such as the United States, there wasn't any legislation in Australia which banned inter-racial marriages (Bagnall, 2011). These inter-racial marriages, although not always accepted by everyone within the community, were legal. The children of these marriages were also considered legitimate. Despite the early discrimination they faced, many Chinese men and their families became valued members of the community.

First Nations people were also excluded

As the new nation was being forged, the image in *The Bulletin* of the typical Australian as the quintessential bushman also excluded First Nations people and those from the Pacific Islands and Africa. The Ballards, like the rest of the population, were subject to the ramifications which arose from this image. The legendary status of the quintessential bushman within the Australian consciousness led to demeaning stereotypes of people who did not fit the image of the roguish, white, male, bushman. These stereotypes included the use of 'blackface' to portray black people. Unfortunately, 'blackface' was a popular feature of theatrical performances during the nineteenth century. 'Blackface', is when a white entertainer paints their face black and they then perform racial caricatures of black culture in order to make the audience laugh. Performers in blackface would sing and dance and act like buffoons or naughty children. They were known as 'Minstrels' (Neklason, 2019).

Minstrels originated in the United States during the civil war and were also very popular in Britain and colonial NSW throughout the second half of the nineteenth century (Neklason, 2019). British and American troupes performed on extended tours around the colony and many colonists found their songs and jokes endlessly entertaining. One such troupe, which came to Glen Innes at the turn of the century and performed at the Town Hall were the 'McAdoo Georgia Minstrels and original Alabama Cake-walkers' ('Local Notes', 6 April 1900, p.2).

Minstrelsy was also the most common form of amateur stage show performed in the late nineteenth century. Local fundraisers, sports socials and church events often included a minstrel show (Waterhouse, 2008). On one occasion, a Grand Plantation Scene was performed by The Black Diamonds at McCormack's Music Hall, as a benefit for the Glen Innes Band. 'Tambo' was played by WC Hodd ('Grand Ethiopian Entertainment', 29

May 1888, p.4). On another occasion an amateur show took place in Glen Innes called 'A Night in Ebony' to raise money for the Jockey Club. This time, Mr JB Wisdom played 'Tambo' and, according to the *Examiner,* 'fairly convulsed the house with laughter by his inimitable rendering of "Duck foot Sue"' ('A Night in Ebony', 2 January 1893, p.2).

Figure 25. Fancy dress, Glen Innes, c1900. Four of the participants at this fancy dress event in Glen Innes are dressed in blackface (Photo courtesy of Glen Innes Historical Society Archives, NSW, Australia, No.3510, 18 August 2022).

As you can see in Figure 25, four of the costumes at this event in Glen Innes included people with their faces painted black. Two of the people in blackface are dressed as minstrels; the other two people in the back row, with their faces painted black, appear to be an Aboriginal tracker and his prisoner. Clearly, having a blackface was seen as funny. The people dressed in Blackface were most probably unaware at the time of the bigotry which was inherent in their costumes, as racism was embedded in colonial society from its very inception. Fancy dress was very popular both for 'Juvenile Balls' and adult 'Plain and Fancy-dress Balls', so no doubt some of the social events at Red Range would have also included people with their faces painted black.

Neklason (2019) argues that minstrel shows were not just harmless fun. They featured demeaning stereotypes of black people as 'dimwitted' and 'uncivilised'. These stereotypes were then used to justify prejudice and oppression. Some scholars, who have analysed minstrelsy, suggest it was a way in which the dominant white society could justify their dominance and reassure themselves that they would retain their social status (Neklason, 2019). This popular form of entertainment was actually reinforcing notions of white supremacy and black oppression in the minds of the audiences as they watched and laughed along at the idiocy of the 'blackfaced' performer.

Social Darwinism was often used to justify the policies and practices of colonisation, racism and inequality. It was expected by many people that First Nations people would soon die out, in what was seen as the inevitable extinction of Aboriginal people and their cultures. According to a paper by the colonial politician and publisher Mr Edward Greville, which was read at a meeting of the Royal Colonial Institute in Sydney, 'Contact with a superior race has been fatal and he (Aborigines) will soon become only a name'. The paper argues that despite attempts by legislation and charity 'there is no practical check to their rapid extinction' ('The Australian Aboriginal: His Origin and Future', 5 February 1891, p.4). The 1891 NSW census included the number of First Nations people who were in contact with the authorities. The figure suggests that the once numerous Aboriginal people living in the Glen Innes district were reduced down to only eighty-seven people ('The Census', 1891, p.2). However, First Nations people proved to be more resilient than the white colonists expected.

Race and gender divisions were deeply embedded in colonial society. The prevailing system of social stratification enabled the exclusion of women, non-white men and men who did not conform to the masculine trope of the Australian bushman. The so called 'typical Australian', which was promoted by the *Bulletin* and other media, was a divisive means of reinforcing existing power structures. The bushman trope promotes a 'typical Australian' who was, in fact, a rarity in the late nineteenth century. In reality, this 'typical Australian', with his roaming, drunken, thieving and uncouth manner, was not someone most people would have chosen to align themselves with had he not been romanticised in fiction by the likes of the *Bulletin*.

The Ballard men may have seen glimpses of themselves in the bushman trope, but they were Christian, family men with very different values. Catherine and the other women in the colony were largely invisible in the narrative of the 'typical Australian'. However, this mute invisibility, whether by chance or intent, came at a time when many women, particularly younger women, were looking for change. We will see in the coming chapters that as the new century appeared on the horizon, many European women in the NSW colony, and around the western world in general, wanted more choice in how they lived. As a result, women were starting to demand a voice in the social and political discourse which shaped their lives.

Chapter 13
Life was Fragile

Many young deaths - death from drowning - the loss of a beloved son - Typhoid - James Cornish - more loss - the Public Health Act 1896 - preventatives and abortion - a lighter side of Thomas Ballard

Death was ever-present

Death by accident, or from illness, was ever-present for families living in the nineteenth century in the NSW colony. However, that didn't make it any easier for those who lost people they loved and cared about. Sadly, on the 8th of June in 1884, Catherine's first grandchild Alfred MacDonald died (Alfred MacDonald, 1884). The cause of his death is unknown. He was just fifteen years old and living with his parents, Ewen and Emily McDonald at Skinners Creek in northern NSW (Herbert Ewen MacDonald, 1892). Alfred's death followed that of his younger brother David James McDonald, who was only eighteen months old when he died two years previously on the 11th of May 1882, in Dungog, before the family left for northern NSW (David James McDonald, 1882).

Then in 1892, just eight years after Alfred had died, tragedy struck again for his family when Ewen and Emily's son, Herbert Ewen McDonald, died at their home at Skinners Creek. Herbert accidentally drowned in a flooded river on the 1st of September 1892. He was just seventeen years old (Herbert Ewen MacDonald, 1892). Ewen and Emily would have been devastated at the loss of a third child in just ten years.

There had been a drowning incident a few years previously at Red Range when Edward Larkin, a young lad of six years old, accidentally drowned. Young Edward's mother had sent him down to the river to fetch a bucket of water from the waterhole. When he lent over the slabs on the edge of the waterhole, he fell into the river. His younger brother saw him fall and alerted his mother and a neighbour, Mrs Goodwin. By the time the women got to the river and found him he couldn't be revived ('Death by Drowning', 18 May 1886, p.2). There is no doubt that the Ballards knew his family.

Another drowning happened in the area just a few years after the death of Catherine's grandson. Thirteen years old Thomas O'Brien from Glen Innes drowned in the Beardy River near where the Red Range Road crossed. A number of teenage boys had gone in to the water to cool off, when young Thomas got into difficulty and couldn't be saved ('Sad Drowning Fatality', 29 November 1898, p.2).

Death by accident, including drowning, was fairly common in the nineteenth century. One in five of the deaths from external causes, including accidents, suicides and homicides, was the result of drowning (de Looper, 2015). In 1892 alone, there were 178 deaths from drowning in the NSW colony ('Inquests and Inquiries', 7 February 1893, p.4). However, this was a drop from previous, even higher occurrences. Towards the end of the century, the number of drownings had started to drop, mostly due to better infrastructure such as bridges. The construction of more bridges enabled people to safely cross rivers, particularly when the rivers were in flood (Staines & Ozanne-Smith, 2017).

Sadly, the year after Alfred died, Catherine's son Malcolm McDonald and his wife Lydia also lost a child. His name was Stuart Beaton McDonald. He was their third child and he was only four years old when he died. His death was registered in Dungog (Stuart B McDonald, 1893). The cause of young Stuart's death is unknown, but Catherine and her family had lost yet another young child.

In 1894, the youngest of Catherine's children, Allan Ballard, married Ellen Oliver Campbell. Allan was thirty and Ellen was twenty-two at the time of the marriage. Ellen was from Wellingrove, which is twenty kilometres north west of Glen Innes (Allan Ballard, 1894). Her mother, Ellen May Oliver, was born in Armidale in NSW; and her father, John Campbell, was from the Isle of Mull in Scotland. However, the joy was short lived when later that year tragedy struck Catherine's family yet again.

In October 1894, Catherine and Thomas's eldest son Thomas Edward Ballard (Edward) died in Glen Innes hospital. Edward had been sick for five weeks with 'Locomotor Ataxy' (Thomas Edward Ballard, 1894). Ataxy is the loss of muscle control and coordination. People with Locomotor Ataxy are unable to walk or speak or pick up objects. It can result from damage to the cerebellum due to a stroke, a tumour, multiple sclerosis, thyroid problems or syphilis ('Ataxia', 2022). Edward was only thirty-six when he died and he was unmarried.

By now there was increasing confidence in the medical profession's ability to administer care that could not be given at home. However, it is unlikely that Dr Wrigley, who was the hospital Medical Officer, would have been able to offer any viable treatment for Edward's condition other than to keep him comfortable. According to his obituary, Edward died peacefully. He is buried in the Glen Innes cemetery (Thomas Edward Ballard, 14 February 2012). Many residents and neighbours from Red Range attended Edward's funeral which, according to the *Examiner,* 'proved he had the respect and esteem of all' ('Local Notes and News', 2 October 1894, p.3). Edward's death must have been a severe loss to Catherine, Thomas and their family.

But that wasn't the end of their losses. As the nineteenth century drew to a close, typhoid fever had become endemic throughout the NSW colony. Typhoid fever is a bacterial infection which is spread through contaminated food, milk or water. Typhoid was most prevalent during the hot summer months. Relentless typhoid epidemics in the colony had resulted in the passing of the *Dairies Supervision Act* in 1886. This legislation was the first of its kind in the colony to be based on the idea of germ-theory.

In 1882 the German physician and scientist, Robert Koch, identified the 'Myobacterium tuberculosis' as the cause of tuberculosis. This was the beginning of the understanding of how bacteria can cause disease (de Looper, 2015). The new *Act* required dairies to be registered and to adhere to standardised practices of sanitation and distribution. Dairies were also required to report all cases of bovine and human disease to the authorities so that the source of the disease could be determined ('Dairies Supervision Act (1886 No22a)', 2023).

Nevertheless, eighteen people died of typhoid in the Glen Innes district in 1899 ('The Typhoid Scare', 20 February 1903, p.2). Sadly, Catherine's son-in-law, James Cornish, was one of those who died. James spent two weeks in the Glen Innes hospital prior to his death ('Death of an Old Resident', 7 February 1899, p.2). He was forty-eight when he died and some of his children were still quite young. Maria and James's daughter, Hilda, was sixteen; the twins, Isabella and Mary were fourteen and their son, Frank, was only eleven years old. Their three older children Kate, Vincent and Eliza were all young adults. James' death meant that Catherine's daughter Maria was a widow for the last thirty-six years of her life.

After James died, the Roseville property was transferred into Maria's name (Historical Lands Record Viewer, 1958(b)) and it continued to be a productive farm for many years. A story in the *Glen Innes Examiner* talked of the prime quality of the Brownell potatoes grown by Maria's oldest son, Vincent Cornish at Roseville. The size and quality were the best the author had seen ('Prime Potatoes', 4 September 1906, p.2). In another article in the *Examiner,* it was suggested that Vincent had sent eight tons of potatoes to the Glen Innes railway station for transportation. Apparently, it had taken '11 horses to shift the consignment of 'Murphys' to Glen Innes' ('Town Talk', 1 October 1917, p.4). 'Murphys' was a colloquial word for potatoes.

Clearly, life was fragile in the NSW colony. Two more young children also died in Catherine's family at this time. In 1899 David and Kitty Ballard, who were living at Bryans Gap near Tenterfield by then, had a son who they named Thomas David Ballard. He was their sixth child. However, tragedy struck again and he died when he was only two months old. He was buried in the cemetery at Tenterfield (Thomas David Ballard, 22 September 2020). Allan and Ellen Ballard also lost a son the following year. His name was

Ewen Alexander Ballard. He was nearly two and a half years old when he died. He is buried in the Red Range cemetery (Ewen Alexander Ballard, 13 December 2016). The cause of the deaths of these two young boys is unknown. However, there was an influenza epidemic in the NSW colony which led to an unusually high number of deaths in very young children over this period. There was also a spike in the number of deaths in young infants from whooping cough in NSW in 1899 (de Looper, 2015).

Declining child mortality rates

In the early 1860s, the death rate of young children aged between one and four years was about fifty percent. By 1901, the rate had fallen to thirty percent. It was still a high number. The overall fall in the rate of childhood deaths was largely attributed to two factors. The first was the decline in communicable diseases, particularly gastroenteritis disease in young children. This was mainly due to improvements in sanitation, particularly in the ever-expanding urban areas. The other reason for the fall in the childhood death rate was a marked decrease in fertility rates, with women having considerably less children (de Looper, 2015).

The identification of squalor as both the cause and transmitter of many diseases led to a transformation in the uptake of cleanliness. One outcome of this increased understanding of the need for improvements in sanitation was the passing of a wide-ranging *Public Health Act* in 1896, which increased the power of the Board of Health. The *Act* brought Municipal Councils under the jurisdiction of the Board of Health in relation to many aspects of public health and included the mandatory reporting of infectious diseases. The NSW colony was criticised for coming late to the idea of instituting public health measures to deal with disease. These measures had already been implemented in other colonies and other countries ('New Public Health Act', 17 November 1896, p.5). Sanitation reforms changed the way individuals and society as a whole thought about health. With the new *Public Health Act,* improving sanitation became a public responsibility.

The second notable reason for the decline in child mortality was a general decrease in the birth rate. Between the years 1880-1901, there was a thirty percent drop in the birth rate in the colony (New South Wales, 1904, vol.1, p.6). As a result of this decline, a Royal Commission was held in NSW in 1903-4, to try to ascertain the cause of the falling number of births. Birth rates were not only falling in NSW, but across the entire western world. However, the Commission was only concerned with the decline of births in Anglo families. The birth rate in First Nations people's families was not even considered. All of the thirteen Commissioners were reputable, professional men. There were another ninety-six witnesses called to testify, but only nine of these were women.

The Commission's report (New South Wales, 1904, vol.1, p.16) said:

> Consideration of the evidence given before us leaves no room for doubt that the trade in materials used for the prevention of conception and the destruction of foetal life has become not merely of great volume, but also of widespread extent, seeing that, in addition to the trade carried on by druggists and others, these articles are carried from house to house by hawkers, and by women (some of whom wear a dress resembling that of a nurse), who find their way into the homes of the people on various pretexts for the purpose of trading in these "preventives", or abortifacients".

The prevention of childbirth was referred to in the report as a flourishing industry.

According to the report (New South Wales, 1904, vol.2, p.58), tonics and poisons were used to bring on abortions, as well as tools for manually inducing miscarriage such as 'Sea-tangle tents'. Sea-tangle tents, also known as 'Laminaria tents', are a 5-10 cm cylinder of dried seaweed with a string attached to one end. The cylinder is inserted into the cervical canal and it slowly expands as it absorbs moisture, dilating the cervix and bringing on labour or miscarriage. The string is used to remove the cylinder (Lawrence, 10 August 2002, p.497).

Abortions were performed by a few medically trained practitioners but mostly they were performed by lay people, often in unsafe conditions.

Women could die or be left permanently damaged. Pre-Federation abortion was illegal under British law, with the exception of saving the mother's life. Then the *Crimes Act of 1900 (NSW)* made abortion illegal under NSW law. Women seeking an abortion could be prosecuted as could anyone performing an abortion or supplying the means to force a miscarriage ('*Crimes Act of 1900 (NSW) – sect82*', 2023).

The number of women dying in childbirth, or postpartum, had also risen significantly despite improvements in gynaecology. The evidence from medical experts to the Commission attributed this increase to the 'direct or indirect effects of abortion'. One medical practitioner suggested that in his practice alone he had treated 150 women over the past five years from the ill-effects of abortion (New South Wales, 1904, vol.1, p.22).

The devices for the prevention of conception referred to by the report included douches, pessaries and syringes. French letters (condoms), the India-rubber *Pessaire Preventif*, Rendell's soluble pessaries and safety sponges were all being imported to Australia and were available in pharmacies from the 1890s. However, many of the preventive measures were relatively expensive and not always available in country areas. For example, a French Letter sold for about 6s a dozen, and soluble pessaries were around 3s a dozen (New South Wales, 1904, vol.2, p.76). As a result, women and rural druggists often made their own preventives.

In his testimony to the Commission, Dr ET Thring (New South Wales, 1904, vol.1, p.25) suggested that women from all classes 'approach the subject quite freely'. He said: 'They recognise that they are not doing exactly the right thing; but still, so long as they themselves get clear, they do not mind'. He then added, 'I suppose that means to say there is a lack of moral sense in the matter'.

Even though many of the working-class men who were interviewed by the Commission expressed support for the idea of smaller families, the Commissioners blamed women for its implementation. The Commissioners denounced women for using preventive and abortive measures to limit the size of their families, calling them 'selfish', 'evil' and 'immoral'. Despite the patriarchal and belittling language which was used by the Commissioners and some of the witnesses, McDonald and Moyle (2018, p.2) argue that, at least in Australia, 'women have been not only active agents but also the principal agents in fertility decision making from the late 19th century onwards.' They posit that the agency of women in limiting the birth rate has been largely understated in the analysis of the transition to smaller families.

According to McDonald and Moyle (2018, p.2), there has generally been an assumption in the twentieth century literature that men were making the choice to limit family size for economic reasons and using withdrawal methods and abstinence as a means to achieve it. However, the Commission found that there wasn't any connection between the decline in the birth rate and an economic cause. They noted that the decline started before, and had continued well after, the economic crisis of 1893 (New South Wales, 1904, vol.1, p.18).

The evidence presented to the Royal Commission implied other factors were at play. Testimony from witnesses such as midwives, doctors and pharmacists suggested the reasons for limiting family size given by women included an 'unwillingness to submit to the strain and worry' of having lots of children. The women had a desire to avoid the physical discomfort of countless pregnancies, births and endless lactation. They were generally seeking the 'social pleasures' of a more comfortable and enjoyable life (New South Wales, 1904, vol.1, p.17).

Despite the possible risks to themselves, many women were prepared to take their chances in order to have an easier life than what their mothers and grandmothers had to endure. Large families put a huge strain on women, physically, mentally and emotionally. The demands of a large family were twenty-four hours a day, seven days a week. As the standard of living improved towards the end of the nineteenth century and women generally became more educated, they started to imagine the possibilities of another way of life. Depending on individual circumstances, this may or may not have been a joint decision which included both the husband and the wife. It is unknown how many women took action to limit the size of their families without their husband's knowledge.

Not surprisingly, the Sydney Chamber of Commerce (New South Wales, 1904, vol.1, p.30) commented to the Commission that 'any action which tends to restrict the growth of population in this country is a menace and a detriment to its prosperity and progress'. Businesses saw population increase as necessary to maintain a productive capitalist system. The Chamber of Commerce didn't mention the idea that the population increase could be achieved by immigration, rather than at the expense of women's lives.

The Commission made a raft of recommendations to stem the decline of the birth rate, based mainly on increased surveillance and the restriction of the means of prevention. Their recommendations were principally intended to limit the choices available to women of child-bearing age. Nevertheless, subsequent generations continued the transition to smaller families.

Despite the fact that birth rates generally remained higher for longer in rural areas (New South Wales, 1904, vol.1, p.34), the trend for smaller families was evident in the Ballard family. Catherine's three youngest sons and their even younger wives were all born into the generation choosing to have less children. These three families had seven, nine and nine children respectively, whereas Catherine had eleven children in total. Catherine's grandchildren then mostly chose to have considerably less children than their parents and their grandparents.

Thomas Ballard

As Catherine and Thomas were getting older, they were presumably slowing down. No doubt losing so many close family members, particularly their son Edward, would have taken its toll on them. They had been married for over forty years and had faced many of life's challenges together - Edwards death being just one of them. There aren't any photos of Thomas Ballard available. However, as we have already established, Thomas was an intelligent, devoutly Christian man, with strong convictions. A little more of his personality and his enduring sense of humour can be gleaned from this courtroom story which took place as the end of the century neared.

On the 9th of October in 1897, two brothers, John and Richard Newby, were charged with stealing and killing a heifer which belonged to Thomas Ballard. John Newby was a neighbour of the Ballard family. To quote one court report, Newby held '22,000 acres of the roughest country in the northern part of the colony, most of it unfenced and, no dividing fence between it and Ballard's' ('Armidale Circuit Court', 23 April 1898, p.2).

According to Thomas's courtroom testimony, the heifer in question was stolen from the Ballard's selection on the Mitchell River where he ran cattle. The heifer carried his family's brand which was D over B (David Ballard) on its hind quarter. Thomas told the court that he looked after the cattle himself, but his son Allan Ballard sold them on his behalf ('Killing Cattle with Intent to Steal', 29 October 1897, p.3). The case was adjourned to be heard in four months. Then, at the next hearing, the case was held over again and moved to the Armidale Circuit Court to be heard in the next session ('Local Notes & News', 8 February 1898, p.2).

After Thomas had given his evidence at the Armidale Circuit Court, the Judge complimented Thomas on his demeanour in the courtroom. The Judge said 'You are an old man, yet you spoke without any effort, and your voice was heard in every part of the court'. Mr Moriarty, the Crown Prosecutor, stated that 'The witness is over eighty years old Your Honour'. To this the Judge replied 'Why he is only a chicken yet'. Thomas then laughingly replied 'A pretty tough chicken Your Honour'. The Judge jovially remarked 'By your appearance I should think people only start to get old when they are ninety'. The accused admitted to killing the beast, but not to stealing it. At the end of the hearing, the jury were sequestered overnight. They couldn't agree on a verdict ('Local Notes & News', 26 April 1898, p.2) and the case was held over yet again. The final outcome of the case is unknown.

Medical care was generally improving at the end of the century. It was a time of enormous epidemiological change. There was a growing understanding that scientific knowledge could be utilised to combat disease and improve health and well-being. However, accidents were prevalent and medical care often wasn't available or it was limited in its scope. There still weren't any antibiotics to treat infections and vaccinations against childhood diseases and influenza weren't yet available.

Early death was common in the nineteenth century, and most families suffered the loss of loved ones, particularly children. Even so, child mortality rates were declining as public health measures improved and women had less children. Many women were taking active steps to limit the size of their families. The declining birth rate meant women did not have to endure the relentless child-bearing of previous generations. But there was still so much loss. Certainly, Catherine and her family suffered their share.

Despite the inevitable grief that follows from the death of so many family members there was still a lighter side to Catherine's husband, Thomas. It is clear from his interaction with the magistrate that Thomas was a strong, outspoken man, with a good sense of humour, even in his later years. He was still riding his horse and rounding up cattle out in the bush, even though he was eighty. He must have been a very resilient, robust man. However, both Catherine and Thomas were getting on in years by this time and ultimately life is fragile.

Chapter 14
The Changing World

Leasing out the farm - Commonwealth of Australia Constitution Act 1900 - Queen Victoria - the motor car - the first Federal election - Immigration Restriction Act 1901 - suffragist movement - Red Range School of Arts - European women vote

The dawn of a new century

Catherine and Thomas were witnessing many rapid changes now that the new century was upon them. It was a world that was becoming more and more unfamiliar to them as they advanced in years. An advertisement appeared in the *Glen Innes Examiner* on the 6th of April 1900, looking for 'Dairymen and Farmers' interested in leasing 300 acres of land. The advertisement suggested anyone interested in taking up the lease should apply to Thomas Ballard, at 'the Farm'. The lease included 300 acres of land which was grassed, fenced and subdivided, seventy or eighty acres of which was under cultivation, and included a dwelling, yards and sheds ('Advertising', 6 April 1900, p.3).

The farm must have been getting to be too much work for Thomas and Catherine. Thomas was by now eighty-one and Catherine was seventy-seven years old. Their eldest daughter, Mary Bignell (nee Ballard) and her family lived over at the coast near Taree. Their daughter, Maria Cornish (nee Ballard) and her family had their own farm to run at Red Range. The Ballard sons all had careers and responsibilities of their own.

Their youngest son, Allan had been appointed by the Governor as a Magistrate (Justice of the Peace) for the NSW colony ('NSW Government Gazette Appointments and Employment', 20 October 1899) and he had land of his own at Kingsgate ('Land Board', 22 March 1892, p.2). Allan had advertised for tenders to erect two miles of fencing in Kingsgate ('Advertising', 3 August 1900, p.3), so presumably he was farming the land.

In 1894, after leaving Fernhill Public School, near Inverell, David Ballard had been assigned as the acting teacher at Amosfield Public School, north of Tenterfield (David Ballard, 1886). Then in 1895, he was employed as a school teacher at Bryans Gap Public School. The school was just outside the town of Tenterfield, which was ninety-one kilometres (fifty-six miles) from Glen Innes ('NSW Government Gazette Appointments and Employment', 7 May 1895). David and his family made their home at Bryan's Gap (David Ballard, 31 March 1901) where they stayed for many years.

Like his brothers, Angus (4) and David, Cyrus Ballard was also a school teacher. He was first appointed in 1890, at the age of twenty-eight. He had been living at Moredun and teaching at Maybole Public School, south west of Glen Innes, for the previous few years (Cyrus Ballard, 1897-1907) (Cyrus Ballard, 31 March 1901). However, Cyrus took up a teaching position at Yarrow Creek Public School in July 1901 (Cyrus Ballard, 1897-1907), and moved back to Red Range. That same month, he was granted permission by the council to build a weatherboard cottage in Red Range ('Glen Innes Municipal Council', 26 July 1901, p.2). It is unclear if the Ballard family managed to lease the family farm, but I assume they did.

Major changes were also taking place at this time on a national level. The Commonwealth of Australia Constitution Bill, had been supported by Australian voters at three referenda, passed by British Parliament and then given Royal Assent on the 9 July 1900. As a result, on the 1st of January in 1901, the Commonwealth of Australia was formed. The six colonies, New South Wales, Queensland, South Australia, Victoria, Tasmania and Western Australia, which until now had acted like six separate countries, all federated under the *Commonwealth of Australia Constitution Act 1900*. However, the newly conceived Federal constitution did not recognise the existence of First Nations people before colonisation, and it did not allow them to be counted in the census. Asian immigrants and people from the Pacific Islands were also not recognised (Williamson, 2017).

Only a few weeks later, on 22 January 1901, Queen Victoria died, ending her reign of nearly sixty-four years. Queen Victoria had begun her reign in 1837, the same year that Catherine had left Skye and sailed to NSW. Queen Victoria reigned over a time of great change in the British Empire, not the least of which was a major part of the industrial revolution. The industrial revolution saw rapid advances in manufacturing and the production of steel, iron, coal and textiles as well as science, art, transportation and technology. Britain consolidated its dominant status on the world stage under Queen Victoria. Her son, Edward VII, succeeded her as the new monarch ('Victoria (r.1837-1901)', 2023).

The *Glen Innes Examiner* contained many tributes, as well as extensive and detailed accounts of her life, death, burial and succession. Queen Victoria's death was felt deeply by many with British heritage, throughout Britain, Australia and the Empire. Glen Innes, and no doubt Red Range, were no exception. Thomas and Catherine would have been touched by her death, which heralded the end of an era.

Political, social and technological changes in society were happening rapidly, and Glen Innes was not immune. For example, up until the turn of the century, women who worked in retail were mostly employed by drapers to sell fabric. However, in the *Glen Innes Examiner* it was suggested that a large grocery firm was going to 'experiment' having women behind the counter in their stores ('Ladies Column', 27 July 1900, p.2).

There was another major change afoot, which in time would reshape how everyone lived their lives and change the landscape in previously unfathomable ways. It was of course, the development of the motor vehicle. Glen Innes, like much of the developed world, was preparing for the appearance of motor vehicles on the streets and into everyday life. In 1901, the Glen Innes Municipal Council adopted a resolution giving Messrs Wood and Winter, who owned an American automobile company, permission to drive their motor vehicles on the streets of Glen Innes ('Glen Innes Municipal Council', 19 April 1901, p.2).

At this time, cars were still few and far between with only a select few people owning one. It was an unusual sight which must have challenged the average resident once they did start to appear on the streets (see Figure 26). It was most probably a sight that Catherine and Thomas never witnessed. Due to their age, it is possible that they no longer travelled to Glen Innes. A trip to Glen Innes would have meant travelling some distance in a horse and buggy, over rough dirt roads. No doubt though, they would have heard about the new motor vehicles from their children and grandchildren. Some of whom would have aspired to own one themselves one day. Apparently, it wasn't until 1916, long after Catherine and Thomas had passed, when the first resident of Red Range, Jack Lawler senior, owned a motor car. He had purchased one of the first Chevrolet cars to be imported into Australia ('Red Range, NSW', 2021).

Figure 26. Grey Street Glen Innes, NSW, Australia, early 1900s. There are no cars to be seen (Photo courtesy of Glen Innes Historical Society Archives, NSW, Australia, no.3965, 26 August 2023).

Following on from Federation, the first Federal election in Australia was held on the 30th of March 1901. The Ballard family would have been very excited to witness the election, which was contested by three parties, the Protectionist Party, the Free Trade Party and the Labor Party. Following the election, the votes were fairly evenly distributed between them. However, the first Federal Government of Australia was formed by the Protectionist Party with the support of the Labor Party. As a result, the leader of the Protectionist Party, Sir Edmund Barton, became the first Prime Minister of the Commonwealth of Australia (Simms, 2001). Women, First Nations people and non-British immigrants still didn't have the right to vote.

Another thing which hadn't changed at the turn of the century was the racism aimed at Chinese immigrants. Anti-Chinese sentiment was still so strong that the '*Immigration Restriction Act*' became Federal legislation in 1901. The *Act* was supposedly to 'protect the Colony from the dangers of Chinese immigration' and was the start of what we now know as the 'White Australia Policy'. The policy was openly racist and designed to severely restrict non-white immigration, and specifically Asian immigration to Australia ('The Immigration Restriction Act 1901'). The *Act* required all people wanting to migrate to Australia to write a passage in any European language which was chosen by an immigration officer ('Chinese on the Goldfields', 2023). This amounted to blatant racial selection.

The suffragist movement

Many women in colonial NSW were hoping to advance the position of women in the new century. The suffragists were early feminists who sought changes in society based on the idea of equal rights for women. The changes sought by early feminists would come too late to make a big difference in Catherine's life, and even for her daughters, but it would be important to her grand-daughters, her great grand-daughters and all the women who came after them.

Women in the nineteenth century were seen as necessarily dependent on a male bread winner. However, many women worked both in the home and outside on the farm. Some women also ran businesses, such as shops and boarding houses. Poor women often worked as servants, housemaids or in factories. Despite this, there was a distinct ideology of separate spheres. Women's lives were part of the private sphere and men were active in the public sphere (Strachan & Henderson 2005). As a result, men maintained financial power. Women's work often went unrecorded or was downplayed. The dominant ideal of the male breadwinner and female dependant was asserted in statistics, the census and on official documents, such as death certificates (Alford, 1986).

However, many women at the turn of the century, were looking to gain more power, at least within their own homes. Russell (1993) argues 'the common experience for the majority of women in the nineteenth century was that their private, as well as their public space, was controlled by men.' The main agenda for feminist activists became advocating for women's suffrage. That is, they were seeking equal voting rights in all government elections. The early feminist suffragists included Henrietta Dugdale, who started the first women's suffrage society in Australia; and Louisa Lawson, who had founded a feminist newspaper in 1888, called 'The Dawn' (Lake, 2020, p.245).

Many women in the Women's Christian Temperance Union (WCTU) also became associated with the first wave of feminism. Women such as Elizabeth Nicholls, Serena Lake, Rosetta Birks, Mary Colton, Jessie Rooke, Elizabeth Brentnall and Margaret Ogg, all of whom held strong Christian beliefs, were also calling for a change in the status of women (Lake, 2020, p.241). Women from the WCTU lectured from soap boxes in parks, in churches and on street corners about the evils of consuming alcohol. They argued that alcoholism led to violence, sexual assault and the abuse of women and children. Even though the main objective of the union remained the prohibition of, or abstinence from alcohol, it became clear that without economic independence, women who suffered at the hands of their husbands had few options but to suffer in silence ('The National Christian Temperance Union of Australia. (1891-)', 2009).

Gradually, the WCTU became involved in a broader platform of reform. Changes such as raising the age of marriage, voluntary motherhood, women's economic independence, equal pay and women's suffrage became part of their agenda. They also supported campaigns to remove prostitutes from the streets, to get women out of factories and to get barmaids out of public houses. They argued that women working in these roles corrupted society, believing it was a Christian woman's duty to uphold high moral standards in society ('The National Christian Temperance Union of Australia. (1891-)', 2009). Good Christian women remained what Caroline Chisholm had termed 'God's Police'.

The WCTU saw women's suffrage, their right to vote in elections, as the best way to influence politicians to support their reform agenda. Lake (2020, p.241) suggests that the WCTU mostly appealed to middle-class women who had a modest education and were devout Christians with an evangelical faith. As discussed earlier, Catherine would have subscribed to the notion that it was a woman's role to maintain high moral standards in society and the ensuing agenda. She also would have supported the temperance movement, as drinking alcohol was not accepted within her devout Presbyterian faith. In fact, in compliance with an edict which was passed by the General Assembly of the Presbyterian church, the Rev Kay preached a special sermon on 'temperance' to the Sunday congregation in Glen Innes ('The Temperance Crusade', 9 June 1893, p.2). He most probably repeated the sermon on one of his regular trips to preach at Red Range. We can only presume that Catherine and her family also supported women's suffrage, although we can't be sure.

By the beginning of the twentieth century, early feminist activists, together with the WCTU and their goal of women's suffrage, had become a strong force on the socio-political landscape of Australia. There was much discussion throughout the country about the pros and cons of women having the right to vote in elections and how it would change society. A commentator in favour of women's suffrage suggested that

> women as a rule, have a keen perception, and when they begin to take a proper interest in politics, we may be sure the aim will be to rid the House of all taint of blackguardism, drunkenness and other evils which are freely alleged to be frequently associated with it ('Female Vote', 4 November 1902, p.2).

However, many men believed that women didn't want to vote, and even that they weren't intelligent enough to have an understanding of politics. Some men were also concerned that it would take women away from their domestic responsibilities, or even 'coarsen' them, undermining the husband's role in the family ('Equal Suffrage', 28 August 1903, p.2). Another popular argument against women's suffrage was that women would vote the same as their husbands, effectively giving a married man two votes ('New South Wales Parliament', 17 November 1900, p.7).

One particularly belittling writer in the *Glen Innes Examiner* suggested that

> ...we fail to see any real desire among rational women to take a leading part in politics. Sensible wives are generally satisfied to leave that kind of business to their husbands...the strength of women's desire for voting influence might be said to exist-if it exists at all-in the ranks of widows and old maids, who are tired of blooming alone, and who may siege upon election day as an excellent opportunity to ogle some unwary ADONIS with a view to matrimonial considerations ('Female Franchise', 20 August 1901, p.2).

Despite the views of some men who were resisting change, suffragists continued to campaign, march, lobby, hold public lectures and organise petitions, demanding voting rights for women.

The 'local option' at Red Range

In early 1902, according to the *Examiner* ('Round About', 7 February 1902, p.1) there was a push from some of the 'younger gentlemen' in the Red Range community for a public house to be opened in the village. The 'pub' was a place where men could 'drink, smoke and swear freely'. They could play cards or dice and enjoy the companionship of other males (Doyle, 2006, p.65). Clearly, it was not a place for good Christian women.

The writer in the *Examiner* ('Round About', 7 February 1902, p.1) described Red Range as the 'jewel in the lotus'. He suggested that it was a 'happy and prosperous village, where the beauty of flower and field, the sweet songs of birds in the bosky foliage, are scenes and harmony sufficient, and should not be disturbed and debased by the revelry of a drinking shop'.

Even though Australia never prohibited the consumption of alcohol, as had happened in the United States of America, there were on-going attempts to curb its pervasiveness. Australian temperance advocates were successful in getting various forms of local laws in place across the colony. The *Licencing Act of 1882* included what was known as a 'Local Option' which gave ratepayers in a particular locality the right to vote either in favour of a public-house in their town or to veto the licence ('Licencing Act of 1882 No 26a', 2023).

However, the law was controversial. Some people disagreed with the Local Option laws, and other people thought the bill did not go far enough in preventing public houses altogether. Some voters believed compensation should be paid to those whose public licence was not renewed, while other people disagreed on paying any compensation ('Women's C.T. Union', 5 November 1901, p.2). There were the 'Licenced Victuallers Association of NSW' on one end of the argument and temperance advocates on the other.

Not surprisingly, a public house in Red Range was not supported by the majority of the residents. Many of the older residents (and no doubt most the women of the district), strongly objected to the idea ('Round About', 7 February 1902, p.1). It is unknown if any of the Ballards supported the opening of the pub, but from what we know of them it seems unlikely as they would have supported the temperance movement.

Equal voting rights, but not for everyone

As a result of the long-concerted campaign by thousands of women, the *Commonwealth Franchise Act 1902* was enacted giving many women in Australia suffrage. Women (over the age of twenty-one) won the right to vote in Australian Federal elections and also to stand as candidates for election. Australia was only the second country in the world, after New Zealand, to give women voting rights. The Australian states soon followed, giving women the right to also vote in state elections ('Electoral Milestones for Indigenous Australians', 2020).

First Nations men and women, together with European women, had previously won the right to vote in state elections in South Australia and technically this now included Federal elections. However, under the *Commonwealth Franchise Act 1902,* which sets out who can vote in elections for the Commonwealth Parliament, Aboriginal men and women had their right to vote in Federal elections removed. People from Asia, Africa and the Pacific Islands were also excluded ('Electoral Milestones for Indigenous Australians', 2020).

First Nations women were not included in the emancipation sought by the early women's movement. Even though 1902 saw a leap forward for many women in the newly federated Commonwealth, it was at the expense of First Nations people who were not recognised or afforded any rights of citizenship in their own country. It wasn't until sixty years later, in 1962, that the *Commonwealth Electoral Act* was amended to give all First Nations people the right to vote ('Electoral Milestones for Indigenous Australians', 2020).

The regulation of First Nations people continued and had become all pervasive with state supervision of their movements, their labour, their children, and their lives generally. Many Aboriginal people were pushed off Country and forced on to government reserves and missions where every aspect of their lives could be controlled. By 1903 in NSW, there were one hundred and thirty-nine reserves covering an area of 25,281 acres which had been set apart for First Nations people ('Crumbs', 8 September 1903, p.2). These reserves totally disregarded connections to Country, sacred sites and the differences in family groups and tribal connections.

White women were no longer invisible

The first annual meeting of the Red Range branch of the Farmers and Settlers Association was held on the 22nd of March 1902, at Mr Ruming's hall. There was a record turnout, with the hall crowded with enthusiastic locals. Allan Ballard was the president and chair of the meeting. Among the proceedings there was correspondence from the Lands Department with a grant of £25 towards improvements at the Red Range cemetery. Another decision taken at the meeting was for the secretary to write to the local member Mr F A Wright about the necessity of fencing the school reserve to 'benefit' children riding their horses to school. There was also a resolution passed to hold a public meeting to establish a School of Arts at Red Range ('Red Range', 28 March 1902, p.3).

As a result of this resolution, a public meeting was held a week later on the 29th of March 1902 at Red Range to discuss the matter. The School of Arts movement, which was also known as the 'Mechanics Institute' movement, was very popular at the time. A School of Arts served as a hub for self-improvement, often providing wider education in the form of culture, art and literature to a local community. The Enlightenment period in Europe had generated an enthusiasm for 'science, rationality and popular improvement'. It is estimated that about 750 'School of Arts' were established in towns across NSW. They were usually founded by volunteers with a small government subsidy (Freyne, 2010).

The Red Range meeting appointed a School of Arts building committee and in no time at all the land was secured. The tender to erect the new building was won by Mr F A Cox. The building was forty feet by twenty feet and situated in close proximity to the Red Range Public School. Cyrus Ballard was the secretary of the building committee. Once the building was completed his work as the secretary was applauded by the *Examiner* ('Red Range', 26 August 1902, p.3). The article said that the completion of the building was due to the 'untiring efforts of the ever-obliging secretary who has done a mammoth share in bringing the project to its present state'. It must be noted that Cyrus was also the secretary of the Red Range Cricket Club at this time ('Red Range Cricket Club', 12 September 1902), so he had his work cut out for him.

Once the School of Arts was completed (see Figure 27), there were seventy-four residents on the members roll. The Ballard family were still very involved in the Red Range community, so I assume that Catherine and Thomas were most likely members even though they were well into older age by now. Cyrus Ballard was the treasurer of the newly formed management committee and Allan Ballard and his nephew Vincent Cornish, were also among the committee members ('Official Opening of the Red Range School of Arts', 16 January 1903, p.2).

Figure 27. Red Range School of Arts, 1920 (Photo courtesy of Glen Innes Historical Society Archives, NSW, Australia, No.06254, 30 August, 2023).

The School of Arts was opened on the 14th of January 1903, with an evening of musical and vocal entertainment. The local Member of Parliament, Mr F A Wright MP, officially opened the building. In his opening speech Mr

Wright stated that 'he would have to face a new element at the next election as the ladies of the district now possessed the right to vote and he hoped, in a political sense, to win their confidence' ('Official Opening of the Red Range School of Arts', 16 January 1903, p.2).

Women were no longer invisible. Men in parliament were realising that they would have to consider the views of the women in their constituency, now that they had the power to vote. Families were increasingly encouraging their daughters to expand their education and move into professions roles. With women being afforded more work and educational opportunities, Australia saw the rise of the intellectual middle-class, white woman (Strachan and Henderson, 2005). No doubt, Catherine's granddaughters would have felt optimistic about the changes in their status and the choices available to them.

Women entered the political process

The first Federal election in Australia which allowed women voting rights was held on the 16 December in 1903. Four women stood at the election. Selina Anderson was the only woman to stand for the House of Representatives. Vida Goldstein, Nellie Martel and Mary Moore-Bentley all stood for the Senate. All four women stood as independents, but none of them was elected. It took another forty years for a woman to be elected to the federal parliament in Australia ('Our Century of Women's Suffrage', July 2009).

According to the 1903 Electoral Roll (Thomas Louis Ballard, 1903), Thomas Ballard was living at Kingsgate. By now Thomas and Catherine may have been living with their son, Allan and his family at Kingsgate, although it is unclear. Catherine was not registered on the electoral roll. It would have been her only chance to ever cast an electoral vote, but she chose not to. As she most likely remained illiterate, she may have felt excluded from the process, or perhaps she was just too frail.

Enrolment and the casting of a vote in the 1903 election was voluntary. Overall, the percentage of women who were enrolled and turned out to vote was less than the number of men. For example, in the NSW Senate, forty-one percent of the women who were enrolled actually cast a vote, and fifty-three percent of the men who were enrolled voted. Nevertheless, hundreds of thousands of women turned out to vote across the country and 'their enfranchisement marked their entry into the political process' ('Our Centenary of Women's Suffrage', July 2009).

The Protectionist Party again formed government with the support of the Labor Party. The vote at Red Range and Grahams Valley combined was 122 votes for Mr Sawer, the Protectionist Party candidate, and 32 votes for Mr Lonsdale of the Free Trade Party ('The Election', 18 December 1903, p.4). The farmers of Red Range were clearly in favour of policies which supported their ability to sell at a fair price and keep out cheaper imported products.

Catherine's granddaughter Kate McKinnon Cornish (1874-1947) was enrolled to vote at Red Range in the 1903 election (Cornish, Kate McKinnon, 1903-1904). At a time when many of the women on the electoral roll were listed as doing 'home duties', Kate's occupation was given as a 'dressmaker', so I assume she was earning her own money (Cornish, Kate McKinnon, 1903-1904). Kate later became a school teacher (Cornish, Kate McKinnon, 1930, 1934 & 1936). Clearly, Kate was an independent woman who seized her chance to vote and saw that there were possibilities for her to have a career and earn her own living. Times were changing, albeit slowly.

Kate's younger sister, one of the twins, Mary Vivian Cornish (1885-1872) was not old enough to vote at the first Federal election in 1903. However, she was later appointed as the postmistress at the Red Range Post Office in December 1924 ('Personal', 22 December 1924, p.4). Mary was very well respected and worked in the post office until December 1965. She was awarded The British Empire medal in 1966 for forty years of service to the community (Chappell, 21 August 2019).

Neither Kate, or Mary, ever married or had children but they did have careers. To have a career and not marry was not previously an option for most respectable white, middle-class women. Catherine, her two daughters, her daughters in law and her granddaughters witnessed the success of the suffrage movement and the changing roles of European women in Australian society. European women were finally able to participate more fully in the democratic processes that shaped the society they lived in.

Incredibly though, Aboriginal women along with Aboriginal men remained without suffrage for six more decades. This effectively left First Nations people marginalised without the political power to influence decisions made in their own country, including those policies which directly affected them and their families. On top of the invasion of their country by Britain, the disenfranchisement of First Nations people has left a legacy of intergenerational trauma which still impacts the lives of many Aboriginal people today.

Also, despite the changes that have improved the lives of women since suffrage was achieved, many of the struggles and inequities which existed during Catherine's lifetime have still not disappeared. Ideals such as equal pay, equal representation in parliament, freedom from sexual harassment and gender-based violence and control, remain elusive for many women to this day. Cultural change has been slow to address these inequities. and First Nations women are particularly at risk from a mix of racial and gender-based violence, discrimination and disadvantage.

Epilogue

On the 14th of February 1904, after being ill for a week, Catherine's husband Thomas died of pneumonia at the age of eighty-six, ('Death of Mr Thomas Ballard', 23 February 1904, p.2). Thomas's death must have been a great loss for Catherine. She had survived many challenges in her lifetime, but she was now elderly and most likely not as strong as she had once been.

Only three months after she buried Thomas, in the late Autumn, Catherine also came down with a bout of pneumonia. Just three days later, on the 16th of May 1904, she passed away. Catherine died of cardiac failure. She was eighty-one. She was survived by nine of her children and her younger sister, Margaret McMillian (nee McKinnon).

Catherine was buried at Red Range Cemetery the following day. The Presbyterian Minister, Rev Cameron, delivered her funeral service (Catherine Ballard, 1904) (Obituary, 1904, p.2). Catherine was buried with her beloved husband Thomas. An elegant headstone was commissioned to mark the grave and a low wrought iron fence was erected around the plot (see Figure 28).

Catherine's sons, David and Allan Ballard, were named as the executors of Thomas's will ('Probate Jurisdiction', 3 June 1906, p.4). The Ballard farm was advertised for sale on the 17th November 1906. The advertisement in the *Glen Innes Examiner* ('Sales by Auction', 13 November 1906, p.4) stated that the auctioneers had been instructed by the Ballard family to sell their 'Well known farm at Red Range'. 'The farm', it was suggested, was suitable for dairying and potato growing and contained one-hundred acres of 'tip top' land.

Interestingly, Allan Ballard had registered a horse and cattle brand in June, only a few months before the sale of the farm ('Stock Act 1901', 21 November 1906, p.6331). The brand DB (the B is lying horizontally under the D. DB = David Ballard) was listed for 'Kendram Farm, Red Range'. Kendram was, of course, the name of the crofting settlement where

Catherine had begun her life in Scotland on the Isle of Skye, and so the story of her life finishes back at Kendram, half way round the world in Red Range.

Figure 28. Catherine and Thomas Ballard's grave, 2023 (Photo by Gail Barnes, Red Range Cemetery, 17 April 2023, NSW, Australia).

There is scant written record of Catherine's life. The first written record of her was on the *Midlothian* passenger list. There is no written record of her first marriage to Angus (2). Even when Angus (2) won the lottery, there was no mention of Catherine in the newspapers. After her son was legally acknowledged as the owner of Underbank in court, Catherine was only referred to as the 'guardian' of young Angus (4) in the 1849 Supreme Court announcement in the *Maitland Mercury*. She wasn't even named. She was referred to as Mrs McDonald in the newspaper, when she was accused of selling cattle which didn't belong to her in 1852. Her name was recorded on their marriage certificate when she married Thomas, although she signed with an X, and she appeared as the 'mother' on the birth certificates of her children.

There weren't any references to Catherine in the *Glen Innes Examiner* from the time of her arrival at Red Range in 1876 until her death. Even her obituary in the *Examiner* (Obituary, 1904, p.2) gave the date of her death, but it didn't give any clue to her interests or her personality. She doesn't appear on any land deeds, for as a woman she had no property rights. She wasn't registered to vote. Her name is not on the NSW census - as women were only given as the number of females in a household - and her attendance is not acknowledged at cricket matches or at meetings which were held in her home. She was not on any committees and she didn't place any advertisements in the newspaper. Apart from the few fleeting mentions stated above, very little was ever recorded about her as an individual.

This was typical of most women in the nineteenth century. Societal norms for women of Catherine's times meant that she was expected to provide comfort and support to her family without standing out. Mrs Susan Nugent Wood (1862 cited in Alford, 1986), wrote about the ideal Australian woman in her book titled, *Woman's Work in Australia*:

> Women do not, must not, live for themselves. It is their mission to combat against the worldly spirit which men too often cherish at home and abroad; it is theirs to soften the hard selfish feelings of business life; to refine, exalt, purify, and strengthen – and all this may be done without giving up the seat by the fireside, without one curtain lecture, without any declamation of 'Women's Rights'... 'Woman's Work' must begin at home, and very often she never need move from the common round of an uneventful life to fulfil her noiseless part.

So it was for Catherine. In the nineteenth century, women's roles mostly revolved around the home and domestic duties. The 'ideal' woman was like Catherine: pious, God fearing and selfless. These were the standards by which society judged her. Yet despite the social and political constraints she experienced as a woman in the nineteenth century, she lived a valued and valuable life.

Like many women of her time, Catherine's life was spent in the home. As Russell (1993, p.28) posits, women in the nineteenth century only had limited ways in which they could claim identity and status in the public world. The private sphere of the home and family offered many women validation. As such, despite Catherine's public 'invisibility' in her private life, she was a central figure in the lives of her two husbands, her eleven children and to many of her seventy-six grandchildren (see Figure 29).

Figure 29. Catherine Ballard c1900 (Photo courtesy of Jan Vizer & Glen Innes Historical Society Archives, NSW, Australia, No.0778_001, 4 March 2021).

Her day-to-day life was lived around the stove, in the kitchen, in the laundry, the milking sheds, the chicken shed and the vegetable garden, tending to sick children, labouring, birthing, feeding, mending, sewing, cooking, serving and nurturing. Farm women often sold milk, butter and eggs, they worked in the paddocks when extra hands were needed and they fed the workers. They made meals, clothes and home comforts out of very little. These things were not documented: they didn't reach the newspapers, or make the government gazettes, yet they were the backbone of families and communities.

By trying to understand more about the historical period in which she lived, hopefully we are able to understand more about Catherine herself. Life isn't lived in a void. The social and political values of the society in which we live shape our choices, our own values and our expectations. By centring the narrative on Catherine, a woman with no formal education who remained illiterate throughout her life, we get a unique perspective on a particular historical period.

Through telling Catherine's story, we are able to make her life visible. This visibility does not give her a voice, as we don't really know what she thought, or how she felt. Without any letters or journals, her thoughts and feelings are only conjecture made from a very different future perspective. What we do know though, is that women like Catherine helped to create the nation. They were the very fabric of colonial life.

Catherine was a survivor and I hope that she lived a fulfilling life. Many of her descendants have been given her name, so it has been carried down through the generations. She was clearly very loved and held in the highest regard by those who knew her best. It has been a great pleasure to get to know Catherine, at least to some extent, through undertaking this project. It has given me enormous pride in my Scottish heritage and my great, great grandmother in particular.

A beautiful handmade black, beaded shoulder cape which was owned by Catherine remains as a tangible link to her (see Figure 30). The cape was passed from Catherine to her daughter Maria Cornish, and then down to Catherine's granddaughter, Isabella Gertrude Sargeant (nee Cornish).

Isabella donated the cape to the Glen Innes Historical Museum and Research Centre in 1969.

The cape is referred to in an article which was written by The Glen Innes and District Historical Society and published in the *Glen Innes Examiner* ('The Gulf Country', 7 July 1969, p.3). The article, titled 'The Gulf Country', suggests the shoulder cape had been made more than a century ago, so it would now be over 150 years old. The cape is made of high-quality cloth, and remains in excellent condition. It is a beautiful piece of functional, historical art which has survived the test of time.

Figure 30. A finely beaded, black shoulder cape which belonged to Catherine Ballard, 2020 (Photo by Gail Barnes, 31 December 2020).

Appendix

Catherine's eldest surviving son from her first marriage, Ewen, and his wife Emily had nine children. They were Alfred, John, William, Herbert, George, David, Catherine, Samuel and Albert. Two years after Catherine and Thomas had died, on the 19th of April 1906, Emily also died at Red Range. She was fifty-nine years old. Emily is buried in an adjoining grave to the left of Catherine and Thomas, in the Red Range cemetery (Emily Weller McDonald, 17 February 2012).

After his wife Emily died, Ewen McDonald went to live in Warwick, in south east Queensland with his son Samuel and was buried there ('Obituary', 14 July 1916, p.6). His only daughter, Catherine Sarah McDonald died in 1911, near Clunes. Catherine was crossing a flooded river on a fallen tree in order to take lunch to her husband who was working on the other side, when she fell into the river. She didn't drown, but she died a week later from pneumonia. She was twenty-eight and had married Robert Kirkland only a couple of years before her death. Catherine is buried in Clunes cemetery (Personal, 7 March 1911, p.3).

Angus McDonald (4) and his wife, Helena had eight children. They were Eldred, George, Victor, Cyrus, Alexander, Frederick, Arthur and Miriam. When Angus and Helena left Gunnedah, they retired to live in Sydney. Helena died in Stanmore in Sydney in 1919 and Angus (4) died eight years later in 1927, when he was eighty-four after a short illness ('Mr. Angus McDonald', 13 June 1927, p.5).

Malcolm McDonald and his wife, Isabella, had seven children: Alexander, Angus, Stuart, Catherine, Lydia, Margaret and Agnes. Most of their children were born near Dungog. Malcolm McDonald died on the 17th of August 1905 in Sydney. He is buried in the Woronora Memorial Park in Sutherland, Sydney (no.9146). He was sixty years old and his wife died in 1946 ('Generation No.3', n.d.).

Catherine's youngest son with her first husband, John McDonald, and his wife Elizabeth had six children: Angus, Clementine, Catherine, Ewen, Neil and Kenneth ('Generation No.3', n.d). John was a farmer and a Senior Elder of the Dungog Presbyterian Church. John had to have his leg amputated in 1916 after a horse kicked him. Apparently, his health was never good after that. He died four years later ('Deaths', 16 January 1920, p.2). John died in Ashfield and is buried at Waverley cemetery in Sydney (John McDonald, 2020). Elizabeth died in 1926 and is also buried at Waverley.

Mary Ballard, Catherine's eldest daughter, and her husband Robert had thirteen children: Robert, Annie, Kate, Clarence, Ellie, Mary, Selina, Thomas, Robert, Alfred, Florence, Cecil and David. Mary and Robert retired to Taree in 1924. Robert died in 1925 and Mary died nine years later in 1934 ('The Late Mrs Mary Bignell', 9 June 1934, p.2).

According to the NSW Electoral Roll (Maria Catherine Cornish, 1930), Catherine's daughter, Maria Cornish, was still living at Red Range in 1930. She was living with her daughter Kate who was a school teacher, her daughter Mary who was the post mistress and her son, Vincent, a farmer. Maria was described as being a cheerful, kind and a very hospitable person ('The Late Mrs M. C. Cornish', 4 May 1935, p.2). She died in 1935 and was buried next to her husband James Cornish in the Glen Innes cemetery (James Cornish, 2012).

David Ballard and his wife Kitty had seven children: Flora, Catherine, Allan, Colina, Laura (Jessie), Thomas (David), and Christina (Minnie). David Ballard continued teaching and was the school teacher at the Bryans Gap school until at least 1921 (David Ballard, 1921). Then, according to the 1930 NSW Electoral roll, David and Kitty moved to Eastwood in Sydney. David later passed away in 1937 at the age of seventy-seven ('Deaths', 9 June 1937, p.14) and Kitty died in 1953, at the same address in Eastwood ('Deaths', 19 March 1953, p.14).

Just four months after Catherine's death, her son Cyrus Ballard, who was forty-three and living at Red Range, married Elsie Beatrice Macleay Cornish. Cyrus was the last of Catherine's children to marry. Elsie was born at Macleay

River in NSW, in 1883. Elsie was twenty-one at the time of their marriage (Elsie B M Cornish, 1883). She was the niece of the late James Cornish, who was married to Cyrus's sister, Maria. Cyrus and Elsie were married in the Presbyterian church at Hamilton in Newcastle in NSW, where Elsie's family lived. After the wedding the couple caught the train to Sydney for their honeymoon ('Local and General', 18 October 1904, p.2).

In late 1905, Cyrus left where he was teaching at Yarrow Creek Public School (near Red Range) to take charge of Dundee Public School, which was forty kilometres away (about twenty-five miles) ('Transfer', 10 November 1905, p.4). Cyrus and Elsie had their first child, a son Cyrus V Ballard, in March 1906. Sadly, he died as a newborn. He is buried in the Glen Innes cemetery (Cyrus V Ballard, 14 February 2012). Cyrus retired from teaching the following year (Cyrus Ballard, 1897-1907), and he and Elsie moved to Nambour in Queensland to take up farming.

Cyrus and Elsie had nine children: Cyrus, Elise, Daphine, Reginald, Dulcie, Dolley, Wilfred, Roy and Lewis. Lewis died when he was only three weeks old. In the 1934 Queensland Electoral Roll Cyrus's occupation was listed as a farmer (Cyrus Ballard, 1934). Cyrus died in 1941 at the age of seventy-nine and Elsie died in 1968 when she was eighty-five.

Catherine's youngest son, Allan Ballard, and his wife Ellen had nine children: Grace, Gertrude, Ewen, Mary, Laura, Elsie (twin), Effie (twin), Archibald and Catherine. As was mentioned earlier, Catherine's two years old grandson Ewen Alexander Ballard, who was the son of Allan Ballard, is also buried in the Red Range cemetery. His grave, which is now unmarked, lies to the left of Emily McDonald's grave. However, Allan and Ellen also lost another child, Effie, in 1908 when she was three years old. She was one of their twins.

Later in 1906, Allan was appointed as a councillor on the first Severn Shire Council. The councillors were initially appointed by the Governor and elections were held later ('C Riding, Shire Council', 30 October 1906, p.6). Allan served on the Severn Shire Council until 1909 ('Severn Shire Council', 10 August 1909, p.5). As well as being a local councillor, Allan was also a farmer and a prominent member of the Red Range Farmers and Settlers

Association since its inception in 1901. He was their first President. Mr Ryall, on Allan's departure from Red Range in 1911, stated that Allan had 'acted as their guide, philosopher and friend in all of their public movements' ('Farewell to Mr Allan Ballard', 15 May 1911, p.2).

Allan was a keen debater and a member of the Red Range Debating Society ('Debate at Red Range', 28 September 1909, p.2). He was said to be a 'formidable personality at the debating table, his lucidity of utterance ever denoting the highly intelligent trend of thought he brought to bear on any subject which came up for discussion' ('Mr Allan Ballard', 5 March 1935, p.4). Presumably, Allan's skill at the debating table would have been ably reflected in his performance on the council and in his other endeavours.

Allan died at the age of seventy-one after a 'long and trying illness' and is buried in the Glen Innes cemetery ('Mr Allan Ballard', 5 March 1935, p.4) (Allan Ballard, 2012). His wife Ellen, who died twenty-eight years later in 1963, is also buried in the Glen Innes cemetery.

Catherine's step daughter from her first marriage, Flora Sherwood (nee Graham) died in 1886 and is buried at the Lawrence Cemetery (Flora Sherwood, n.d.). At the time of writing, it is unknown where and when Flora's husband William Sherwood died. Her brother, Murdoch Graham, died in 1891 and is also buried in the Lawrence Cemetery ('The Late Mr M Graham', 11 April 1891, p.8).

Catherine's younger sister, Margaret McMillan (nee McKinnon) was her only sibling to outlive her. Margaret lived to be eighty-five years old. She died in 1912 at Woodford Leigh and is buried in the Maclean cemetery ('Obituary', 9 July 1912, p.2) with her husband John who had died in 1896 (John McMillan, 3 March 1896). Margaret signed her last will and testament with an X the year before she died, so she remained illiterate ('MacLean Will Case', 5 December 1912, p.5).

Mr Langton Parker Esq who purchased Underbank Estate in 1878 ('Latest Telegrams', 28 February 1878, p.5) kept the Estate for just over ten years.

Theophilis Cooper then bought Underbank in 1889 ('Maitland District Court', 24 June 1890, p.8). Cooper sold Underbank about ten years later to Mr JK McKay ('Death of a Pioneer', 27 February 1912, p.2). Trustees for the estate of McKay later subdivided the area around Quart Pot Creek and Tunnybuck Mountain Country. Mr J R Fulton bought 2,300 acres including the Underbank homestead. The remaining land became known as 'Tunnebuc Station' ('Dungog and Round About', 17 May 1910, p.3).

In 1913, the property was advertised for sale again. By this time, it was approximately 2000 acres, and was divided into eleven smaller farms. The small farms were each between 11 and 405 acres ('Unsold portions of Underbank Estate', 4 March 1913, p.4), but it didn't sell. Mr Fulton advertised Underbank again in 1919. Underbank was advertised as 1865 acres which was divided into 11 blocks, ranging in area between 86 acres and 457 acres on the homestead block ('Advertising' 4 April 1919, p.8). The Underbank Estate was bought, sold and divided many times over the years. However, around 1960, John McDonald a Director of the Dungog Co-operative Dairy Co, who was a great, great grandson of Catherine and Angus's (2) bought 1,770 acres of the original Underbank Estate, which had previously been subdivided into smaller lots (Forster, 1979, p.2).

In more recent times the estate was under threat for a number of years from the Tillegra Dam proposal, which was first suggested as far back as the 1950s. The dam was to be built on the Upper Williams River, seven miles from Dungog. The dam would have flooded some of the original Underbank property, as well as other local properties, many of which are owned by McDonald descendants. It would also have flooded the original cemetery of Quart Pot where some of the ancestors are buried. Fortunately for Underbank, the dam proposal was fought by locals and their supporters and finally withdrawn in 2010 (History in the Williams River Valley, n.d.).

Bibliography

'Aborigines', *The Sydney Morning Herald (NSW: 1842-1954)*, 11 September 1882, p.4, https://trove.nla.gov.au/newspaper/article/13524856

'About Crofting', 2024, *Scottish Crofting Federation.*

'About Glen Innes', *Land of the Beardies*, 2016-2022, https://www.beardieshistoryhouse.info

'About Parliament', 2022, *Australian Parliament House.*

Abstract of Individuals, Midlothian, 1837, Assisted Immigrant Passenger Lists, NSWSA: NRS 5313/4_4780/Midlothian_12 Dec 1837, [online] *NSW State Archives*, Sydney.

'Abstract of Sales by Auction This Day', *The Sydney Morning Herald (NSW:1842-1954)*, 2 March 1847, p.2, https://trove.nla.gov.au/newspaper/article/12897098

'Acclimatisation Society of New South Wales Annual Report, 1861, *Trove*, https://catalogue.nla.gov.au/Record/2988772

'Advertisement', *Glen Innes Examiner and General Advertiser (NSW: 1874 - 1908)*, 8 December 1885, p.5, https://trove.nla.gov.au/newspaper/rendition/nla.news-article217771000

'Advertising', *Sydney Herald (NSW: 1831-1842)*, 13 April 1840(a), p.2, https://trove.nla.gov.au/newspaper/article/12858762

'Advertising', *Sydney Herald (NSW: 1831 - 1842)*, 26 December 1840(b), p.4, https://trove.nla.gov.au/newspaper/rendition/nla.news-article12867250

'Advertising', *The Sydney Morning Herald (NSW:1842-1954)*, 30 April 1845, p.4, https://trove.nla.gov.au/newspaper/article/12879153

'Advertising', *The Sydney Morning Herald (NSW:1842-1954)*, 13 August 1846, p.4, https://trove.nla.gov.au/newspaper/article/12889106

'Advertising', *The Sydney Morning Herald (NSW: 1842-1954)*, 1 February 1849, p.1, https://trove.nla.gov.au/newspaper/article/12912368

'Advertising', *The Sydney Morning Herald (NSW:1842-1954)*, 2 February 1849, p.1, https://trove.nla.gov.au/newspaper/page/4094329

'Advertising', *The Sydney Morning Herald (NSW: 1842-1954)*, 31 March 1849, p.3, https://trove.nla.gov.au/newspaper/article/12913115

'Advertising', *The Sydney Morning Herald (NSW: 1842-1954)*, 21 April 1849, p.3, https://trove.nla.gov.au/newspaper/article/12910748

'Advertising', *The Sydney Morning Herald (NSW: 1842-1954)*, 29 October 1851, p.3, https://trove.nla.gov.au/newspaper/article/12931638

'Advertising', *The Sydney Morning Herald (NSW: 1842-1954)*, 26 August 1854, p.1, https://trove.nla.gov.au/newspaper/article/30940853

'Advertising', Sydney Morning Herald (NSW: 1842-1954), 30 December 1856, p.8, https://trove.nla.gov.au/newspaper/article/12990721

'Advertising', *The Maitland Mercury and Hunter General Advertiser (NSW: 1843-1893)*, 25 December 1875, p.4, https://trove.nla.gov.au/newspaper/article/18801647

'Advertising', *Glen Innes Examiner and General Advertiser (NSW: 1874 - 1908)*, 12 January 1876, p.1, https://trove.nla.gov.au/newspaper/article/217827847

'Advertising', *The Maitland Mercury and Hunter River General Advertiser (NSW: 1843-1893)*, 29 March 1877, p.1, https://trove.nla.gov.au/newspaper/article/18817055

'Advertising', *The Maitland Mercury and Hunter General advertiser (NSW: 1843-1893)*, 30 June 1877, p.2, https://trove.nla.gov.au/newspaper/article/18820243

'Advertising', *Glen Innes Examiner and General Advertiser, (NSW: 1874-1908)*, 2 March 1880, p.4, https://trove.nla.gov.au/newspaper/article/217784116

'Advertising', *Glen Innes Examiner and General Advertiser, (NSW: 1874-1908)*,10 February 1880, p.1, https://trove.nla.gov.au/newspaper/article/217783871

'Advertising', *Glen Innes Examiner and General Advertiser, (NSW: 1874-1908)*, 21 December 1880, p.1, https://trove.nla.gov.au/newspaper/article/217784266

'Advertising', *Glen Innes Examiner and General Advertiser, (NSW: 1874-1908)*, 1 March 1881, p.5, https://trove.nla.gov.au/newspaper/article/217833084

'Advertising', *Glen Innes Examiner and General Advertiser, (NSW: 1874-1908)*, 30 August 1881, p.2, https://trove.nla.gov.au/newspaper/page/23897459

'Advertising', *Glen Innes Examiner and General Advertiser, (NSW: 1874-1908)*, 6 September 1881, p.5, https://trove.nla.gov.au/newspaper/article/217831819

'Advertising', *Glen Innes Examiner and General Advertiser, (NSW: 1874-1908)*, 2 October 1883, p.4, https://trove.nla.gov.au/newspaper/article/217839906

'Advertising', *Glen Innes Examiner and General Advertiser, (NSW: 1874-1908)*, 3 November 1885, p.5, https://trove.nla.gov.au/newspaper/article/217771822

'Advertising', *Glen Innes Examiner and General Advertiser, (NSW: 1874-1908)*, 8 December 1885, p.5, https://trove.nla.gov.au/newspaper/article/217771000

'Advertising', *Glen Innes Examiner and General Advertiser (NSW: 1874 - 1908)*, 12 October 1886, p.6, https://trove.nla.gov.au/newspaper/article/217877102

'Advertising', *Glen Innes Examiner and General Advertiser (NSW: 1874 - 1908)*, 6 September 1887, p.1, https://trove.nla.gov.au/newspaper/article/217818788

'Advertising', *Glen Innes Examiner and General Advertiser (NSW: 1874 - 1908)*, 1 May 1888, p. 1, https://trove.nla.gov.au/newspaper/article/217772748

'Advertising', *Glen Innes Examiner and General Advertiser (NSW: 1874 - 1908)*, 8 May 1888, p.5, https://trove.nla.gov.au/newspaper/article/217774726

'Advertising', *Glen Innes Examiner and General Advertiser (NSW: 1874 - 1908)*, 16 October 1888, p. 5, https://trove.nla.gov.au/newspaper/article/217774015

'Advertising', *Glen Innes Examiner and General Advertiser (NSW:1874-1908)*, 2 August 1895, p.5, https://trove.nla.gov.au/newspaper/rendition/nla.news-article217811570

'Advertising', *Glen Innes Examiner and General Advertiser (NSW: 1874-1908)*, 6 April 1900, p.3, https://trove.nla.gov.au/newspaper/article/217838346

'Advertising', *Glen Innes Examiner and General Advertiser (NSW: 1874-1908)*, 1 May 1900, p.3, https://trove.nla.gov.au/newspaper/article/217838778

'Advertising', *Glen Innes Examiner and General Advertiser (NSW: 1874-1908)*, 3 August 1900, p.3, https://trove.nla.gov.au/newspaper/article/217838451

'Advertising', *The Maitland Daily Mercury (NSW: 1894-1939)*, 4 April 1919, p.8, https://trove.nla.gov.au/newspaper/article/123292143

'AKF: Shocking Figures Reveal the Devastating Impacts of the Koala Fur Trade', 25 August 2015, *Australian Koala Foundation*.

Alford, K., 1986, 'Colonial Women's Employment as Seen by Nineteenth-Century Statisticians and Twentieth-Century Economic Historians', *Labour History*, no. 51, pp.1-10.

Alfred McDonald, 14 May 1869, NSW Birth Certificate, Registration No.10260/1869, Dungog, *NSW Registry of Births, Deaths and Marriages*, Sydney, Australia.

Alfred MacDonald, 8 June 1884, Certified copy of NSW Death Certificate, Registration No. 13232/1884, *NSW Registry of Births, Deaths and Marriages*, Sydney, Australia.

Allan Ballard, 2012, *Find a Grave*, New South Wales, Glen Innes General Cemetery, https://www.findagrave.com/cemetery/2437433

Allan Ballard, 1894, Australia, Marriage Index, 1788-1950, *Ancestry.com*

'An Abundance of Honey', *The Maitland Mercury and Hunter River General Advertiser (NSW: 1843-1893)*, 2 May 1871, p.3, https://trove.nla.gov.au/newspaper/article/18753709

Andrew Lang, 19 Jany [sic] 1848, 'Letter applying to have the Dunmore school placed under the general system', NRS 15051-1-20[1088]-7, *NSW State Archives & Records*, Sydney.

Angus Cameron, 1881, Snizort North, Inverness, Ref: Census 117/1 2/8, Scotland's People, *National Records of Scotland*.

Angus Macdonald, 3 August 1837, Old Parish Registers Marriages, Ref. no. 117/ 1013 2, Snizort, p.132, Scotland's People, *National Records of Scotland*.

Angus MacDonald, 7 January 2023, Text Message, 'The McKinnons of Kendram' Facebook Group Page.

Angus McDonald, 1837, Midlothian, Assisted Immigrant Passenger Lists, NSWSA: NRS 5313/4_4780/Midlothian_12 Dec 1837, p.1, *NSW State Archives,* Sydney.

'Angus McDonald', *Dungog Chronicle: Durham and Gloucester Advertiser (NSW: 1894-1954),* 17 June 1927, p.2, https://trove.nla.gov.au/newspaper/article/138213945

Angus McKinnon, 6 June 1851, Emperor, Assisted Immigrants Shipping Lists, NRS5316/4_4790/Emperor_6 Jun 1851, p. 7-9, *NSW State Archives,* Sydney.

Angus McKinnon, 9 June 1851, 'Emperor', Immigration Board, *NSW State Archives,* Sydney.

Angus McKinnon, 17 April 1863, Certified copy of NSW Marriage Certificate No.2092, 1853, *NSW Registry of Births, Deaths & Marriages,* Sydney, Australia

Angus McKinnon, Correspondence to 'The Under Secretary, Department of Public Instruction, Sydney', 2 April 1885, p.1.

'A Night in Ebony', *Glen Innes Examiner and General Advertiser (NSW: 1874-1908),* 2 January 1893, p.2, https://trove.nla.gov.au/newspaper/article/217784855

Ann MacLeod, 1851, Kilmuir, Inverness, Ref: Census 112/1/16, Scotland's People, *National Records of Scotland.*

Ann MacLeod, 25 December 1856, Statutory Registers Marriages, 112/1/13, Kilmuir (Inverness), Scotland's People, *National Records of Scotland.*

Ann MacLeod, 1861, Kilmuir, Inverness, Ref: Census 112/1 6/10, Scotland's People, *National Records of Scotland.*

Ann Macleod, 1871, Kilmuir, Inverness, Ref: Census 112/1 6/11, Scotland's People, *National Records of Scotland.*

Ann Macleod, 1881, Kilmuir, Inverness, Ref: Census 112/1 7/6, Scotland's People, *National Records of Scotland.*

Ann MacLeod, 4 May 1881, Statutory Registers Deaths, 112/1 16 Kilmuir (Inverness), p.6, Scotland's People, *National Records of Scotland.*

Ann McKinnon, 1834, Old Parish Registers Births, 112/Kilmuir, p.3, Scotland's People, *National Records of Scotland.*

Anne Ross, 4 August 1917, Statutory Registers Deaths, 112/1/8, Kilmuir (Inverness), p.3, Scotland's People, *National Records of Scotland.*

'Another Lottery Scheme', *The Sydney Morning Herald (NSW: 1842-1954)*, 22 January 1849, p.2, https://trove.nla.gov.au/newspaper/article/28647279

'A Plea for the Blacks', *The Maitland Mercury and Hunter River General Advertiser (NSW: 1843 - 1893)*, 2 April 1863, p.2, https://trove.nla.gov.au/newspaper/rendition/nla.news-article18694620.3

'Application from the Emigrants per Ship Midlothian to be Located in One District', 29 December 1837, Summary Extract from Minute of Council, No.37/47, *NSW State Archives*, [research by Evelyn Smith].

'Appointments and Employment', *NSW Government Gazette (Sydney, NSW:1832-1900)*, 16 September 1884, p.6205, https://trove.nla.gov.au/newspaper/article/221675705

'Appointments and Employment', *NSW Government Gazette (Sydney, NSW:1832-1900)*, 12 March 1889, p.1923, https://trove.nla.gov.au/newspaper/article/223990674

Archer, C. & Sullivan, J., 2004, '*A History of St Ann's Presbyterian Church Paterson*', Paterson Historical Society Inc, p.30.

'A Red Range Witness', *Glen Innes Examiner and General Advertiser (NSW: 1874-1908)*, 26 April 1898, p.2, https://trove.nla.gov.au/newspaper/article/217880951

'Armidale', *The Maitland Mercury and Hunter General advertiser (NSW: 1843-1893)*, 4 April 1876, p.6, https://trove.nla.gov.au/newspaper/article/18805202

'Armidale Circuit Court', *The Armidale Chronicle (NSW: 1894-1929)*, 23 April 1898, p.2, https://trove.nla.gov.au/newspaper/article/188366242

'Arrival and Despatch of Mails in the Hunter', *The Maitland Mercury and Hunter General advertiser (NSW: 1843-1893)*, 13 January 1847, p.2, https://trove.nla.gov.au/newspaper/article/687103

'Ataxia', 2022, Diseases & Conditions, *Mayo Clinic*.

Attwood, B., 13 July 2017 'Denial in a Settler Society: The Australian Case', *History Workshop Journal*, vol.84, iss.1, pp.24-43.

'Australian Literature', n.d. *Britannica [online]*.

Australian Museum Business Services (AMBS), 2010, *Glen Innes Severn LGA Aboriginal Heritage Study*, Consultancy Report to Glen Innes Severn Council.

'Australian Voting History in Action', 16 September 2020, *Australian Electoral Commission*.

Author Unknown, 1924, *The Martin's of Skye: A Short Family History*, Alex Maclaren and Sons, Glasgow, https://catalogue.nla.gov.au/Record/7459407

'A Wonderful Old Horse', *Glen Innes Examiner, (NSW: 1908-1954)*, 20 January 1913, p.2, https://trove.nla.gov.au/newspaper/article/180175471

A written return for NSW, 18 October 1863 - 18 October 1864, re: the number of highway robberies and other robberies under arms reported to the police of the colony, *Justice & Police Museum*, Sydney.

Background Map, 1840's-1880's boundaries, County: Inverness-shire Parish: Kilmuir, 'Reproduced with the permission of the National Library of Scotland', https://maps.nls.uk/geo/boundaries

Bagnall, K., 2011, 'Rewriting the history of Chinese families in nineteenth-century Australia', *Australian Historical Studies*, vol.42, iss.1, pp.62-77,

Bagnall, K., 9 August 2016, 'From Canton to the Colonies: Chinese Women in 19th Century NSW', Speaker Connect Program, *History Council NSW*.

Baker, D.W.A., 2006, 'Lang, John Dunmore (1799-1878)', *Australian Dictionary of Biography*, https://adb.anu.edu.au

'Bank of Australia', *The Sydney Morning Herald (NSW: 1842-1954)*, 8 September 1843, p.3, https://trove.nla.gov.au/newspaper/article/12422216

Bank of Australia, 1848, *Schedule of the lots in the plan of partition of the Bank of Australia: the drawing to commence on Monday, January 1st, 1849* [Sydney, s.n.] http://nla.gov.au/nla.obj-278367156

'Bank of Australia Lottery [?]', *The Argus (Melbourne, Vic: 1848-1957)*, 23 January 1849, p.2, https://trove.nla.gov.au/newspaper/article/4764747

'Bank of Australia Result of the Drawing of the Lots', *The Sydney Morning Herald (NSW: 1842-1954)*, 6 January 1849, p.3, https://trove.nla.gov.au/newspaper/page/1514620

'Bank of Australia Result of the Drawing of the Lots', *The Sydney Morning Herald (NSW: 1842-1954)*, 7 January 1849, p.3, https://trove.nla.gov.au/newspaper/page/1514624

Bard, K., 1983, p.71 cited in Gifford, M., 2020, 'Vaudeville: The Last Theatre of the Working Class', *The University of NSW*, PhD Thesis.

Bassin, E., 1977, '*The Old Songs of Skye: Frances Tolmie and her Circle*' edited by Derek Bowman, Routledge and Kegan Paul.

'Bathurst Free Press-*Magna est veritas et prvalebt*', 20 February 1891, *Bathurst Free Press and Mining Journal (NSW: 1851-1904)*, p.2, https://trove.nla.gov.au/newspaper/article/64219195

Bell, R.,1973, *Mateship in Australia: Some Implications for Female-male Relationships*, La Trobe University Bundoora, Victoria.

Bennett, G., 1964, 'The Earliest Inhabitants: Aboriginal Tribes of Dungog, Port Stephens and Gresford', *Chronicle Print*, Dungog, http://wonnarua.org.au

Blackadder, J., 1800, 'Survey and Valuation of Lord MacDonald's Estate 1800', *Macdonald Estate Papers* DDBM/27/3 [from Transcript copy held at the Museum of the Isles Library at Clan Donald Centre, Armadale Castle, Skye].

Blackadder, J., 1811, 'Report Relating to the Value and Division of Lord MacDonald's Estate in Skye 24 December 1811', *Macdonald Estate Papers* NRAS3273/5912 [from original copy held at the Museum of the Isles Library at Clan Donald Centre, Armadale Castle, Skye].

'Black Tommy', *Glen Innes Examiner and General Advertiser (NSW: 1874 - 1908),* 10 April 1878, p.2, https://trove.nla.gov.au/newspaper/article/ 217825986

Boom, K., Ben-Ami, D., Croft, D., Cushing, N., Ramp, D. and Boronyak, L., January 2012, ''Pest' and Resource: A legal History of Australia's Kangaroos', *Animal Studies Journal*, vol.1, iss.1.

'Boundaries of the Hunter Valley Aboriginal People', 2021, *Wonnarua Aboriginal Corporation.*

'Bounty Immigrants', *The Sydney Herald (NSW: 1831-1842),* 3 February 1842, p.2, https://trove.nla.gov.au/newspaper/article/12873535

"Braemar", 1939, Australia's First Gaelic Church Service-Link with the Hunter Valley, *Newcastle Morning Herald & Miners Advocate*, 18 February 1939, p.12, https://trove.nla.gov.au/newspaper/article/135480605

Brissette, A., 2022, Microhistory: Looking at History under a Microscope, *University of New Mexico.*

Brown, N., 2024, 'History of NSW', *Britannica [online].*

Bubacz, B., 2007, 'The Female and Male Orphan Schools in New South Wales 1801-1850', PhD Thesis *University of Sydney*.

Buchanan, J. L., 1793, *Travels in the Western Hebrides: From 1782-1790*, Printed for G.G.J. and J. Robinson, Pater Noster-Row; and J. Debrett, opposite to Burlington House, Piccadilly, London.

'Bushrangers' Act', *The Sydney Monitor (NSW: 1828-1838)*, 21 June 1834, p.2, https://trove.nla.gov.au/newspaper/article/3214655.

'Bushrangers of NSW', 2021, [online] NSW *State Library*, Sydney.

'Bushranging on the Williams', *Sydney Herald (NSW: 1831 - 1842)*, 10 December 1840, p.2, https://trove.nla.gov.au/newspaper/rendition/nla.news-article12866974

Butlin, S.J., 1968, *Foundations of the Australian Monetary System: 1788–1851*. Sydney: Sydney University Press.

Byron, J., 1883-4, New South Wales Census of 1881, Presented to Parliament, pursuant to Act 44 vic. No.2, sec.11, Sydney: Thomas Richards, Government Printer.

Callanan, J., 2019, Giving Birth in the Bush: Colonial Women of Victoria and the Challenges of Childbirth, 1850-1880, *Provenance: The Journal of Public Record Office Victoria*, Iss.17, https://prov.vic.gov.au

Cameron Family Index, PEI Family Lineages, *Island Register*, 2021, https://www.islandregister.com/cameron.html.

Campbell, Donald Roderick (Rory), 'An Episode of the Ship Midlothian', *The Clarence and Richmond Examiner and New England Advertiser*, (Grafton, NSW: 1859-1889), 27 September 1879, p.3 https://trove.nla.gov.au/newspaper/article/62087602

Case, L., 'Fusing traditional culture and the violin: how Aboriginal musicians enhanced and maintained community in 20th century Australia', 27 July 2023, *The Conversation*, https://theconversation.com

Castle Moil, 2016, CastlesFortsBattles, United Kingdom.

Catherine Ballard, 16 May 1904, Certified copy of NSW Death Certificate, Registration No.5307/1904, *NSW Registry of Births, Deaths and Marriages*, Sydney, Australia.

Catherine Ballard, 1913, NSW Electoral Rolls, 1903-1980, *Ancestry.com*

Catherine (Mary) Ballard, 1890, 'The NSW Pioneers Index: Federation Series 1889-1918', Australian Birth Index, Reg No.17115, *Ancestry.com*

Catherine's Ballard Family, n.d., *Angus McDonalds Genealogy Pages*, http://www.members.iinet.net.au

Catherine MacDonald, 23 June 1853, Certified copy of NSW Marriage Certificate, no.123, vol.81, 1853, *NSW Registry of Births, Deaths & Marriages*, Sydney, Australia.

Catherine Matheson, 1851, Kilmuir, Inverness, Ref: Census 112/7/12, Scotland's People, *National Records of Scotland.*

Catherine McDonald, 1837, Midlothian, Assisted Immigrant Passenger Lists, NSWSA: NRS 5313/4_4780/Midlothian_12 Dec 1837, *NSW State Archives*, Sydney.

Catherine McKinnon, 1837, Midlothian, Assisted Immigrant Passenger Lists, NSWSA: NRS 5313/4_4780/Midlothian_12 Dec 1837, *NSW State Archives*, Sydney.

Catherine McKinnon's Family, n.d., *Angus McDonalds Genealogy Pages*, http://www.members.iinet.net.au

Catherine Munro, 27 August 1917, Tenterfield Cemetery, Tenterfield Shire, *Find a Grave*, https://www.findagrave.com/memorial/215920453

Catherine Munro, 27 August 1917, Certified copy of NSW Death Certificate, Registration No.403/1917, *NSW Registry of Births, Deaths and Marriages*, Sydney, Australia.

'1828 Census', p.510, [online] *NSW State Archives & Records*, Sydney.

'Census Returns', 2023, Scotland's People, *National Records of Scotland*.

Chappell, E., 21 August 2019, 'Postmistress dedicated to serving her community', History Matters, *Glen Innes Examiner*, https://www.gleninnesexaminer.com.au/story/6336413

Chappell, E., 14 September 2021, 'First Banks to Open in Glen Innes', History Matters, *Glen Innes Examiner*, https://www.gleninnesexaminer.com.au/story/7427671

Charles MacKinnon, 1864, Statutory Registers Deaths, 112/1 30, Kilmuir (Inverness), p.10, Scotland's People, *National Records of Scotland*.

Charles McKinnon, 1841, Kilmuir, Inverness, Ref: Census 112/7/3, Scotland's People, *National Records of Scotland*.

Charles McKinnon, 1851, Kilmuir, Inverness, Ref: Census 112/7/9, Scotland's People, *National Records of Scotland*.

'Chinese Coolies', *The People's Advocate and New South Wales Vindicator (NSW: 1848-1856)*, 3 March 1849, p.6, https://trove.nla.gov.au/newspaper/page/27923043

'Chinese Immigration', *The Maitland Mercury and Hunter General advertiser (NSW: 1843-1893)*, 29th November, 1851, p.2, https://trove.nla.gov.au/newspaper/article/677362

'Chinese Immigration', *The Sydney Morning Herald (NSW: 1842-1954)*, 27 March 1852, p.2, https://trove.nla.gov.au/newspaper/article/12935434

'Chinese Immigration', *Empire (Sydney, NSW:1850-1875)*, 10 July 1858, p.4, https://trove.nla.gov.au/newspaper/article/60423526

'Chinese Immigration Act', *The Maitland Mercury and Hunter General advertiser (NSW: 1843-1893)*, 28 November 1861, p.2, https://trove.nla.gov.au/newspaper/article/18685277

'*Chinese Immigrants Regulation and Restriction Act 1861 No28a*', 22 November 1861, UTS and UNSW Faculties of Law, *Australasian Legal Information Institute (AustLII)*.

'Chinese on the Goldfields', 2023, *Sydney Living Museums*.

Christina McKinnon, 24 July 1873, Certified copy of NSW Death Certificate, Registration No. 4389/1873, Grafton, NSW, *NSW Registry of Births, Deaths and Marriages*, Sydney, Australia.

Christy Cameron, 12 March 1828, Old Parish Registers Marriages, Ref. no. 117/ 10 107, Snizort, p.107, Scotland's People, *National Records of Scotland*.

'Church of Scotland', 2022, *Wikipedia*.

'Church Registers', 2022, Scotland's People, *National Records of Scotland*.

'Claims to Leases of Crown Lands', *The Maitland Mercury and Hunter River General Advertiser (NSW: 1843-1893)*, 26 August 1848, p.4, https://trove.nla.gov.au/newspaper/article/709756

'Claims to Leases of Crown Lands Beyond the Settled District', *The Maitland Mercury and Hunter River General Advertiser (NSW: 1843 - 1893)*, 30 September 1848, p.2, https://trove.nla.gov.au/newspaper/article/ 708877/125742

'*Clandestine Marriages Act 1836No10a*', 5 August 1836, UTS and UNSW Faculties of Law, *Australasian Legal Information Institute (AustLII)*.

Clark, A., 2022, *Making Australian History*, Vintage, Australia

Clarkson, C., Jacobs, Z., Marwick, B., 2017, 'Human Occupation of Northern Australia by 65,000 Years Ago', *Nature*, 547, pp.306-310.

'Classified Advertising', *The Sydney Gazette and New South Wales Advertiser (NSW: 1803-1842)*, 9 January 1830, p.1, https://trove.nla.gov.au/ newspaper/article/2194262

268

'Classified Advertising', *The Maitland Mercury and Hunter River General Advertiser (NSW: 1843 - 1893)*, 17 April 1852, p.1, https://trove.nla.gov.au/newspaper/article/671033

'Classified Advertising', *The Maitland Mercury and Hunter River General Advertiser (NSW: 1843-1893)*, 14 January 1854, p.3, https://trove.nla.gov.au/newspaper/article/678675

'Classified Advertising', *The Maitland Mercury and Hunter River General Advertiser (NSW: 1843-1893)*, 15 March 1854, p.3, https://trove.nla.gov.au/newspaper/article/686799

'Clearing off the Aborigines', *Glen Innes Examiner and General Advertiser (NSW: 1874-1908)*, 16 June 1885, p.3, https://trove.nla.gov.au/newspaper/article/217770797

'Colonial Politics', *The Colonial Observer (Sydney, NSW: 1841-1844)*, 9 December 1841, p.1, https://trove.nla.gov.au/newspaper/article/226360418

'Colonial Secretary's Office', *New South Wales Government Gazette (Sydney, NSW: 1832 - 1900)*, 20 September 1837 (No.294), p. 652, https://trove.nla.gov.au/newspaper/rendition/nla.news-article230670651.3

Colonial Secretary Town Purchases, 1855 7/650, 16 April 1855, NSW Land Grants, *State Records Authority of NSW*, Reel 1772, Series 1216.

'Compulsory Education', *The Newcastle Chronicle (NSW:1866-1876)*, 11 December 1869, p.2, https://trove.nla.gov.au/newspaper/article/111159019

'Conditional Purchase of Crown Land Guide', 2023, [online] *NSW State Archives & Records*, Sydney.

'Conflicts with the Natives', *Wingham Chronicle and Manning River Observer (NSW: 1898 - 1954)*, 25 April 1922, p.2, https://trove.nla.gov.au/newspaper/article/166220492

'Confirmation of Parish Roads', *New South Wales Government Gazette, (Sydney, NSW:1832-1900)*, 11 March 1890, iss. no.136, p.2058, https://trove.nla.gov.au/newspaper/article/222113268

'Convicts Guide', 2024, [online] *NSW State Archives and Records*, Sydney.

'Cook to the Officer in Command Maitland Police', 29 January 1836, Dungog Magistrates Letterbook, *Trove*, https://nla.gov.au/nla.obj-232856734

'Cook to Thomson', 14 December 1837, Dungog Magistrates Letter Book, *Trove*, https://nla.gov.au/nla.obj-232787744

Cornish, Kate McKinnon, 1903-1904, Australia Electoral Rolls 1903-1980, Red Range, Gough, Glen Innes Division, p.13, no.801, *Ancestry.com*

Cornish, Kate McKinnon, 1930, Australia Electoral Rolls 1903-1980, Red Range, New England, Glen Innes South, p.13, no.703, *Ancestry.com*

Cornish, Kate McKinnon, 1934, Australia Electoral Rolls 1903-1980, Red Range, New England, Glen Innes South, p.4, no.204, *Ancestry.com*

Cornish, Kate McKinnon, 1936, Australia Electoral Rolls 1903-1980, Red Range, New England, Glen Innes South, p.5, no.224, *Ancestry.com*

Correspondence from The Honourable Colonial Secretary to the Immigration Office, Sydney, 8 February 1838, Re: Settlement of Highland Immigrants, *NSW State Archives & Records*, Sydney.

Correspondence to the Board of the Orphan Schools, December 1837, re: 'Applicants to the Orphan School per the Midlothian Immigrants', Colonial Secretary's Correspondence, 1826-1894, *NSW State Archives & Records*, Sydney.

'Cricket', *Glen Innes Examiner and General Advertiser (NSW: 1874 - 1908)*, 26 April 1898, p.2, https://trove.nla.gov.au/newspaper/rendition/nla.news-article217880954

'Crimes Act of 1900 (NSW) – sect82', 2023, UTS and UNSW Faculties of Law, *Australasian Legal Information Institute (AustLII)*.

'Criminal Sittings', *Australasian Chronicle (Sydney, NSW: 1839-1843)*, 25 February 1841, p.2, https://trove.nla.gov.au/newspaper/article/31730988

'C Riding, Shire Council', *Glen Innes Examiner and General Advertiser (NSW: 1874-1908)*, 30 October 1906, p.6, https://trove.nla.gov.au/newspaper/article/217796628

'Crown Lands', *The Sydney Herald (NSW:1831-1842)*, 7 November 1838, p.2, https://trove.nla.gov.au/newspaper/article/12861179

'*Crown Lands Alienation Act 1861 No26a*', 18 October 1861, UTS and UNSW Faculties of Law, *Australasian Legal Information Institute (AustLII)*.

'*Crown Lands Occupation Act 1861 No27a*', 18 October 1861, UTS and UNSW Faculties of Law, *Australasian Legal Information Institute (AustLII)*.

'Crown Land Sale', *Glen Innes Examiner and General Advertiser (NSW: 1874-1908)*, 26 April 1901, p.2, https://trove.nla.gov.au/newspaper/article/217865922

'Crumbs', *Glen Innes Examiner and General Advertiser (NSW: 1874 - 1908)*, 8 January 1897, p.3, https://trove.nla.gov.au/newspaper/article/217922589

'Crumbs', *Glen Innes Examiner and General Advertiser (NSW: 1874-1908)*, 8 September 1903, p.2, https://trove.nla.gov.au/newspaper/article/217889350

Cunningham, P.M., 1827, Two Years in New South Wales: A series of letters, comprising sketches of the actual state of society in that colony, of its peculiar advantages to emigrants, of its topography, natural history, vol.2, Henry Colburn, London.

'Currency Crises', 2023, Online Exhibitions, *Reserve Bank of Australia Museum*.

Cyrus Ballard, 1897-1907, School Teachers Rolls 1869-1908, No. INX-73-406, Series: NRS 4073, p.1082 & 1090, Reel No. 1991, Roll 1, Index 73, *NSW State Archives and Records,* Sydney.

Cyrus Ballard, 31 March 1901, NSW Census, Ben Lomond, Inverell, NSW, Australia, *Ancestry.com*

Cyrus Ballard, 1903-1904 Electoral Roll, Red Range, Kookabookra, Gough, NSW, Australia, *Ancestry.com*

Cyrus Ballard, 1934, *Australia, Electoral Rolls 1903-1980,* Mooloolah, Landsborough, Wide Bay, Queensland, Australia, *Ancestry.com*

Cyrus EDA McDonald, 1882, Glen Innes, NSW, Reg16056, Australia, Birth Index, 1788-1922, *Ancestry.com*

Cyrus V Ballard, 14 February 2012, Glen Innes Cemetery, Glen Innes Severn Council, NSW, Australia, *Find a Grave,* https://www.findagrave.com/memorial/84960748

'*Dairies Supervision Act (1886 No22a)*', 2023, UTS and UNSW Faculties of Law, *Australasian Legal Information Institute (AustLII)*.

David Ballard, 1886, Teachers' Rolls, 1869-1908, No. INX-73-407, Series NRS 4073, p.624, Reel No.1993, Roll 4, Index 73, *NSW State Archives and Records,* Sydney.

David Ballard, 1888, No.5644, Inverell, Australia, *Marriage Index, 1788-1950, Ancestry.com*

David Ballard, 31 March 1901, NSW Census, Tenterfield, Clive, NSW, Australia, *Ancestry.com*

David Ballard, 1921, 'New South Wales Public Service Lists (Blue Books)', *State Records Authority of NSW, Sydney.*

David James McDonald, 11 May 1882, Certified copy of NSW Death Certificate, Registration No. 7890/1882, *NSW Registry of Births, Deaths and Marriages*, Sydney, Australia.

Davidson, B.R., 'The Development of the Pastoralist Industry during the Nineteenth Century in Australia', in Chang, C. & Koster H.A., (eds), 1994, *Pastoralists at the Periphery*, The University of Arizona Press, Tucson.

Dayton, L., 5 September 2022, 'Chlorodyne: The Quadruple Threat', *Australian Pharmacist*.

'Death by Drowning', *Glen Innes Examiner and General Advertiser (NSW: 1874 - 1908)*, 18 May 1886, p.2, https://trove.nla.gov.au/newspaper/article/217876781

'Death of an Old Resident', *Glen Innes Examiner and General Advertiser, (NSW: 1874-1908)*, 7 February 1899, p.2, https://trove.nla.gov.au/newspaper/page/23892194

'Death of a Pioneer', *Dungog Chronicle: Durham and Gloucester Advertiser (NSW: 1894-1954)*, 27 February 1912, p.2, https://trove.nla.gov.au/newspaper/article/136135473

'Death of Dr Lang', *Glen Innes Examiner and General Advertiser, (NSW: 1874-1908)*, 14 August 1878, p.2, https://trove.nla.gov.au/newspaper/article/217825439

'Death of Mr T. G. Hewitt', Northern Star (Lismore, NSW :1876-1954), 28 January 1915, p.2, https://trove.nla.gov.au/newspaper/article/72108102

'Death of Mr Thomas Ballard', *Glen Innes Examiner and General Advertiser (NSW: 1874-1908)*, 23 February 1904, p.2, https://trove.nla.gov.au/newspaper/article/217899264

'Death of Thunderbolt – Additional Particulars', *The Goulburn Herald and Chronicle (NSW:1864-1881)*, 4 June 1870, p.2, https://trove.nla.gov.au/newspaper/article/101470682

'Deaths', John McDonald, *Dungog Chronicle: Durham and Gloucester Advertiser (NSW: 1894-1954)*, 16 January 1920, p.2, https://trove.nla.gov.au/newspaper/article/137996687

'Deaths', *The Sydney Morning Herald*, 9 June 1937, p.14, https://trove.nla.gov.au/newspaper/page/1133989

'Deaths', *Sydney Morning Herald*, 19 March 1953, p.14, https://trove.nla.gov.au/newspaper

'Debate at Red Range', *Glen Innes Examiner (NSW: 1908 - 1954)*, 28 September 1909, p. 2, https://trove.nla.gov.au/newspaper/rendition/nla.news-article180118568.3

de Looper, M., 2015, *Death Registration and Mortality in Australia 1856-1906*, PHD thesis, The Australian National University, Canberra.

Denham Pinnock, J., 1838, 'Remarks on the passengers on the Midlothian to the Immigration Office', Evelyn Smith researcher, *State Records Authority of NSW*, Sydney.

Denham Pinnock, J., 'Report from J Denham Pinnock, Esquire, Colonial Agent for Immigration, to His Excellency Governor Sir George Gipps, on the Progress of Immigration Generally', *The Sydney Monitor and Commercial Advertiser (NSW: 1838-1841)*, 3 July 1839, p.2, https://trove.nla.gov.au/newspaper/article/32164730

'Department of Lands/164955', n.d., Research Data Australia, *NSW State Records Authority, Sydney*.

'Department of Lands, Sydney, 11/03/1890', *New South Wales Government Gazette (Sydney, NSW: 1832-1900)*, 11 March 1890, iss. 136, p.2060, https://trove.nla.gov.au/newspaper/article/222113266

'Department of Lands, Sydney, 25/07/1893', *New South Wales Government Gazette (Sydney, NSW: 1832-1900)*, 25 July 1893, iss. 528, p.5848, https://trove.nla.gov.au/newspaper/page/13187089

Descendants of Edward Ballard, n.d., *Angus McDonalds Genealogy Pages*, http://www.members.iinet.net.au

Dettre, M., 23 August 2022, 'How 24 Rabbits Took Over Australia: DNA Confirms Invasion's Origins', *Sydney Morning Herald*, https://www.smh.com.au/national/how-24-rabbits-took-over-australia-dna-study-confirms-what-caused-invasion-20220823

'Documenting a Democracy', 2011, *Museum of Australian Democracy*, https://www.foundingdocs.gov.au

'Domestic Intelligence', *The Sydney Times (NSW:1834-1838)*, 13 January 1838, p.2, https://trove.nla.gov.au/newspaper/article/252637160

'Domestic Intelligence', *The Colonist (Sydney, NSW: 1835-1840)*, 7 March 1838, p.2, https://trove.nla.gov.au/newspaper/article/31720553

'Domestic Intelligence', *The Sydney Gazette and New South Wales Advertiser (NSW: 1803-1842)*, 24 November 1838, p.2, https://trove.nla.gov.au/newspaper/article/2541796

'Domestic Intelligence', *The Sydney Morning Herald (NSW:1842-1954)*, 26 April 1844, p.2, https://trove.nla.gov.au/newspaper/article/12425539

Donald, J.K., 1987, *Exploring the North Coast and New England*, Kangaroo Press, Kenthurst, NSW.

Donald Macleod, 1891, Kilmuir, Inverness, Ref: Census 112/1 7/7, Scotland's People, *National Records of Scotland*.

Donald Munro, 1865, Death Index 1836-1988, *The Victorian Registry of Births, Deaths and Marriages*, Melbourne, Victoria, *Ancestry.com*

Dorcas Ross, 1851, Kilmuir, Inverness, Ref: Census 112/7/13, Scotland's People, *National Records of Scotland*.

Dorcas Gormhail Ross, 18 June 1855(a), Statutory Register of Deaths, 112/1/ 23, Kilmuir, Inverness, Scotland's People, *National Records of Scotland*.

Dorcas Gormhail Ross, 18 June 1855(b), Statutory Register, Births, 112/ 1 /27, Kilmuir Inverness, Scotland's People, *National Records of Scotland*.

Dorcas Gormhail Ross, 24 October 1859, Statutory Register, Deaths, 112/ 1/ 29, Kilmuir Inverness, Scotland's People, *National Records of Scotland.*

Doukakis, A., 2006, The Aboriginal People, Parliament and "Protection" in New South Wales, 1856-1916, The Federation Press, Sydney.

Doyle, S., 2006, *Common Pleasures: Low Culture in Sydney 1887-1914*, PhD Thesis, University of Technology Sydney.

'Dreadful Coach Accident', Sydney, January 8', *South Australian Register*, [By Telegraph], Special Telegrams, 9 Jan 1884, p.5, https://trove.nla.gov.au/ newspaper/title/41

'Dreadful Coach Mishap', *Australian Town and Country Journal (Sydney, NSW: 1870 - 1919)*, 12 January 1884, p.11, https://trove.nla.gov.au/ newspaper/rendition/nla.news-article71007425.3

'Dr Lang's Immigration Lecture', *The Maitland Mercury and Hunter River General Advertiser, (NSW: 1843-1893)*, 9 November 1850, p.2, https://trove.nla.gov.au/newspaper/article/688459

'Dr Lang on Squatting', *The People's Advocate and New South Wales Vindicator (Sydney, NSW:1848-1856)*, 13 January 1849, p.5, https://trove.nla.gov.au/newspaper/article/251538134

Dunakin/ Casteal Maol, *Clan McKinnon Society*, 2021, https://www.themackinnon.com/ancientseats.html

Dunbavin, P., 1998, *Picts and Ancient Britons: An exploration of Pictish Origins*, Third Millenium Publishing, London.

'Dungog and Round About', *Dungog Chronicle: Durham and Gloucester Advertiser (NSW: 1894-1954)*, 17 May 1910, p.3, https://trove.nla.gov.au/ newspaper/article/137993575.3

'Dungog', *The Maitland Mercury and Hunter River General Advertiser, (NSW: 1843-1893)*, 31 January 1849, p. 2, https://trove.nla.gov.au/ newspaper/article/705950

'Dungog', *The Maitland Mercury and Hunter River General Advertiser,* (*NSW: 1843-1893*), 24 June 1876, p.7, https://trove.nla.gov.au/newspaper/article/18808022

'Dungog', *The Maitland Mercury and Hunter River General Advertiser,* (*NSW: 1843-1893*), 7 December 1878, p.16, https://trove.nla.gov.au/newspaper/article/18825153

'Dungog, NSW', 2020, *Aussie Towns.*

Dunmore House, 2018, NSW State Heritage Register, *Office of Environment & Heritage HO1887.*

Dunmore Lang College, 2023, https://www.dunmorelangcollege.nsw.edu.au

Dunmore Lang, J., 'The Dunmore Highlanders', *The Sydney Herald (NSW: 1831-1842),* 7 September 1841, p.2, https://trove.nla.gov.au/newspaper/article/12871006

Dunmore Lang, J., Private letter to Bowie, J., 'Condition of a Cluster of Highland Emigrants in New South Wales', in *The Sydney Herald,* 1 March 1842, p.4, https://trove.nla.gov.au/newspaper/article/12873944

Dunn, M., May 2021, *Benjamin Boyd's Role in 19th Century Blackbirding in the Pacific for Labour in New South Wales: Historical Analysis and Evaluation Report,* NSW National Parks and Wildlife Service.

'Early Dungog 1868', *Dungog Chronicle: Durham and Gloucester Advertiser (NSW: 1894-1954*), 10 July 1923, p.2, https://trove.nla.gov.au/newspaper/page/15598156

'Early European Settlement in New England', 2018, https://gardenhistorysociety.org.au

'Editorial', *The Sydney Herald (NSW: 1831-1842),* 14 September 1838, p. 2, https://trove.nla.gov.au/newspaper/article/28653472

'Editorial', *The Newcastle Chronicle (NSW: 1866-1876)*, 16 October 1869, p.2, https://trove.nla.gov.au/newspaper/article/111156822

'Education', *The Sydney Morning Herald (NSW:1842-1954)*, 16 September 1881, p.8, https://trove.nla.gov.au/newspaper/article/13524949

Edward Ballard, 1838, Woodbridge, *NSW Assisted Immigrants (digital) Shipping Lists*, RS5313/4_4780/Woodbridge_15 Sep 1838, p.2, http://indexes.records.nsw.gov.au

'*Electoral Act of 1880 No 34a*', 1880, UTS and UNSW Faculties of Law, *Australasian Legal Information Institute (AustLII)*.

'Electoral Milestones for Indigenous Australians', *Australian Electoral Commission*, 12 November 2020.

Elsie B M Cornish, 1883, Macleay River, NSW, no.21868, Australia Birth Index 1788-1922, *Ancestry.com*

Emma Ballard, 1878, Certified copy of NSW Marriage Certificate No.3567, 1878, *NSW Registry of Births, Deaths & Marriages*, Sydney, Australia.

'Emigration – New South Wales', *The Inverness Courier and General Advertiser*, 14 July 1838, p.2.

Emily Weller McDonald, 17 February 2012, Red Range Cemetery, Glen Innes Severn Shire Council, NSW, Australia, *Find A Grave*, https://www.findagrave.com/memorial/85096309

'Evidence on Immigration', *The Sydney Morning Herald (NSW:1842-1954)*, 5 March 1844, p.2, https://trove.nla.gov.au/newspaper/article/12418361

Ewen Alexander Ballard, 13 December 2016, Red Range Cemetery, Glen Innes Severn Council, NSW, Australia, *Find a Grave*, https://www.findagrave.com/memorial/173826608

Ewen Cameron, 16 November 1824, Old Parish Registers Marriages, Ref. no. 117/ 10 102, Snizort, p.102, Scotland's People, *National Records of Scotland*.

Ewen Mackinnon, 1861, Statutory Registers Deaths, 112/1 3 Kilmuir (Inverness), p.1, Scotland's People, *National Records of Scotland*.

Ewen McKinnon, 1841, Kilmuir, Inverness, Ref: Census 112/7/1, Scotland's People, *National Records of Scotland*.

'Equal Suffrage', *Glen Innes Examiner and General Advertiser (NSW: 1874 - 1908)*, 28 August 1903, p.2, https://trove.nla.gov.au/newspaper/article/217887031

'Extracts from letters transmitted by Clergymen, Magistrates and others, relative to the present destitution in the Highlands and Islands of Scotland', 1837, Papers of the MacKenzie Family, Earls of Seaforth, Reference: GD 46/13/199/8, *National Records of Scotland,* http://catalogue.nrscotland.gov.uk

Eyre-Todd, G., 1923, *The Highland Clans of Scotland: Their history and traditions*, Appleton, New York.

'Family History', 2000-2012, *Australian Postal History and Philately*, http://www.auspostalhistory.com

'Family Notices', *Glen Innes Examiner and General Advertiser (NSW: 1874 - 1908)*, 1 March 1881, p.2, https://trove.nla.gov.au/newspaper/article/217833068

'Farewell to Mr. Allan Ballard', *Glen Innes Examiner (NSW: 1908 - 1954)*, 15 May 1911, p.2, https://trove.nla.gov.au/newspaper/rendition/nla.news-article180148414

'Fatal Accident', *The Maitland Mercury and Hunter River General Advertiser, (NSW: 1843-1893)*, 7 Apr 1849. p. 2, https://trove.nla.gov.au/ newspaper/page/125989

'*Felons Apprehension Act 1865 No11*', 8 April 1865, UTS and UNSW Faculties of Law, *Australasian Legal Information Institute (AustLII)*.

'Female Franchise', *Glen Innes Examiner and General Advertiser (NSW: 1874 - 1908)*, 20 August 1901, p.2, https://trove.nla.gov.au/newspaper/article/217869362

'Female Orphan School', 2017, *Western Sydney University*, https://www.westernsydney.edu

'Female Vote', *Glen Innes Examiner and General Advertiser, (NSW: 1874-1908)*4 November 1902, p.2, https://trove.nla.gov.au/newspaper/article/217924760

Feng, J., Anti-Chinese Prejudice in Australia 1850-1919: Content Analysis of Newspaper Articles, 2017, *Middle States Geographer*, 50: p.1-6.

Finding your Family, 2024, *The Hebrides People Genealogical Database.*

Fitz-Gibbon, B. & Gizycki, M., October 2001, A History of Last Resort Lending and other Support for Troubled Financial Institutions in Australia, *Reserve Bank of Australia*, https://rba.gov.au

Fitzmaurice, A., 2007, 'The Genealogy of Terra Nullius', *Australian Historical Studies*, vol.38, iss.129, p.14.

Fletcher, B., 25 May 2001, 'Man of the People', [A speech delivered at the naming ceremony for the Parkes Room], *NSW Parliament House*, https://parkesfoundation.org.au

Flora MacKinnon, 1870, Statutory Registers Deaths, 112/1 1 Kilmuir (Inverness), p.1, Scotland's People, *National Records of Scotland.*

Flora McKinnon, 1861, Kilmuir, Inverness, Ref: Census 112/1 6/10, Scotland's People, *National Records of Scotland.*

Flora Sherwood, n.d., *Find a Grave*, Lawrence, Clarence Valley Council, NSW, https://www.findagrave.com/memorial/1822677622

'Forenames', 2021, Scotland's People, *National Records of Scotland.*

Foster, A.P., 'Our Earliest Lottery', 21 November 1979, *Dungog Chronicle.*

Freyne, C., 2010, 'The School of Arts Movement', The Dictionary of Sydney, *NSW State Library*, https://dictionaryofsydney.org

'From a Lady Correspondent in Sydney', *Goulburn Herald (NSW: 1881-1907)*, 7 December 1889, p.3, https://trove.nla.gov.au/newspaper/article/100118132

Frost, L.,1984, *'No Place for a Nervous Lady: Voices from the Australian Bush'*, Penguin, Australia.

Gallacher, L., Jokiranta, M. and Marie, S., 'The History Listen', 4 November 2022, Australian Broadcasting Commission Radio National.

Gammage, B., 2011, *The Biggest Estate on Earth: How Aborigines made Australia*, Allen & Unwin, Sydney.

Gardner, W., 1854, Production and Resources of the Northern and Western Districts of New South Wales, vol.1, ref. 954586, *State Library of NSW*.

'General Intelligence', *Glen Innes Examiner and General Advertiser (NSW: 1874 - 1908)*, 10 October 1877, p.3, https://trove.nla.gov.au/newspaper/rendition/nla.news-article217809152.3

Generation No.1, n.d., *Angus McDonalds Genealogy Pages*, http://www.members.iinet.net.au

Generation No.2, n.d., *Angus McDonald's Genealogy Pages*, http://www.members.iinet.net.au

Generation No.3, n.d., *Angus McDonalds Genealogy Pages*, http://www.members.iinet.net.au

Gibson, R., 2020, *The Highland Clearances Trail*, Luath Press Ltd.

Gilpin, J., 'On the Wrong Track', *The Maitland Mercury and Hunter General advertiser (NSW: 1843-1893)*, 29 October 1889, p.3, https://trove.nla.gov.au/newspaper/article/18976935

Gittings, B.M., 2012, *The Gazetteer for Scotland*, https://www.scottish-places.info

'Glencoe v Red Range', *Glen Innes Examiner and General Advertiser (NSW: 1874 - 1908)*, 13 December 1881, p.2, https://trove.nla.gov.au/newspaper/article/217831669

'Glen Innes Land Board', *Glen Innes Examiner and General Advertiser (NSW: 1874 - 1908)*, 8 September 1885, p.2, https://trove.nla.gov.au/newspaper/article/217771528

'Glen Innes Municipal Council', *Glen Innes Examiner and General Advertiser (NSW: 1874 - 1908)*, 19 April 1901, p.2, https://trove.nla.gov.au/newspaper/article/217862910

'Glen Innes Municipal Council', *Glen Innes Examiner and General Advertiser (NSW: 1874 - 1908)*, 26 July 1901, p.2, https://trove.nla.gov.au/newspaper/article/217863792

'Glen Innes Protection Union', *Glen Innes Examiner and General Advertiser (NSW: 1874-1908)*, 28 August 1888, p.2, https://trove.nla.gov.au/newspaper/article/217773137

'Glen Innes Protection Union', *Glen Innes Examiner and General Advertiser (NSW: 1874-1908)*, 2 October 1888, p.2, https://trove.nla.gov.au/newspaper/article/217773249

Goodall, H., 2008, *Invasion to Embassy: Land in Aboriginal Politics in New South Wales, 1770-1972*, Sydney University Press, St Leonards NSW.

'Gossip', *The Australasian (Melbourne, Vic:1864-1946)*, 23 November 1889, p.42, https://trove.nla.gov.au/newspaper/article/139138370

'Government Gazette Notices', *NSW Government Gazette, Sydney (NSW: 1832-1900)*, 31 Oct 1879, iss. 390, p.4877, https://trove.nla.gov.au/newspaper/article/223123215

282

'Government Gazette Notices', *NSW Government Gazette, Sydney (NSW: 1832-1900)*, 24 January 1882, iss. 35, p.467, https://trove.nla.gov.au/newspaper/article/221701459

'Government Order', *The Sydney Gazette and New South Wales Advertiser (NSW: 1803-1842)*, 17 October 1829, p.1, https://trove.nla.gov.au/newspaper/article/2193642

'Government Order', *Sydney Morning Herald (NSW: 1831-1842)*, 8 August 1831, p.1, https://trove.nla.gov.au/newspaper/article/12843374

Governor Bourke's Proclamation 1835 (UK), *Museum of Australian Democracy*, https://www.foundingdocs.gov.au/item-did-42.html

'Grand Ethiopian Entertainment', *Glen Innes Examiner and General Advertiser (NSW: 1874-1908)*, 29 May 1888, p.4, https://trove.nla.gov.au/newspaper/page/23887008

'Grants of Land', *The Sydney Gazette and NSW Advertiser (NSW: 1803-1842)*, 24 December 1836, p.4, https://trove.nla.gov.au/newspaper/page/502986

Gregoire, P. & Nedim, U., 9 March 2021, 'Policing the Poor: The History of Vagrancy Laws and the Criminalisation of the Homeless', *Sydney Criminal Lawyers*, NSW Courts.

Grehan, M., 2009, '"A Most Difficult and Protracted Labour Case": Midwives, Medical Men and Coronial Investigations into Maternal Deaths in Nineteenth-Century Victoria, *Provenance: The Journal of Public Record Office Victoria*, iss.8.

Greig, A., 2023, *The Road to Batemans Bay: Speculating on the South Coast During the 1840s Depression*, ANU Press, Canberra.

'Gwydir Highway: History and Development', n.d., *National Route 38-Ozroads*, https://www.ozroads.com.au

Hansen, G., 10 May 2019, 'Australia for the White Man', *National Library of Australia*, https://www.nla.gov.au/stories/blog/exhibitions/2019/05/10

Hardy, K. & Wildgoose, M., 2019, *'Travelling Through Time: Archaeological Walks in Skye, Raasay and Lochalsh'*, Archaeologywalks, United Kingdom.

Herbert Ewen MacDonald, 1 September 1892, Certified copy of NSW Death Certificate, Registration No. 2308/1892, *NSW Registry of Births, Deaths and Marriages,* Sydney, Australia.

'Highland Clearances', 2018, *Crann Tara: Preserving and maintaining the culture, history, heritage and future of Scotland.*

'Highland Clearances', 2024, *Undiscovered Scotland.*

Hirsch, J., 2019, 'Wild Country: Australian Masculinity from the Frontier to the Social Front', Research Paper, *The University of Sydney.*

Historical Lands Record Viewer, 1893, Parish of Underbank, County of Glouchester, Severn Shire, Glen Innes, Historical Land Records, *NSW Land Registry Service.*

Historical Lands Record Viewer, 1958 (a), Parish of Mitchell, County of Gough, Severn Shire, Glen Innes, 6th edition, Historical Land Records, *NSW Land Registry Service.*

Historical Lands Record Viewer, 1958 (b), Parish of Rusden, County of Gough, Severn Shire, Glen Innes, 6th edition, Historical Land Records, *NSW Land Registry Service.*

Historic Britain, 2017, *'Singing for your Supper'*, https://blog.historicenvironment.scot/2017/05/scottish-work-songs.

History in the Williams River Valley, n.d., https://williamsvalleyhistory.org/historical-overview

'History of Clarence', *Daily Examiner (Grafton, NSW: 1915-1954)*, 13 January 1925, p.2, https://trove.nla.gov.au/newspaper/article/195365905

'History of Democracy in NSW', 2023, [online] *Parliament of NSW*.

'History of Scottish Surnames from the Isle of Skye', 14 January 2016, The Newsroom, *The Scotsman*, https://www.scotsman.com/whats-on/arts-and-entertainment/history-of-scottish-surnames-from-the-isle-of-skye-1485586

'Hospital Annual Meeting', *Glen Innes Examiner and General Advertiser (NSW: 1874-1908)*, 25 January 1895, p.3, https://trove.nla.gov.au/newspaper/article/217813173

Howell, M., Howell, R. & Brown, D., 1989, *The Sporting Image, A Pictorial History of Queenslanders at Play*, Brisbane: University of Queensland Press.

Hradsky, D., 9 July 2021, 'Invasion or Reconciliation: What matters in the Australian Curriculum', *Monash University*.

Hughes-de'Aeth, T., 15 June 2018, 'Friday Essay: Dark Emu and the Blindness of Australian Agriculture', *The Conversation*, https://theconversation.com/friday-essay-dark-emu-and-the-blindness-of-australian-agriculture-97444

'Hunter River District News', *The Maitland Mercury and Hunter General advertiser (NSW: 1843-1893)*, 21 November 1846, p.2, https://trove.nla.gov.au/newspaper/article/685749

Huntsman, L., 2002, Bounty Emigrants to Australia, *Clogher Record*, vol.17, no.3, pp.801-812, https://doi.org/10.2307/27699475

Hussain, A., 9 February 2023, *'The McKinnons of Kendram, Skye'*, Facebook Group, https://facebook.com.au

Iltis, J., 2006, 'Chisholm, Caroline (1808-1877)', *Australian Dictionary of Biography*, https://adb.anu.edu.au/biography/chisholm-caroline-1894

'Immigration', *The Australian (Sydney, NSW: 1824-1848)*, 4 July 1839, p.3, https://trove.nla.gov.au/newspaper/article/36859918

'Inquests and Inquiries', *Clarence and Richmond Examiner (Grafton, NSW: 1889-1915)*, 7 February 1893, p.4, https://trove.nla.gov.au/newspaper/article/61248949

'Insolvency Act 1841 No.17a', 29 December 1841, UTS and UNSW Faculties of Law, *Australasian Legal Information Institute (AustLII)*.

'Insolvency Proceedings', *The Sydney Morning Herald (NSW:1842-1954)*, 20 July 1843, p. 2, https://trove.nla.gov.au/newspaper/article/12420942

'Insolvency Proceedings', *The Maitland Mercury and Hunter River General Advertiser (NSW: 1843 - 1893)*, 7 August 1852, p.2, https://trove.nla.gov.au/newspaper/article/665235

Irby, E. & Irby, L., 1908, 'Memoirs of Edward and Leonard Irby, 1841', William Brooks and Co, Sydney, https://nla.gov.au/nla.obj-2604939357/view?partId=nla.obj-2604972588

'Iron Age Ruins of Dun Ringill', 2020, *Scotland.com*.

Isle of Skye, 2021, *Gazetteer of Scotland*, https://www.scottish-places.info

Isle of Skye, 6 Oct 2021, *Britannica [online]*.

'Isle of Skye', 2024, https://www.isleofskye.com

James Cornish, 2012, Glen Innes General Cemetery Memorials, New South Wales, *Find a Grave*, https://www.findagrave.com/cemetery/2437433

John MacLeod, 5 January 1883, Statutory Registers Deaths, 112/1/1 Kilmuir (Inverness), p.1, Scotland's People, *National Records of Scotland*.

John McDonald, 2020, Waverley Council, New South Wales, Plot W 21GESL 5538, *Find a Grave*, https://www.findagrave.com/memorial/218633307

John MacKinnon, 21 March 1839, 'Letter to the Colonial Secretary', Index to Colonial Secretary Letters Received, INX-106-40727, Citation [4/

2457.1], Letter No. 39/3359, Reel No. 2218, *NSW State Archives & Records*, Sydney.

John McKinnon, 1837, Midlothian, Assisted Immigrant Passenger Lists, NSWSA: NRS 5313/4_4780/Midlothian_12 Dec 1837, *NSW State Archives & Records*, Sydney.

John McKinnon, 9 January 1872, Certified copy of NSW Death Certificate, Registration No. 4162/1872, Grafton, *NSW Registry of Births, Deaths and Marriages*, Sydney, Australia.

John McMillan, 3 March 1896, NSW Death Registration Transcript, No. 1696/2614, Maclean, *NSW Registry of Births, Deaths and Marriages*, Sydney, Australia.

John Ross, 16 August 1863, 112/1/22, Kilmuir, (Inverness), Scotland's People, *National Records of Scotland,*

Johnson, S., 1773, Journey to the Western Isles, cited in Highland Clearances, *Crann Tara: Preserving and maintaining the culture, history, heritage and future of Scotland.*

Johnston, W & A.K., 1850, Johnston's Map of the Island of Skye, https://maps.nls.uk/counties/rec/7255

Jonathan Campbell, 4 March 1888, Statutory Registers Deaths, 112/1 7, Kilmuir (Inverness), p.3, Scotland's People, *National Records of Scotland.*

Jones, B.T., 1 March 2017, Currency Culture: Australian Identity and Nationalism in New South Wales Before the Gold Rushes, *Australian Historical Studies*, vol.48, iss.1, pp.68-85.

'Jottings by the Way-New England', *Australian Town and Country Journal (Sydney, NSW:1870-1919)*, 26 August 1871, p.18, https://trove.nla.gov.au/newspaper/page/4763308

'Journeys to Australia', 2024, *Immigration Museum*, https://museumsvictoria.com.au

Jowett, S., Carpenter, B. and Tait, G., 2018, 'Determining a Suicide Under Australian Law', *UNSW Law Journal*, vol.41, iss.2, pp.355-379.

Judah, B., 15 December 2015, 'The Highland Clearances and Land Reform in Scotland: The Country's Semi Feudal Great Estates Face Reform', *Independent*.

Justice Jagot, 20 October 2017, 'The Rule of Law and Reconciliation', *Federal Court of Australia*.

Karskens, G., March 1986, *Dungog Shire Heritage Study-Thematic History*, Dungog Shire Council - Heritage Council of NSW.

Karskens, G., 2009, *The Colony: A History of Early Sydney*, Allen & Unwin, Sydney, NSW.

Karskens, G., 2020, *People of the River*, Allen & Unwin, Sydney, NSW.

Kendram Rental Table, 1718-1823, *MacDonald Estate Papers*, Museum of the Isles Library, Clan Donald Centre, Armadale Castle, Isle of Skye.

Kendram Rental Table, 1823-1855, *MacDonald Estate Papers*, Museum of the Isles Library, Clan Donald Centre, Armadale Castle, Isle of Skye.

'Killing Cattle with Intent to Steal', *Glen Innes Examiner and General Advertiser, (NSW: 1874-1908)*, 29 October 1897, p.3, https://trove.nla.gov.au/newspaper/article/217919330

'Kilmuir Estate', 2015, *Christie and Ferguson Solicitors Records 1835-1952*, GB3219/Acc:230 Ref: D123, Skye & Lochalsh Archive Centre, Portree, Scotland.

'Kilmuir Estate Rental Book', 1875-1879, HRA/D123/9(b), p.140, *Christie and Ferguson Solicitors Records 1835-1952*, Skye and Lochalsh Archive Centre, Portree, Scotland.

'Kilvaxter Soutterain', 2024, *Undiscovered Scotland*.

Kingston, B., 'Women in Nineteenth Century Australian History', *Labour History*, No.67(Nov 1994), pp.84-96.

Knight, R.L., 2006, 'Boyd, Archibald (1801-1864)', Australian Dictionary of Biography, National Centre of Biography, Australian National University, https://adb.anu.edu.au/biography/boyd-archibald-1814

'Ladies Column', *Glen Innes Examiner and General Advertiser, (NSW: 1874-1908)*, 27 July 1900, p.2, https://trove.nla.gov.au/newspaper/article/217835038

Lake, M., 2020, *The Bible in Australia*, NewSouth Publishing, Sydney, Australia.

Lamb, P.N., 2015, 'Spread of Railways', *Royal Australian Historical Society*, https://www.rahs.org.au

'Lambing Flat', *The Sydney Morning Herald (NSW: 1842-1954)*, 18 December 1860, p.7, https://trove.nla.gov.au/newspaper/article/13050333

'Land Board' *Glen Innes Examiner and General Advertiser, (NSW 1874-1908)*, 22 March 1892, p.2, https://trove.nla.gov.au/newspaper/article/217777159

'Land of the Beardies', 2016-2021, https://www.beardieshistoryhouse.info/glen-innes

Lang, John Dunmore, 1834, *An Historical and Statistical Account of New South Wales, Both as a Penal Settlement and as a British Colony*, Cochrane & McCrone, London, vol.2.

Lang, John Dunmore, 1837, *An Historical and Statistical Account of New South Wales, Both as a Penal Settlement and as a British Colony*, AJ Valpy, London, vol.1, https://nla.gov.au/nla.cat-vn902574

Lang, John Dunmore, 1852, *The Australian Emigrants Manual, or a Guide to the Gold Colonies of New South Wales and Port Phillip*, Partridge and Oakley, Paternoster Row, London, https://nla.gov.au/nla.obj-501106160

Lang, John Dunmore, 1854, 1799-1878 & Lang Testimonial Fund, *Presentation of the testimonial to the Rev. Dr. Lang. s.n.,* Sydney, http://nla.gov.au/nla.obj-99614801

'Language and Culture', 2023, *Britannica [online].*

'Large Scale Emigration to Australia after 1832', 2023, *Electricscotland.*

'Latest News from the Barrington Diggings', *The Maitland Mercury and Hunter General advertiser (NSW: 1843-1893),* 18 July 1876, p.3, https://trove.nla.gov.au/newspaper/article/18808765

'Latest Telegrams', *The Maitland Mercury and Hunter General advertiser (NSW: 1843-1893),* 28 February 1878, p.5, https://trove.nla.gov.au/newspaper/article/18826998

'Law Intelligence', *The Sydney Herald (NSW: 1831-1842),* 1 July 1833, p.3, https://trove.nla.gov.au/newspaper/article/12847165

Lawrence, G., 10 August 2002, 'Laminaria tents', *The Lancet,* vol.360, iss.9331, p.497.

'Lawrence Head Master', Correspondence to 'The Under Secretary Department of Public Instruction, Sydney', 10 August 1885.

'Legislative Council', *The Sydney Morning Herald (NSW:1842-1954),* 24 December 1844, p.2, http://nla.gov.au/nla.news-article12419135

'Legislative Council', *The Sydney Morning Herald (NSW:1842-1954),* 2 October 1847, p.2, https://trove.nla.gov.au/newspaper/article/12896661

'Legislative Council', *The Sydney Morning Herald (NSW:1842-1954),* 15 December 1852, p.2, https://trove.nla.gov.au/newspaper/page/1506713

Lewis, M.J., 7 July 2014, 'Medicine in Colonial Australia, 1788-1900', *The Medical Journal of Australia,* vol.201, iss.1.

'Licencing Act of 1882 No 26a', 2023, UTS and UNSW Faculties of Law, *Australasian Legal Information Institute (AustLII).*

'Local & General Items', *Glen Innes Examiner and General Advertiser (NSW: 1874-1908)*, 26 May 1891, p.2, https://trove.nla.gov.au/newspaper/article/217808126

'Local & General News', *Glen Innes Examiner and General Advertiser (NSW: 1874-1908)*, 21 September 1886, p.2, https://trove.nla.gov.au/newspaper/article/217877627

'Local & General News', *Glen Innes Examiner and General Advertiser (NSW: 1874 - 1908)*, 19 April 1887, p.2, https://trove.nla.gov.au/newspaper/article/217818177

'Local & General News', *Glen Innes Examiner and General Advertiser (NSW: 1874 - 1908)*, 10 May 1887, p.2, https://trove.nla.gov.au/newspaper/article/217816709

'Local & General News', *Glen Innes Examiner and General Advertiser (NSW: 1874 - 1908)*, 9 August 1887, p.2, https://trove.nla.gov.au/newspaper/article/217816209

'Local & General News', *Glen Innes Examiner and General Advertiser (NSW: 1874 - 1908)*, 29 May 1888, p.2, https://trove.nla.gov.au/newspaper/article/217775265

'Local & General News', *Glen Innes Examiner and General Advertiser (NSW: 1874-1908)*, 11 December 1888, p.2, https://trove.nla.gov.au/newspaper/article/217774155

'Local & General', *Dungog Chronicle: Durham and Gloucester Advertiser, (NSW: 1894-1954)*, 18 October 1904, p.2, https://trove.nla.gov.au/newspaper/article/137751512

'Local Notes', *Glen Innes Examiner and General Advertiser (NSW: 1874-1908)*, 6 April 1900, p.2, https://trove.nla.gov.au/newspaper/article/217838290

'Local Notes & News', *Glen Innes Examiner and General Advertiser (NSW: 1874-1908)*, 8 February 1898, p.2, https://trove.nla.gov.au/newspaper/article/217885580

'Local Notes & News', *Glen Innes Examiner and General Advertiser (NSW: 1874-1908)*, 26 April 1898, p.2, https://trove.nla.gov.au/newspaper/article/217880951

'Local & Other Notes', *Glen Innes Examiner and General Advertiser (NSW: 1874-1908)*, 14 January 1879, p.2, https://trove.nla.gov.au/newspaper/article/217826530

'Local & Other Notes', *Glen Innes Examiner and General Advertiser (NSW: 1874 - 1908)*, 10 June 1879, p.2, https://trove.nla.gov.au/newspaper/article/217826709

'Local and Other Notes', *Glen Innes Examiner and General Advertiser (NSW: 1874 - 1908)*, 20 January 1880, p.2, https://trove.nla.gov.au/newspaper/article/217784061

'Local and Other Notes', *Glen Innes Examiner and General Advertiser (NSW: 1874 - 1908)*, 23 August 1881, p.2, https://trove.nla.gov.au/newspaper/article/217832092

'Local Intelligence', *Glen Innes Examiner and General Advertiser, (NSW: 1874-1908)*, 5 April 1876, p.2, https://trove.nla.gov.au/newspaper/article/217828585

'Local Intelligence', *Glen Innes Examiner and General Advertiser, (NSW: 1874-1908)*, 19 July 1876, p.2, https://trove.nla.gov.au/newspaper/article/217827678

'Local Notes & News', *Glen Innes Examiner and General Advertiser (NSW: 1874-1908)* 2 October 1894, p.3, https://trove.nla.gov.au/newspaper/article/217831288

'Local & Numeral News', *Glen Innes Examiner and General Advertiser (NSW: 1874 - 1908)*12 July 1887, p.2, https://trove.nla.gov.au/newspaper/article/217818113

'Local & Other Notes', *Glen Innes Examiner and General Advertiser (NSW:1874-1908)*, 6 February 1878, p.2, https://trove.nla.gov.au/newspaper/article/217826067

'Local & Other Notes', *Glen Innes Examiner and General Advertiser, (NSW: 1874-1908)*, 9 November 1880, p.2, https://trove.nla.gov.au/newspaper/article/217783346

'Local & Other Notes', *Glen Innes Examiner and General Advertiser, (NSW: 1874-1908)*, 1 March 1881, p.2, https://trove.nla.gov.au/newspaper/article/217833075

'Local & Other Notes', *Glen Innes Examiner and General Advertiser (NSW:1874-1908)*, 31 May 1881, p.4, https://trove.nla.gov.au/newspaper/article/217833046

'Local & Other Notes', *Glen Innes Examiner and General Advertiser (NSW:1874-1908)*, 4 Dec 1883, p.2, https://trove.nla.gov.au/newspaper/article/217840399

Lord MacDonald Rental Valuation Records, 1837/38, *Museum of the Isles Library at Clan Donald Centre*, Armadale Castle, Isle of Skye.

'Lord Stanley Despatch to Sir George Gipps', 17 May 1845, *Historical Records of Australia*, series 1, vol.24, https://nla.gov.au/nla.obj-496380980

'Lower Clarence-MacLean, Friday', *Clarence and Richmond Examiner (Grafton, NSW:1889-1915)*, 7 March 1896, p.4, https://trove.nla.gov.au/newspaper/article/61310012

Lydia Kingston Smith, 21 May 2016, *Find a Grave*, https://www.findagrave.com/memorial/162864988

MacDonald, A. & MacDonald, A., 1896-1904, *The Clan Donald*, vol.3, Northern Counties Publishing Co. Ltd, Inverness, pp. 41-48.

MacKenzie, E., 1852, *Memoirs of Mrs Caroline Chisholm, with an account of her Philanthropic Labours in India, Australia and England; to which is added A History of the Family Colonisation Loan Society; Also, the Question who ought to Emigrate? Answered.* Webb, Millington & Co, London, 2nd Edition, p.115, https://nla.gov.au/nla.obj-52866095

MacKenzie, A., 1881, *History of the MacDonalds and Lords of the Isles; with Genealogies of the Principal Families of the Name*, Aberdeen, A. King & Co., https://digital.nls.uk/histories-of-scottish-families/archive/96862054

MacKinnon Clan, 1999-2021, *Scots Connection*.

MacKinnon, D., 1899, *Memoirs of Clan Fingon*, Lewis Hepworth and Co. Ltd., Tunbridge Wells.

MacKinnon Gazetteer, 2024, http://www.emackinnon.com/gazetteer

'MacLean Will Case', *Clarence and Richmond Examiner (Grafton, NSW: 1889-1915)*, 5 December 1912, p.5, https://trove.nla.gov.au/newspaper/article/61668806

MacPherson, H., 21 July 2020, 'How the Potato Famine Hit Scotland Hard', *The National*, https://www.thenational.scot/news/1859535

'Mail Robbery', *Glen Innes Examiner and General Advertiser (NSW:1874-1908)*, 29 May 1883, p.2, https://trove.nla.gov.au/newspaper/article/217841230

'Maitland Circuit Court', *Empire (Sydney, NSW:1850-1875)*, 24 August 1853, p.2, https://trove.nla.gov.au/newspaper/article/61327270

'Maitland District Court', *The Maitland Mercury and Hunter General Advertiser (NSW: 1843-1893)*, 24 June 1890, p.8, https://trove.nla.gov.au/newspaper/article/18988798

'Maitland Stock Reports', *The Maitland Mercury and Hunter General Advertiser (NSW: 1843-1893)*, 11 December 1875, p. 7, https://trove.nla.gov.au/newspaper/article/18801231

Malcolm Cameron, 1841, Snizort North, Inverness, Ref: Census 117/1 2/2, Scotland's People, *National Records of Scotland*.

Malcolm Camron [sic], 1861, Snizort North, Inverness, Ref: Census 117/7/ 3, Scotland's People, *National Records of Scotland*.

Malcolm MacDonald, 2010, Australia Marriage Index, 1788-1950, No. 4472 MacLean, NSW, *Ancestry.com*

'Male Orphan School', 2012, *State Library of New South Wales*, Sydney.

Margaret Mackinnon, 1828, Old Parish Registers Births 112/ 10 4 Kilmuir, p.4 of 55, Scotland's People, *National Records of Scotland*.

Margaret McKinnon, 6 June 1851, Emperor, Assisted Immigrants (digital) Shipping Lists, NRS5316/4_4790/Emperor_6 Jun 1851, p.7-9, *NSW State Archives*, Sydney.

Margaret McKinnon, 9 June 1851, 'Emperor', Immigration Board, *NSW State Archives*, Sydney.

Margaret McKinnon, 28 August 1851, NSW Marriage Transcription (early church records), *NSW Births, Deaths and Marriages*, ref no.326, vol.80, transcribed by Marilyn Rowan, 1 December 2003.

Maria Ballard, 1874, Australia, Marriage Index, 1788-1950, *Ancestry.com*

Maria Catherine Cornish, 1930, *Australian Electoral Rolls 1903-1980*, New England, Glen Innes, *Ancestry.com*

Marion MacLeod, 1881, Kilmuir, Inverness, Ref: Census 112/1 7/6, Scotland's People, *National Records of Scotland*.

Marr, D., 2023, *Killing for Country: A Family Story*, Black Inc, Victoria.

'Marriages', *The Sydney Morning Herald*, 25 February 1875, p.1, ttps://trove.nla.gov.au/newspaper/page/1445529

Mary Ross, 11 April 1926, Statutory Register of Deaths, 112/1 5, Kilmuir, Inverness, Scotland's People, *National Records of Scotland*.

McDonald, B., 2000, '*You Can Dig All You Like, You'll Never Find Aboriginal Culture There'. Relational Aspects of the History of Aboriginal Music of New England New South Wales 1830-1930*, PHD thesis, University of New England, Armidale, NSW.

McDonald, P.F., August 1972, *Age at First Marriage and Proportions Marrying in Australia 1860-1971*, PHD Thesis ANU.

McDonald, P. & Moyle, H., 2018, 'Women as Agents in Fertility Decision-Making: Australia 1870- 1910', *Population and Development Review*, vol.44, no.2, pp.203-230.

'McDonald v Elliott and Another', Civil Side, Maitland Circuit Court, The *Maitland Mercury and Hunter River General Advertiser (NSW: 1843 – 1893)*, 8 September 1852, p.1, https://trove.nla.gov.au/newspaper/page/127512

McKenzie, S., 22 May 2013, 'The Crofters War and the Napier Commission', *BBC News*.

McKinnon, L., 1973, *The Illawarra McKenzie Family*, 'The Scottish Potato Famine of 1836', https://themckenziefamilyillawarra.wordpress.com

McSwan, E.H. & Switzer, M., March 2006, *A Thematic History vol.2*, Maclean Shire, Community Based Heritage Study.

'Meeting of the Teachers', *The Manning River News and Advocate for the Northern Coast Districts of New South Wales (Tinonee, NSW: 1865-1873)*, 4 July 1868, p.2, https://trove.nla.gov.au/newspaper/article/266389955

'Melancholy Fatality', *The Manning River Chronicle (Wingham, NSW (:1886-1888)*, 4 August 1887, p.2, https://trove.nla.gov.au/newspaper/article/267809996

'Memorandum of Agreement between Mr Andrew Lang and Donald Gillis and Donald McMillan', 19 January 1838, Dunmore Hunter River, *NSW State Archives*, Sydney, [research by Evelyn Smith].

Miller, J., 1985, *Koori, A Will to Win: The Heroic Resistance, Survival and Triumph of Black Australia*, Angus & Robertson, Sydney.

'Minutes of Evidence Taken Before the Select Committee on Monetary Confusion', *The Sydney Morning Herald (NSW: 1842-1954)*, 21 November 1843, p.4, https://trove.nla.gov.au/newspaper/page/1520976

'Missions, Stations and Reserves', 2022, *The Australian Institute of Aboriginal and Torres Strait Islander Studies (AIATSIS)*.

Molony, J.N., 2000, *'The Native-born: the First White Australians'*, Melbourne University Press, Victoria

Monckton, W. & Pratt, A., 1910, *Three Years with Thunderbolt*, The States Publishing Co., Sydney, *National Library Australia*, http://nla.gov.au/nla.obj-52861897

Morris, E. E., 1898, *Austral English: A Dictionary of Australasian Words, Phrases and Usages*, Project Gutenberg Australia eBook, http://gutenberg.net.au/ebooks09/0900231h.html

'Mr. Allan Ballard', *Glen Innes Examiner (NSW: 1908 - 1954)*, 5 March 1935, p.4, https://trove.nla.gov.au/newsarticle/184619473

Mr & Mrs Ballard, 1921, Wedding Invitation, *Barnes Family Collection*.

'Mr. Angus McDonald', *The Daily Telegraph, (Sydney NSW: 1883-1930)*, 13 June 1927, p.5, https://trove.nla.gov.au/newspaper/article/247370383

'Mr. Archibald Boyd and the Squatocracy', *Morning Chronicle (Sydney, NSW :1843-1846),* 7 May 1845, p.2, https://trove.nla.gov.au/newspaper/article/31745338

'Mr. Martin's Vindication of the Patriotic Lottery', *The Sydney Morning Herald (NSW: 1842-1954),* 21 February 1849, p.2, https://trove.nla.gov.au/newspaper/article/28646856

'Mr. Merewether's Immigration Report for 1841', *The Australian (Sydney, NSW:1824-1848),* 4 June 1842, p.2, https://trove.nla.gov.au/newspaper/article/37113530

'Mrs Cockburn' telegram to 'The Minister for Public Instruction, Sydney', 30 May 1884.

'Mudgee Quarter Sessions', *Sydney Morning Herald, (NSW: 1842-1954),* 9 October 1861, p.3, https://trove.nla.gov.au/newspaper/page/1483562

Munro, Donald, 1853, *Hercules Passenger List,* 1853, no.400, https://www.angelfire.com/ns/bkeddy/HIES/hercules3.html

'Murder', Maitland Circuit Court, *The Maitland Mercury & Hunter River General Advertiser, (NSW: 1843-1893),* 24 April 1869, p.4, https://trove.nla.gov.au/newspaper/page/143416

Murdo Campbell, 1841, Kilmuir, Inverness, Ref: Census 112/7/3, Scotland's People, *National Records of Scotland.*

Murdoch Graham, *Find a Grave,* New South Wales, Lawrence, Clarence Valley Council, https://www.findagrave.com/memorial/182266781

Murray, L., 2013, 'Death and Dying in Nineteenth Century Sydney', *Dictionary of Sydney,* https://dictionaryofsydney.org

Murrie, L., 1998, The Australian Legend: Writing Australian Masculinity/ Writing 'Australian' Masculine, *Journal of Australian Studies,* vol.22, iss.56, pp.68-77.

'Myles to the Colonial Secretary', 20 May 1836, *Dungog Magistrates Letterbook*, https://nla.gov.au/nla.obj-232867499

Napier Commission, 1883, vol.1, p.109, *University of the Highlands and Islands*, Inverness, Scotland, https://www.uhi.ac.uk/en/research-enterprise/cultural/centre-for-history/research/research-alliances/the-napier-commission

'Native Blacks', *The Sydney Monitor and Commercial Advertiser (NSW:1838-1841)*, 24 December 1838, p.2, https://trove.nla.gov.au/newspaper/article/32162320

Neklason, A., 17 February 2019, 'Blackface was Never Harmless', *The Atlantic*, https://www.theatlantic.com/582733

'New Enactments', *The Sydney Gazette and NSW Advertiser* (NSW: 1803-1842), 4 August 1836, p.2, https://trove.nla.gov.au/newspaper/article/2205837

'New England (NSW)', 2022, *Wikipedia*.

'New Magistrates', *The Maitland Mercury and Hunter General Advertiser (NSW: 1843-1893)*, 9 September 1873, p.2, https://trove.nla.gov.au/newspaper/article/18777200

'New Public Health Act', *The Sydney Morning Herald (NSW: 1842-1954)*, 17 November 1896, p.5, https://trove.nla.gov.au/newspaper/article/14075786

'News of the World', *Clarence and Richmond Examiner and New England Advertiser (Grafton, NSW: 1859-1889)*, 15 October 1887, p.3, https://trove.nla.gov.au/newspaper/article/62107134

New South Wales, 1904, Royal Commission on the Decline of the Birth-Rate and on the Mortality of Infants in New South Wales, Parliament, Legislative Assembly, *Report on the Royal Commission on the Decline of the Birth-Rate and on the Mortality of Infants in New South Wales*, vol.1 & vol.2, Government Printer, Sydney, http://nla.gov.au/nla.obj-2625267063

'New South Wales Constitution Act 1855 (UK)', 16 July 1855, [transcript] *New South Wales Government*, https://www.foundingdocs.gov.au

'New South Wales Parliament', *The Sydney Morning Herald (NSW: 1842-1954)*, 17 November 1900, p.7, https://trove.nla.gov.au/newspaper/article/14372608

'New South Wales Police', *The Sydney Morning Herald (NSW:1842-1954)*, 16 July 1870, p.4, https://trove.nla.gov.au/newspaper/article/13222498

'New South Wales Public Service Lists (Blue Books)', n.d., Microfiche, 13 fiche [807–819], *State Records Authority of NSW*, Sydney.

'New Squatting Regulations', *The Citizen (Sydney, NSW:1846-1847)*, 9 January 1847, p.1, https://trove.nla.gov.au/newspaper/article/252637412

'No Sydney Mail', *Glen Innes Examiner and General Advertiser (NSW: 1874-1908)*, 2 March 1880, p.2, https://trove.nla.gov.au/newspaper/article/217784124

'Notes on a Trip from Bandon Grove to Bindera', *Maitland Mercury and Hunter River General Advertiser (NSW: 1843 - 1893)*, 20 April 1872, p.5, https://trove.nla.gov.au/newspaper/article/18762903

'Notice to remove tenants of Tallanantain, Peinvraid and Balnacnock', 1865, SL/D123/19, [Transcript], *Skye & Lochalsh Archive Centre*, Portree, Isle of Skye, Scotland.

'No Title', *The Hobart Town Advertiser (Tas:1839-1861)*, 14 November 1848, p.2, https://trove.nla.gov.au/newspaper/article/264524718

'No Title', *Glen Innes Examiner and General Advertiser (NSW: 1874-1908)*, 4 August 1875, p.2, https://trove.nla.gov.au/newspaper/article/217833511

'No Title', *Glen Innes Examiner and General Advertiser (NSW: 1874-1908)*, 29 September 1885, p.2, https://trove.nla.gov.au/newspaper/article/217771285

Noyce, D., 2021, 'A Taste of Progress: The temperance Movement and its Influence on Food and Drink and the Urban Landscape at the time of the International Exhibitions in the Australian Colonies', *Australasian Journal of Victorian Studies*, https://openjournals.library.sydney.edu.au

'NSW Government Gazette, 1832-2001', *Trove*, https://trove.nla.gov.au

'NSW Government Gazette Appointments and Employment', 7 May 1895, *New South Wales Government Gazette, (Sydney, NSW:1832-1900)*, iss.307, p.2918, https://trove.nla.gov.au/newspaper/article/222223129

'NSW Government Gazette Appointments and Employment' 20 October 1899, *New South Wales Government Gazette, (Sydney, NSW:1832-1900)*, iss.843, p.7953, https://trove.nla.gov.au/newspaper/article/221010193

'Obituary', *Glen Innes Examiner and General Advertiser (NSW: 1874-1908)*, 20 May 1904, p.2, https://trove.nla.gov.au/newspaper/article/217891085

'Obituary', *Clarence and Richmond Examiner (Grafton, NSW: 1889-1915)*, 9 July 1912, p.2, https://trove.nla.gov.au/newspaper/article/61661212

'Obituary', *Dungog Chronicle: Durham and Gloucester Advertiser (NSW: 1894-1954)*, 14 July 1916, p.6, https://trove.nla.gov.au/newspaper/article/136010912

'Obituary' *Dungog Chronicle: Durham and Gloucester Advertiser (NSW: 1894-1954)*, 20 February 1925, p.2, https://trove.nla.gov.au/newspaper/article/137744717

'Official Opening of the Red Range School of Arts', *Glen Innes Examiner and General Advertiser (NSW: 1874 - 1908)*, 16 January 1903, p.2, https://trove.nla.gov.au/newspaper/rendition/nla.news-article217929219

Ohlsson, T., '"Better than Nothing": Eurasian Labour in New South Wales', 1853-54', *Labour History*, Nov 2013, pp.153-70.

Old Friend, 1941, 'The Emigrant Ship "Midlothian"', *The Wingham Chronicle*, 22 July 1941, https://trove.nla.gov.au/newspaper/article/168516927

'Old Parish Registers Marriages', 1837, Ref. no. 117/ 1013 2, Snizort, p.132, Scotland's People, *National Records of Scotland*.

'One Hundred Victorian Boys Names and Meanings', 2023, *Mum Loves Best*, https://momlovesbest.com/victorian-boy-names

O'Neill, A, 10 September 2019, *Child Mortality in Australia 1860-2020*, Statista, https://www.statista.com/statistics/1041779

'Opening of the Great Northern Railway', *Glen Innes Examiner and General Advertiser (NSW: 1874-1908)*, 21 August 1884, p.4, https://trove.nla.gov.au/newspaper/article/18934981

'Order-in-Council Ending Transportation of Convicts', 22 May 1840 (UK), Museum of Australian Democracy, *NSW State Archives & Records*, SRNSW: 4/1310, https://www.foundingdocs.gov.au

Ordnance Survey Field Notebooks, Inverness-shire – Isle of Skye (Kilmuir), 1875, *Skye & Lochalsh Archive Centre*, https://www.highlifehighland.com/skye-and-lochalsh-archive-centre/1893-plan-kilmaluag-inn-skye

Ordnance Survey Map, Inverness Shire - Isle of Skye, IV.6, (Kilmuir), 1878, *National Library of Scotland*, https://maps.nls.uk/view/75105205.

Ordnance Survey Name Book, 1876-78, Inverness-shire, (Skye) vol.7, OS1/16/7/30, *National Records of Scotland,* https://scotlandsplaces.gov.uk

'Original Correspondence', *The Sydney Morning Herald (NSW: 1842-1954)*, 19 February 1849, p.3, https://trove.nla.gov.au/newspaper/article/12910257

'Original Correspondence', *The Maitland Mercury and Hunter General Advertiser (NSW: 1843-1893,)* 25 August 1877, p.10, https://trove.nla.gov.au/newspaper/article/18831954

'Our Centenary of Women's Suffrage', July 2009, The office for the Status of Women, *Dept of the Prime Minister and Cabinet*, https://www.dss.gov.au

'Our Member', *Glen Innes Examiner and General Advertiser (NSW: 1874 - 1908)*, 20 June 1899, p.2, https://trove.nla.gov.au/newspaper/article/217820567

'Our Social Prospects', *People's Advocate and New South Wales Vindicator (Sydney, NSW:1848-1856)*, 3 March 1849, p.6, https://trove.nla.gov.au/newspaper/page/27923042

'Our Third, Upon Mr. Wentworth's Last', *The Sydney Morning Herald (NSW: 1842-1954)*, 15 February 1849, p.2, https://trove.nla.gov.au/newspaper/article/12909622

'Papers relating to sale of part of the McDonald Estates in Skye and North Uist', Macdonald Family, Barons Macdonald, 1846-1848, Reference: NRAS3273/55, Code: 800001, *The National Register of Archives for Scotland*, http://catalogue.nrscotland.gov.uk

Parkinson, A., 'Largs School celebrates 175', *The Maitland Mercury*, 14 September 2013, https://www.maitlandmercury.com.au/story/1774782/largs-school-celebrates-175-years

'Partition of the Bank of Australia', *The Maitland Mercury & Hunter River General Advertiser (NSW: 1843-1893)*, 6 January 1849, p.2, https://trove.nla.gov.au/newspaper/article/706486

Pascoe, B., 2018, *Dark Emu*, Magabala Books Aboriginal Corporation, Broome.

'Pastoral News', *The Maitland Mercury & Hunter River General Advertiser (NSW: 1843-1893)*, 28 December 1875, p.3, https://trove.nla.gov.au/newspaper/article/18801710

'Paterson', *The Maitland Mercury & Hunter River General Advertiser (NSW: 1843-1893)*, 2 February 1875, p.3, https://trove.nla.gov.au/newspaper/article/18791666

'Personal', *Glen Innes Examiner and General Advertiser, (NSW: 1874-1908)*, 22 December 1924, p.4, https://trove.nla.gov.au/newspaper/article/184449539

'Personal', *Northern Star (Lismore, NSW:1876-1954)*, 7 March 1911, p.3, https://trove.nla.gov.au/newspaper/article/72271979).

Pettegree, J., 11 May 2022, 'Francis Tolmie's Skye Songs: manuscript sources from the National Library of Scotland', *Soundyngs Conversations on the History of Scottish Music*, https://soundyngs.wp.st-andrews.ac.uk

Picken, A. & Nicolson, S., 21 May 2019, 'Who Owns Scotland? The Changing Face of Scotland's Landowners', *BBC Scotland News*.

'Pic-nic at Red Range', *Glen Innes Examiner and General Advertiser (NSW: 1874 - 1908)*, 12 May 1893, p.2, https://trove.nla.gov.au/newspaper/rendition/nla.news-article217786841.3

Plevey, T., 'A light in the darkness': the history and hope of Myall Creek, *The Guardian*, 16 July 2022.

'Port Macquarie', *Sydney Mail and NSW Advertiser (NSW:1871-1887)*, 20 August 1887, p.417, https://trove.nla.gov.au/newspaper/article/165226733

Potts, A. & Lester, M., 2002, *In That Beautiful Land*, Lennox Head, Karma Press.

Prebble, John, 1982, *The Highland Clearances*, Penguin Books, London.

Preston, R., 'The Australian Woman Movement, 1880-1914: Sexuality, Marriage and Consent', 2014, *The ANU Undergraduate Research Journal*, vol.6, ANU Press.

'Prevalence of Sickness in the Town of Sydney', *The Sydney Herald (NSW: 1831-1842)*, 15 May 1841, p.2, https://trove.nla.gov.au/newspaper/page/3923418

'Prime Potatoes', *Glen Innes Examiner and General Advertiser (NSW: 1874 - 1908)*, 4 September 1906, p.2, https://trove.nla.gov.au/newspaper/article/217796228

'Prince of Wales's Birthday', *Glen Innes Examiner and General Advertiser (NSW: 1874 - 1908)*, 11 November 1874, p.2, https://trove.nla.gov.au/newspaper/article/217834004

'Probate Jurisdiction', *Glen Innes Examiner and General Advertiser (NSW: 1874 - 1908)*, 3 June 1904, p.5, https://trove.nla.gov.au/newspaper/rendition/nla.news-article217888575

'Provisional School at Red Range', *Glen Innes Examiner and General Advertiser (NSW: 1874 - 1908)*, 3 June 1879, p.2, https://trove.nla.gov.au/newspaper/rendition/nla.news-article217826510

'Public Funeral of the Rev. John Dunmore Lang, *Evening News (Sydney, NSW: 1869-1931)*, 12 August 1878, p.3, https://trove.nla.gov.au/newspaper/article/107935452

'Public Instruction Act 1880', 5 November 2019, *NSW Government*, https://education.nsw.gov.au

Purser, J., 20 July 2020, 'What we can learn from Gaelic Rowing and Waulking Songs', *The National*, https://www.thenational.scot/news/18593134

Radford, N., 2017, 'Australia's First Lottery', *Dictionary of Sydney*, https://dictionaryofsydney.org/entry/australias_first_lottery

Ranald Ross, 1 June 1875, Statutory Registers Deaths, 112/01 0023 Kilmuir (Inverness), p.8, Scotland's People, *National Records of Scotland.*

'Re Angus McDonald, an Infant', Supreme Court, Sydney News, *The Maitland Mercury and Hunter River General Advertiser, (NSW: 1843 – 1893)*, 19th May 1849, p.4, https://trove.nla.gov.au/newspaper/article/703104

'Red Range Cricket Club', *Glen Innes Examiner and General Advertiser (NSW: 1874 - 1908),* 12 September 1902, p.2, https://trove.nla.gov.au/newspaper/article/217929276

'Red Range', *Glen Innes Examiner and General Advertiser (NSW: 1874 - 1908),* 21 August 1883, p.2, https://trove.nla.gov.au/newspaper/rendition/nla.news-article217840832.3

'Red Range', *Glen Innes Examiner and General Advertiser (NSW: 1874 - 1908),* 28 March 1902, p.3, https://trove.nla.gov.au/newspaper/article/217928310

'Red Range', *Glen Innes Examiner and General Advertiser (NSW: 1874 - 1908),* 26 August 1902, p.3, https://trove.nla.gov.au/newspaper/rendition/nla.news-article217923586.3

'Red Range', *Glen Innes Examiner and General Advertiser (NSW: 1908 - 1954),* 5 April 1923, p. 4, https://trove.nla.gov.au/newspaper/rendition/nla.news-article183651226.3

'Red Range, NSW', 2023, *Wikipedia.*

'Red Range, NSW', n.d, *Wikiwand.*

'Red Range, Old hands Return', *Glen Innes Examiner (NSW: 1908 - 1954),* 5 April 1923, p. 4, https://trove.nla.gov.au/newspaper/rendition/nla.news-article183651226.3

'Red Range Picnic', *Glen Innes Examiner and General Advertiser (NSW: 1874 - 1908),* 13 November 1894, p.3, https://trove.nla.gov.au/newspaper/rendition/nla.news-article217830474.3

'Red Range Public School', *Glen Innes Examiner and General Advertiser (NSW: 1874 - 1908),* 9 February 1886, p.2, https://trove.nla.gov.au/newspaper/article/217877780

'*Registration Act 1855 No34a*', 30 December 1855, UTS and UNSW Faculties of Law, *Australasian Legal Information Institute (AustLII).*

'Registry Records', 2021, *NSW Government*, https://www.nsw.gov.au/topics/family-history-search/registry-records

Reid, E, 2013 'The Sheriff in the Heather: Beaton v Ivory', Working Papers, School of Law, *University of Edinburgh*, https://doi.org/10.2139/ssrn.2330752

'Reminisces of Early Glen Innes', *Glen Innes Examiner and General Advertiser, (NSW: 1908-1954)*, 12 July 1917, p.2, https://trove.nla.gov.au/newspaper/article/183271777

'Reminiscences of Maitland and the District', No.13 1849, *The Maitland Weekly Mercury (NSW: 1894-1931)*, 20 January 1894, p.13, https://trove.nla.gov.au/newspaper/page/13713516

'Reminiscences of Maitland and the District', No.14 1851, *The Maitland Weekly Mercury (NSW: 1894-1931)*, 17 February 1894, p.16, https://trove.nla.gov.au/newspaper/article/126612871

Rental ledger, 1837/38/39, *MacDonald Estate Papers NRAS3273/5973*, [from original held at the Museum of the Isles Library at Clan Donald Centre, Armadale Castle, Isle of Skye].

'Report on Comparative Kelp Prices', c1805, Ambaile Highland History and Culture, *Macdonald Estate Papers*, Museum of the Isles Library at Clan Donald Centre, Isle of Skye.

Reynolds, H., 1996, *Frontier: Reports from the Edge of White Settlement*, Allen & Unwin, St Leonards, Australia.

Reynolds, H., 2006, *The Other Side of the Frontier: Aboriginal Resistance to the European Invasion of Australia*, UNSW Press, Sydney.

Reynolds, H., 2013, *Forgotten War*, UNSW, NewSouth Publishing, Sydney.

Richards, N., Australian Museum Business Services (2013), *Tenterfield LGA Aboriginal Heritage Study*, Report to Tenterfield Shire Council

Riley, K., 'Cobb & Co Coaches: Historical Transport', 18 October 2011, *Australian Geographic*.

Ritchie, J., 1940, *'A Keg of 'Bog Butter' from Skye and its Contents: Proceedings of the Society of Antiquities of Scotland*, vol.75, pp.5-22.

Rolls, E., 1981, *A Million Wild Acres: 200 years of Man and an Australian Forest*, Angus & Robertson, Sydney.

Ross, D, 2024, Captain Fraser's Folly, *Britain Express*.

'Round About', Glen Innes Examiner and General Advertiser (NSW: 1874-1908), 7 February 1902, p.1, https://trove.nla.gov.au/newspaper/article/217931351

Russell, P., 'In search of Women's Place: An Historical Survey of Gender and Space in Nineteenth -Century Australia', 1993, *Australian Historical Archaeology*, vol.11, pp.28-32.

'Sad Drowning Fatality', *Glen Innes Examiner and General Advertiser (NSW: 1874 - 1908)*, 29 November 1898, p.2, https://trove.nla.gov.au/newspaper/article/217885798

'Sales by Auction', Advertising, *The Maitland Mercury and Hunter General Advertiser (NSW: 1843-1893)*, 27 December 1877, p.8, https://trove.nla.gov.au/newspaper/article/18832190

'Sales by Auction', *Glen Innes Examiner and General Advertiser (NSW: 1874 - 1908)*, 13 November 1906, p.4, https://trove.nla.gov.au/newspaper/rendition/nla.news-article217804775.3

'School Inspector's Report to the Under Secretary', 21 April 1885.

'Scottish Gaelic', n.d., *Wikipedia*.

Seal, G., 1996, *The Outlaw Legend: A Cultural tradition in Britain, America and Australia,* Cambridge University Press, Cambridge.

'Separation', *Glen Innes Examiner and General Advertiser (NSW: 1874 - 1908)*, 23 August 1887, p. 2, https://trove.nla.gov.au/newspaper/rendition/nla.news-article217818907.3

'Separation Meetings, Red Range', *Glen Innes Examiner and General Advertiser (NSW: 1874 - 1908)*, 10 May 1887, p. 4, https://trove.nla.gov.au/newspaper/article/217816705

'Severn Shire Council', *Glen Innes Examiner (NSW: 1908-1954)*, 10 August 1909, p.5, https://trove.nla.gov.au/newspaper/article/180127913

'Ship News', *The Sydney Gazette and New South Wales Advertiser (NSW: 1803-1842)*, 19 December 1837, p.2, https://trove.nla.gov.au/newspaper/article/2214537

'Shocking Suicide at Port Macquarie', *The Mercury (Hobart, Tas: 1860 - 1954)*, 2 August 1887, p.3, https://trove.nla.gov.au/newspaper/page/818309

Shultz, R.J., 21 December 1971, *'The Assisted Immigrants, 1837-1850'*, PhD Thesis, Australian National University, Canberra, ACT.

Sims, L., 2014, Donald Munro & Catherine MacGillivray, *Clan Munro (Association) Australia*, http://www.clanmunroassociation.org.au

Simms, M., 17 August 2001, '1901: The Forgotten Election', *Lecture presented in the Department of the Senate Occasional Lecture Series at Parliament House.*

Singley, B., 26 January 2017, 'Parrot Pie and Possum Curry- how Colonial Australian Embraced Native Food', *The Conversation*, https://theconversation.com/parrot-pie-and-possum-curry-how-colonial-australians-embraced-native-food-59977

'Sir Henry Parkes at Tenterfield', *The Sydney Morning Herald (NSW: 1842-1954)*, 25 Oct 1889, p.8, https://trove.nla.gov.au/newspaper/article/13746899

Skene, W.F., 1837, '*The Highlanders of Scotland: Their Origins, History, And Antiquities*', London, John Murray, p.258-260.

Smout, T.C., 1986, *A Century of Scottish People 1830-1950*, Fontana Press, London.

'Some Facts About Suicide', *Glen Innes Examiner and General Advertiser (NSW: 1874 - 1908)*, 13 October 1885, p.5, https://trove.nla.gov.au/newspaper/article/217771874

'Something New', *The Sydney Morning Herald (NSW: 1842-1954)*, 19 October 1848, p.2, https://trove.nla.gov.au/newspaper/article/12907728

'Southward Ho!', *Glen Innes Examiner and General Advertiser (NSW: 1874 - 1908)*, 12 November 1878, p. 2, https://trove.nla.gov.au/newspaper/article/217825812

Spillman, J., 2015, '*Queensland Lords: Edward and Eliza Lord's Colonial Family*', Boolarong Press, Tingalpa Queensland.

'Squattocracy', 2023, Australian Agriculture and Rural Life, [online] *State Library of NSW*, Sydney.

Staines, C. & Ozanne-Smith, J., 1 March 2017, 'Drowning deaths between 1861-2000 in Victoria', Australia, *Bulletin of the World Health Organisation*, vol.95, iss.3, pp.174-181.

State Lotteries Act No.511930, 1930, *NSW Legislation*, https://legislation.nsw.gov.au

Stephen, M.D., 2006, 'Mosman, Archibald (1799-1863)', *Australian Dictionary of Biography*, Australian National University, https://adb.anu.edu.au/biography/mosman-archibald-2485

Stewart, T., 2017, *Historic UK*, https://www.historic-uk.com/HistoryUK/HistoryofScotland/The-Highland-Clearances

'Stock Act 1901', *Government Gazette of the State of New South Wales (Sydney, NSW: 1901 - 2001)*, 21 November 1906 (No.259), p. 6331,

https://trove.nla.gov.au/newspaper/rendition/
nla.news-article226477235.3

Strachan, G., 2001(a), 'Caught in the community: Teachers lives in rural schools 1880-1900', *2001 Australian Society for the Study of Labour History Conference.*

Strachan, G. 2001(b), Present at the Birth: Midwives, 'Handywomen' and Neighbours in Rural New South Wales, 1850-1900, *Labour History,* (81), p.13-28.

Strachan, G. & Henderson, L., 2005, 'Assumed but rarely documented: women's entrepreneurial activities in late nineteenth century Australia', *The Past is Before Us: The Ninth National Labour History Conference.*

Strachan, G. & Henderson, L., December 2008, Surviving widowhood: Life alone in Australia in the second half of the nineteenth century, *Continuity and Change,* 23 (03), pp.487-508.

Strachan, G., Jordan, E. & Carey, H., 14 June 1997, 'Women's Work in a Rural Community: Dungog and the Upper Williams Valley 1880-1900', *Paper presented at Labour & Locality Conference,* Sydney, NSW.

Stuart B McDonald, 1893, Dungog, Australia, no.5663, Australia Death Index 1787-1985, *Ancestry.com.*

Stubbs, B.J., 2001, "From 'Useless Brutes' to National Treasures: A Century of Evolving Attitudes towards Native Fauna in New South Wales, 1860s to 1960s", *Environment and History,* vol.7, no.1, pp.23-56.

Summers, A., 2016, *Damned Whores and God's Police: The Colonisation of Women in Australia,* New South Publishing, Sydney Australia.

'Supreme Court', *Australasian Chronicle (Sydney, NSW:1839-1843),* 18 March 1841, p.3, https://trove.nla.gov.au/newspaper/article/31731207

'Supreme Court', *The Maitland Mercury and Hunter River General Advertiser (NSW: 1843 – 1893)*, 14 July 1849, p2, https://trove.nla.gov.au/newspaper/article/701807

'Surnames', 2022, Scotland's People, *National Records of Scotland*.

Sutton, P. & Walshe, K., 2021, *Farmers or Hunter-Gatherers? The Dark Emu Debate*, Melbourne University Press.

Sykes, T., 1998, *Two Centuries of Panic: A History of Corporate Collapses in Australia*. Sydney: Allen & Unwin.

Syron, R. & Russell, L., 15 August 2018, *Special Collections, Hunter Living Histories*, University of Newcastle, https://hunterlivinghistories.com/2018/08/15/the-kabook-watoo

Tallanantain Rental Table, 1718-1823, *MacDonald Estate Papers*, Museum of the Isles Library, Clan Donald Centre, Armadale Castle, Isle of Skye.

Tallanantain Rental Table, 1823-1855, *MacDonald Estate Papers*, Museum of the Isles Library, Clan Donald Centre, Armadale Castle, Isle of Skye.

'Taree Literary Society', *The Manning River News and Advocate for the Northern Coast Districts of New South Wales (Tinonee, NSW: 1865-1873)*, 2 March 1867, p.3, https://trove.nla.gov.au/newspaper/article/266386950

Taylor, G., 2022, 'Love the Sinner: The Crime of Attempted Suicide in late Nineteenth Century Australia', *Australian Bar Review*, vol.51, iss.1, pp.129-160.

Taylor, L., March 2020, 'Researching Unspeakable Crimes: Buggery, Law, and Community Surveillance in New South Wales, 1788-1838', *Law and History Review*.

'Tenders for the erection of a Presbyterian Church at Taree', *The Manning River News and Advocate for the Northern Coast Districts of New South Wales (Tinonee, NSW: 1865-1873)*, 19 September 1868, p.3, https://trove.nla.gov.au/newspaper/article/266390291

'The Anti-transportation Movement', *Maitland Mercury and Hunter River General Advertiser (NSW: 1843 - 1893)*, 15 January 1851, p.3, https://trove.nla.gov.au/newspaper/page/126792

'The Australian Aboriginal: His Origin and Future', *The Sydney Morning Herald (NSW: 1842-1954)*, 5 February 1891, p.4, https://trove.nla.gov.au/newspaper/article/13812799

'The Bank of Australia', *The Sydney Morning Herald (NSW: 1842-1954)*, 2 March 1843, p.2, https://trove.nla.gov.au/newspaper/article/12416480

The Battle of Culloden', 2023, *National Trust for Scotland*, https://www.nts.org.uk

'The Big Flood', *Dungog Chronicle: Durham and Gloucester Advertiser (NSW: 1894-1954)*, 1 September 1931, p.5, https://trove.nla.gov.au/newspaper/page/16354611

'The Birth of Scottish Clan Culture', 2023, [online] *Scotland Magazine*.

'The Bulletin', 2017, The Colonial Newspapers and Magazines Project, *The University of Queensland*, https://www.austlit.edu.au/austlit/page/C278241

'The Census', Local and General News, *Glen Innes Examiner and General Advertiser (NSW: 1874-1908)*, 28 April 1891, p.2, https://trove.nla.gov.au/newspaper/article/217807907

'The Convict Experience', 2021, [online] *State Library of NSW*, Sydney.

'The Coolie Immigrants per "Orwell"', *The Spectator (Sydney, NSW :1846)*, 11 April 1846, p.134, https://trove.nla.gov.au/newspaper/article/250084607

'The Dunmore Highlanders', *The Sydney Herald (NSW: 1831-1842)*, 7 September 1841, p.2, https://trove.nla.gov.au/newspaper/article/12871006

'The East', *Glen Innes Examiner (NSW: 1908-1954)*, 12 October 1939, p.2, https://trove.nla.gov.au/newspaper/article/178522890

'The Election', *Glen Innes Examiner and General Advertiser (NSW: 1874 - 1908),* 18 December 1903, p.4, https://trove.nla.gov.au/newspaper/article/217896643

'The Emigrants, Residents in the Government Domain', *The Sydney Monitor (NSW: 1828-1838),* 26 February 1838, p.2, https://trove.nla.gov.au/newspaper/article/32159173

'The Empire', 8 May 1865, p.4, *Empire (Sydney, NSW: 1850-1875),* https://trove.nla.gov.au/newspaper/article/64137796

'The Famous Underbank Estate', Advertising, *The Sydney Morning Herald (NSW: 1842-1954),* 22 Feb 1878, p.7, https://trove.nla.gov.au/newspaper/article/13408285

'The Felons' Apprehension Act', *The Maitland Mercury and Hunter River General Advertiser (NSW: 1843-1893),* 20 April 1865, p.4, https://trove.nla.gov.au/newspaper/article/18703343

'The Female Factory', *Colonial Times (Hobart, Tas.: 1828-1857),* 18 May 1841, p.2, https://trove.nla.gov.au/newspaper/article/8751732

'The Finish of the Great Strike', *Glen Innes Examiner and General Advertiser (NSW: 1874 - 1908),* 16 September 1890, p.2, https://trove.nla.gov.au/newspaper/article/217781401

'*The Gazetteer for Scotland*', 2021, https://www.scottish-places.info

'The General Election 1887-Results of the Polling', *The Sydney Morning Herald (NSW: 1842-1954),* 28 February 1887, p.12, https://trove.nla.gov.au/newspaper/page/1398233

'The Glen Innes Show', *Glen Innes Examiner and General Advertiser (NSW: 1874 - 1908),* 24 February 1885, p.2, https://trove.nla.gov.au/newspaper/article/217770464

'The Gold Fields', *The Maitland Mercury and Hunter General Advertiser (NSW: 1843-1893)*, 1 December 1852, p.4, https://trove.nla.gov.au/newspaper/article/660236

'The Gold Fever', *Bathurst Free Press (NSW: 1849-1851)*, 17 May 1851, p.4, https://trove.nla.gov.au/newspaper/article/62215988

'The Government Railway Proposals', *Glen Innes Examiner and General Advertiser (NSW: 1874-1908)*, 28 October 1884, p.2, https://trove.nla.gov.au/newspaper/article/217878512

'The Gulf Country', *Glen Innes Examiner*, 7 July 1969, p.3.

The Highland Clearances, 2016, *The Scottish History Society*.

'The Immigration Restriction Act 1901', *National Archives of Australia 1961-2021*, http://naa.gov.au

'The Indian "Hill Coolies"', *The Sydney Monitor (NSW: 1828-1838)*, 28 February 1838, p.2, https://trove.nla.gov.au/newspaper/article/32159201

'The Late Mr McKinnon', *Macleay Argus*, 30 July 1887, p.2, https://trove.nla.gov.au/newspaper/article/234175802

'The Late Mr M Graham', *Clarence and Richmond Examiner* (Grafton, NSW: 1889-1915), 11 April 1891, p.8, https://trove.nla.gov.au/newspaper/page/5357377

'The Late Mrs Mary Bignell', *Glen Innes Examiner (NSW: 1908 - 1954)*, 9 June 1934, p. 2, https://trove.nla.gov.au/newspaper/rendition/nla.news-article183584493

'The Late Mrs M. C. Cornish', *Glen Innes Examiner (NSW: 1908 - 1954)*, 4 May 1935, p. 2, https://trove.nla.gov.au/newspaper/rendition/nla.news-article184626213.3

'The Lords of the Soil', *The Colonist (Sydney, NSW: 1835-1840)*, 12 December 1838, p.2, https://trove.nla.gov.au/newspaper/article/31722188

'The Lottery Scheme', *The People's Advocate and New South Wales Vindicator (Sydney, NSW: 1848-1856)*, 27 January 1849, p.6, https://trove.nla.gov.au/newspaper/article/251539915

'The Lottery System', *The Maitland Mercury and Hunter General Advertiser (NSW: 1843-1893)*, 24 February 1849, p.2, https://trove.nla.gov.au/newspaper/article/705237

'The "Manning Times"', *The Port Macquarie News and Hastings River Advocate (NSW: 1882-1950)*, 13 April 1889, p.2, https://trove.nla.gov.au/newspaper/page/13210352

'The Marsupial Plague: Meeting of Stock Owners', *Glen Innes Examiner and General Advertiser (NSW: 1874 - 1908)*, 4 September 1878, p.2, https://trove.nla.gov.au/newspaper/rendition/nla.news-article217825158.3

'The Mid-Lothian', Domestic Intelligence, *The Sydney Herald (NSW: 1831-1842)*, 18 December 1837, p.2, https://trove.nla.gov.au/newspaper/article/12862945

'The National Christian Temperance Union of Australia. (1891-)', 2009, *Trove*, https://trove.nla.gov.au/people/762051

'The New Australian Staple', *The Sydney Morning Herald (NSW: 1842-1954)*, 24 June 1843, p.2, https://trove.nla.gov.au/newspaper/article/12424320

'The Present Drought', 4 April 1876, p.4, *The Maitland Mercury and Hunter General Advertiser (NSW: 1843-1893)*, https://trove.nla.gov.au/newspaper/article/18805222

'The Runrig System of Land Tenure', 2022, *Hebridean Connections*, https://www.hebrideanconnections.com/stories-reports-and-traditions/16868

'The Shearer Family', *Daily Examiner (Grafton, NSW: 1915-1954)*, 2 January 1940, p.2, https://trove.nla.gov.au/newspaper/article/192343936

'The Steam Service', *The Telegraph (Brisbane, Qld: 1872-1947)*, 28 August 1880, p.2, https://trove.nla.gov.au/newspaper/article/174851096

'The Temperance Crusade', *Glen Innes Examiner and General Advertiser (NSW: 1874-1908)*, 9 June 1893, p.2, https://trove.nla.gov.au/newspaper/article/217786681

'The Transportation Committee [?]', *The Sydney Gazette and NSW Advertiser (NSW: 1803-1842)*, 7 March 1839, p.2, https://trove.nla.gov.au/newspaper/article/2551099

'The Treaty of Perth: 109716', 2024, *Hebridean Connections*, https://hebrideanconnections.com/record/historical-events/109716

'The Typhoid Scare', *Glen Innes Examiner and General Advertiser (NSW: 1874-1908)*, 20 February 1903, p.2, https://trove.nla.gov.au/newspaper/article/217931627

'The Wheatsheaf Inn', n.d., *Free Settler or Felon*.

Thomas David Ballard, 22 September 2020, Tenterfield Cemetery, Tenterfield Shire, NSW, Australia, *Find a Grave*, https://www.findagrave.com/memorial/215918525

Thomas Edward Ballard, 1894, Certified copy of NSW Death Certificate, Registration No. 5463/1894, *NSW Registry of Births, Deaths and Marriages*, Sydney, Australia.

Thomas Edward Ballard, 14 February 2012, Glen Innes General Cemetery Memorials, New South Wales, *Find a Grave*, https://www.findagrave.com/memorial/84960751

Thomas Lewis Bignell, 2010, Australia, Birth Index, 1788-1922, *Ancestry.com*

Thomas Louis Ballard, 1903, Electoral Division of Gough, Kookabookra, *NSW Electoral Roll*.

'Timber and Other Licenses', *NSW Government Gazette (Sydney, NSW (1832-1900),* 17 April 1877, iss.126 (Supplement), p.1546, https://trove.nla.gov.au/newspaper/article/223759051

'To Builders', *Glen Innes Examiner and General Advertiser (NSW: 1874-1908),* 6 April 1886, p.2, https://trove.nla.gov.au/newspaper/page/23896194

Tolmie, F., 1911(a), 'Preface', *Journal of the Folk-Song Society*, vol.4, iss.16, pp.iii.

Tolmie, F., 1911(b), 'A Singers Memories of Life on Skye', *Journal of the Folk-Song Society*, vol.4, iss.16, pp.147-149.

'Towards Responsible Government-1843 to 1855', 2023, *Parliament of NSW*, https://www.parliament.nsw.gov.au

'Town Talk', *Glen Innes Examiner (NSW: 1908-1954),* 1 October 1917, p.4, https://trove.nla.gov.au/newspaper/article/183265060

'Transfer', *Glen Innes Examiner and General Advertiser (NSW: 1874-1908),* 10 November 1905, p.4, https://trove.nla.gov.au/newspaper/article/217794982

'Transfer of Runs', *New South Wales Government Gazette (Sydney, NSW: 1832-1900),* iss.111, 7 August 1849, p.1165, https://trove.nla.gov.au/newspaper/article/230391789

'Transfer of Runs', *The Sydney Morning Herald (NSW: 1842-1954),* 10 August 1849, p.4, https://trove.nla.gov.au/newspaper/article/12913906

Treaty of Perth, 2024, *Hebridean Connections*, https://www.hebrideanconnections.com/historical-events/109716

Tsicalas, P., 2017, 'Early Settlement of Tyagarah, Ewingsdale, Coorabell and St Helena', *Brunswick Valley Historical Society*.

Turnbull, L., 2008, 'The End of Transportation', *The Dictionary of Sydney*, https://dictionaryofsydney.org

Turner, J. W. and Sullivan, J., 1979, *Photos of Old Newcastle*, Hunter History Publications Stockton, NSW, https://catalogue.nla.gov.au/Record/1363081

'Underbank Estate', Advertising, *The Maitland Mercury and Hunter General Advertiser (NSW: 1843-1893)*, 29 January 1876, p.1, https://trove.nla.gov.au/newspaper/article/18802801

'Under the Colonnade', *Glen Innes Examiner and General Advertiser (NSW: 1874 - 1908)*, 4 August 1875, p.2, https://trove.nla.gov.au/newspaper/article/217833524

'Union Church', 2022, *Merriam-Webster Dictionary*.

'Unmarried Male Immigrants', 1837, Midlothian, *Assisted Immigrants (digital) Shipping Lists*, p.1, *NSW State Archives*, Sydney.

'Unsold Portions of Underbank Estate', *Dungog Chronicle: Durham and Gloucester Advertiser (NSW: 1894-1954)*, 4 March 1913, p.4, https://trove.nla.gov.au/newspaper/article/136135532

'Updated NSW Syllabuses to Include Indigenous Perspectives', 1 August 2023, *Special Broadcasting Service*, https://www.sbs.com.au/nitv/article/updated-nsw-syllabuses-to-include-indigenous-perspectives/o5jz4z5au

'*Vagrancy Act 1835* No11a', 25 August 1835, UTS and UNSW Faculties of Law, *Australasian Legal Information Institute (AustLII)*.

'Victoria (r.1837-1901)', 2023, *The Royal Household*, https://www.royal.uk/queen-victoria

Walker, R.B., 1966, *Old New England*, Methuen, London.

Walsh, B., 2020, *Toil and Trouble from Maitland to Moreton Bay-John Eales Convicts*, Paterson Historical Society, NSW.

Ward, R., 1958, *The Australian Legend*, Oxford University Press, Melbourne.

'Ward, The Bushranger – Close Pursuit, and Escape', *The Maitland Mercury and Hunter River General Advertiser, (NSW: 1843-1893)*, 23 February 1864, p.2, https://trove.nla.gov.au/newspaper/page/139212

'Warwicks v Red Range', *Glen Innes Examiner and General Advertiser (NSW: 1874 - 1908)*, 15 November 1881, p.4, https://trove.nla.gov.au/newspaper/rendition/nla.news-article217832586

Waste Lands, Australia Act 1846 9 & 10 Vict, c104, 28 August 1846, Queensland Law, *Queensland University of Technology*, https://digitalcollections.qut.edu.au/4669

Waterhouse, R., 'Minstrel Show and Vaudeville House: The Australian Popular Stage, 1838-1914', 30 September 2008, *Australian Historical Studies*, p.366-385.

Watson, D., 1984, *'Caledonia Australis: Scottish Highlanders on the Frontier of Australia'*, Vintage, Random House, Australia.

Watson, J., Captain Thunderbolt: Hero or Villain, *Gloucester Advocate*, 9 November 2016, https://www.gloucesteradvocate.com.au/story/4278516

West, S. C., 2005, 'The Role of the 'Bush' in 1860's Bushranging', *Royal Australian Historical Society*.

Weston, K.M., Gallagher, W.C., & Branley, J.M., 17 March 2014, 'Smallpox Vaccination, Colonial Sydney and Serendipity', *The Medical Journal of Australia*, vol.200, iss.5, pp.295-297.

Wilkie, B., *'Scottish Migrants in Western Victoria'*, 19 May 2018, https://thescottishaustralian.wordpress.com

'William Fraser of Culbokie', 2023, *Legacies of British Slavery database*, http://wwwdepts-live.ucl.ac.uk/lbs/person/view/8584

William MacLeod, 1841, Kilmuir, Inverness, Ref: Census 112/6/13, Scotland's People, *National Records of Scotland*.

Williams, M., April 2012, *A History in Three Rivers, Dungog Shire Heritage Study Thematic History*, NSW Government.

Williams, M., August 2014, *A History in Three Rivers, Dungog Shire Heritage Study Thematic History*, NSW Government.

Williamson, B., 30 May 2017, South Australia's History of Voting Rights for Aboriginal Australians, *Australian Broadcasting Commission*.

'Women in Print', 19 December 1922, *Evening Post*, vol.cc, no.147, p.7, https://paperspast.natlib.govt.nz

'Women's C.T. Union', *Glen Innes Examiner and General Advertiser (NSW: 1874 - 1908)*, 5 November 1901, p.2, https://trove.nla.gov.au/newspaper/article/217864662

About the Author

Gail lives in the Northern Rivers area of New South Wales, Australia. After completing her studies, Gail taught in the arts, humanities and social sciences at Southern Cross University. She also taught for a number of years at colleges in Dubai in the United Arab Emirates, and in Ghangzhou China. Gail continues to read, write and travel widely. She can be contacted at <gbarnes2@msn.com>